sound
bites

50 YEARS OF HI-FI NEWS
KEN KESSLER & STEVE HARRIS

ipc
COUNTRY
& LEISURE
— MEDIA —
A Part of the IPC Media group of Companies
Distributed by MarketForce
ABC Member of the Audit Bureau of Circulations

Published by IPC Focus Network, part of the IPC Media
Group. Distributed by Marketforce (UK) Ltd, Kings
Reach Tower, Stamford Street, London SE1 9LS.

ISBN 0-86296-242-0

Printed and bound in Great Britain by
Portobello Press, London

Contents

The Contributors

The authors would like to thank all the contributors to this book for their generosity and enthusiasm. They include:

John Atkinson; Arnis Balgalvis; Tom Barron; Robert Becker; Janet Belton; John Borwick; Christopher Breunig; Richard Colburn; John Crabbe; Laura Dearborn; Jim Dovey; Allen Edelstein; Gordon Hill; Geoffrey Horn; Arthur Khoubessarian; Bascom H King; Gene Lyle; Arturo Manzano; Kostas Metaxas; Clement Perry; Bill Peugh; Howard Popeck; John Reddington; Alastair Robertson-Aikman; Karen Sumner; Robert J Reina; Colin Walker; David A Wilson; Be Yamamura.

Acknowledgements

'The Life and Achievements of P G A H Voigt' by Geoffrey Horn (Chapter 1) has been reprinted with the kind assistance of the *British Vintage Wireless Society Bulletin*. 'Percy Wilson: a Gramophone Man' (Chapter 1) by Geoffrey Horn first appeared in *The Gramophone: 75 Years* and is reprinted with the kind permission of Tony Pollard and *The Gramophone*. 'Raymond Cooke remembers Gilbert Briggs' (Chapter 1), 'An Interview With Stanley Kelly' (Chapter 3) and 'An Interview with Peter Walker' (Chapter 4) by Ken Kessler originally appeared in *Audio* magazine. 'Stanley Kelly: in his own words' (Chapter 3) is from G A Briggs' *Audio Biographies*, 1961; 'Edgar Villchur: The Golden Years' by Roy Allison (Chapter 5) is reprinted with the permission of Audio Amateur Press from *Multi Media Manufacturer*, Vol 1, Issue 1. 'An interview with Edgar Villchur' by Laura Dearborn (Chapter 5) first appeared in *Hi-Fi News*, February 1989 and 'A Little Legend' by Trevor Butler (Chapter 7) in *Hi-Fi News*, January 1989. 'KK's high end odyssey (Chapter 12) first appeared as 'Living in the USA' in *Hi-Fi News*, December 1984 and January 1985. Cover photo: www.photos.com.

Special thanks

We'd like to record special thanks to Flick Ekins (Art Direction & Design); Christopher Breunig (architect in InDesign) for page design and production; Rene Andrew and Steve Bailey for further design assistance; Liz Briggs and Janet Belton for research assistance; David Harris for additional proof-reading.

Preface

Simple, like all good ideas. We'd get the audio industry to tell its own stories – the stories that had never been told before. And the timing was perfect. Our 'oral history of an aural medium' could also celebrate the upcoming 50th anniversary of the oldest, most respected audio magazine. We'd intersperse anecdotes – amusing, eye-opening, even shocking – with the history of hi-fi and the story of *Hi-Fi News*.

So here it is. Thanks to our distinguished contributors (and to the great writing and amazing powers of persuasion of my co-author/editor), *Sound Bites* is, I think, easily the most entertaining hi-fi book ever.

Not long ago, I received a letter from a gentleman who'd been reading *Hi-Fi News* since the very first issue, and he said he was still enjoying it. When you're aware that the first issue was published in June 1956, that says something about the lasting value and integrity of the magazine.

I was privileged to be Editor of *Hi-Fi News* for 19 of its first 50 years, and for most of that time, I was well aware that I had the best job in the industry. *Hi-Fi News* had a certain ethos, a sense of duty to its readers and to the truth, that underpinned everything. It was, in fact, an ethos that went right back to Volume 1, issue 1. From the very start, the magazine's contributors included the leading experts in the field, and I'm glad to say that is still true today.

In early 2005 I decided it was time for a change. The latest 'improvements' to the South West Trains timetable were a factor, but mainly, I just had to escape those crushing monthly deadlines and start doing all those things I'd wanted to do for years. This book was one of them.

Our biggest problem with *Sound Bites* was having too much material, and our only regrets were over what we had to leave out. And that's why, you'll notice, it's a somewhat foreshortened view of hi-fi history. We've devoted more space to the great pioneers of audio, the great days of the high end and the excitement of analogue discovery, than we have to the more recent developments in digital audio, for example. In fact, you can read about them elsewhere. What you'll find in *Sound Bites* is unique.

And if, when reading this book, you find yourself wondering where the last 20 years have gone, I can truthfully say, 'So do I.' But it's been fun!

Steve Harris

Who's been who in *Hi-Fi News*

Donald Aldous (Technical Editor, ARR,
to 1970), Technical Editor 1970-79,
Consulting Editor 1979-1989
René Andrew, Art Editor 2000 on
John Atkinson, News Editor 1976-1978,
Deputy Editor 1978-1982, Editor 1982-1986
Emma Axbey, Art Editor 1994-1995
Rex Baldock, Technical Adviser 1971-1999
Gary Bellamy, Editorial Assistant 1973-1974,
News Editor 1974-1976
Julian Berrisford, Assistant Editor 1958-1960
John Borwick, Technical Editor 1959-1962
Christopher Breunig, Musical Adviser
1970-1986, Music Editor 1986-2000
Elizabeth Briggs, Editorial Assistant 2004 on
Anthony Burton-Brown, Assistant Editor
1959-1961
Trevor Butler, Editorial Assistant 1988-1989,
News Editor 1989-1994
Ray Carter, Features Editor, 1974-1976
Andrew Cartmel, Assistant Editor 1994-1997
Mike Cavenett, Production Editor 2003-2004
Martin Colloms, Technical Adviser 1983 on
Peter J Comeau, Contributing Editor 1993-1999
Peter Clayton, Musical Adviser 1970-1982
John Crabbe, Technical Editor 1962-1965,
Editor 1965-1982, Consulting Editor
1982-2004
Karen Douthwaite, Sub-Editor 1989-1990
Flick Ekins, Design Consultant 1989-1994
Steve Fairclough, Editor 2005 on
Linda Fieldhouse, Production Editor
1984-1988, 1993-1994
Patrick Fraser, Production Editor 2004 on
Peter Gammond (Editor ARR to 1970),
Music Editor 1970-1979
John Gash, Art Editor 1982-1989
Mitchell Gaynor, Art Editor 1995-2000
Mike Gleeson, Production Editor 1993
Malcolm Hawksford, Technical Adviser 1988 on
Steve Harris, Editor 1986-2005
Andrew Harrison, Technical Editor 1988-2000,
Deputy Editor 2000 on
Miles Henslow (Founder), Editor 1956-1965
Keith Howard, Consultant Technical Editor
2000 on
Ivor Humphreys, News Editor 1978-1979,
Music Editor 1979-1982, Deputy Editor
1982-1986

Arthur Jackson, Musical Adviser 1970-1975
Arthur Jacobs, Musical Adviser 1972-1998
Burnett James (Music Editor ARR to 1970),
Musical Adviser 1970-1972
Geoff Jeanes, Editorial Assistant 1972-1974,
Record Reviews Editor 1974-1982
Gareth Jefferson, Record Reviews Editor
1971-1972, Assistant Editor 1972
Frank Jones, News & Features Editor
1967-1972
Stanley Kelly, Technical Adviser 1956-2002
Ken Kessler, Assistant Editor 1984-1988,
Contributing Editor 1988-1998,
Senior Contributing Editor 1998 on
Angus McKenzie, Technical Adviser 1988-2005
Paul Messenger, Deputy Editor 1976-1978,
Editor-At-Large 1983-1985
Paul Miller, AV Tech Editor 2004,
Technical Director 2005 on
James Moir, Technical Adviser 1959-1988
Felicity Mulgan, Production Editor 1983-1984
Adrian Orlowski, Features Editor 1983-1984
R S Roberts, Technical Adviser 1956-1961
Marc Sagar, Production Editor 2001-2002
Christine Stapleton, Art Editor 1979-1982
Mark Stevens, Art Editor 1973-1979
Nathalie Thorne, Editorial Assistant 2004
Mike Thorne, Editorial Assistant 1972-1973,
Features Editor 1973-1974
Ralph West, Technical Adviser 1957-1983

Equipment reviewers and regular columnists
(other than those listed above) who made a
major contribution over the years, listed very
roughly in chronological order:
George Tillett, Granville Cooper, Alec Tutchings,
Reg Williamson, Gordon J King, Bert Webb,
Trevor Attewell, Denys Killick, Noel Keywood,
John Freestone, Douglas Brown, Maurice
Taggart, Austin Uden, Bill Newman, David
Pickett, Barry Fox, Ben Duncan, Jimmy
Hughes, Chris Bryant, Alvin Gold, Tony
Faulkner, Ifan Payne, John Nelson, Ben Watson,
David Allcock, David Berriman, Tony Bolton

Unsung heroines: Editorial Secretaries in
chronological order Jennifer Scotland, Barbara
Driver, Sabita Sarran, Penelope Keogh, Sarah
Middleton, Rebecca Payne, Francesca Cheetham

Introduction

'Because the valve revival was in full swing – Michaelson & Austin's TVA amplifiers were among those selling by the truckload and burning the odd carpet – John Atkinson had no problem with publishing a series of articles about retro-gear.' **Ken Kessler**

A marketing type would hype *Sound Bites* as 'Fifty years in the making!' And while it exists to celebrate *Hi-Fi News'* first half-century, that's not quite accurate because, back in the mid-1950s when *HFN* first appeared, specialty audio was too new to have provoked an historical approach. Indeed, it's doubtful that any of the hi-fi community's members – consumers, retailers, reviewers or manufacturers – were wondering about posterity in 1956.

Instead, this book is 22 years in the making, its roots to be found in a word coined in 1983 by John Atkinson: 'anachrophile'.

I had only been with *Hi-Fi News & Record Review* for a few months, after a year with *Stereo-The Magazine*, when I begged John to allow me to indulge in my passion, which was vintage hi-fi. Although audio *per se* was only 30-or-so-years old in 1983, a few of us were already collecting vintage gear with some enthusiasm. But it was a hobby pursued mainly in Japan and France. It seemed that, as far as British and American audiophiles were concerned, vintage audio equipment was interesting, but hardly noteworthy, collectible or even useful when set against current offerings.

Quite why I was obsessed with old equipment is unclear beyond a general interest in antiques, but it was the valve revival that drew me to early audio gear. Because the valve revival was in full swing – Michaelson & Austin's TVA amps were among those selling by the truckload and burning the odd carpet – John had no problem with publishing a series of articles about retro-gear.

He named the column 'The Anachrophile' and let me loose on Radford and Dynaco amps, Decca cartridges, Thorens TD-124s and the like. And a wide cross-section of readers, it turned out, loved it because of a totally unexpected side-benefit: it offered them a way to put together systems at sane, second-hand prices. Well, they were sane at the time. Who knew then that something called 'eBay' would feature a hi-fi collection in 2005 with an entry bid of $165,000? Another pleasant surprise was that older readers enjoyed 'The Anachrophile', too, because it was their nostalgia, their formative years being covered. And the 'Establishment'? They were finally being shown some recognition and respect. It's the only reason I can imagine why people like David Hafler, Stan Kelly, Alastair Robertson-Aikman, Raymond Cooke, Peter Walker, Donald Aldous and many others suffered my presence at hi-fi shows.

It was like this: hi-fi is, or was, an industry unique in its ability to ignore its past. Unlike motoring or fashion or watches or the film industry or even shoes, for goodness sake, we have no museums preserving our 'classics', there are no shelves full of hi-fi history books, we don't get grants to keep valve manufacturers going.

And that distressed me, even as far back as 1983. 'The Anachrophile' was a deliberate if minor attempt at setting the record straight. It even managed to prove nearly life-threatening, when a certain turntable manufacturer took umbrage at my pointing out in print that Edgar Villchur's masterpiece, the AR turntable, preceded the Linn LP12 by a decade. But that confrontation can wait for my memoirs.

When John moved the USA in 1986 and Steve Harris took over as Editor, we realised that we shared a common love of vintage equipment. Indeed, Steve still thinks that 78s are the only way to hear Louis Armstrong or Charlie Parker. Along the way, we nursed a little dream we dubbed 'the *Hi-Fi News* Bookshelf.'

Our inspiration was published in 1961, G A Briggs's *Audio Biographies*. It was flawed, to be sure, filled as it was with Gilbert's buddies, some of whom were so peripheral to audio that it was comical. And Briggs seemed to have an aversion to Americans, only a few of whose profiles were deemed worthy enough for inclusion, despite the USA clearly contributing as much if not more to recorded sound and its playback as did the British. (Edison? DeForest? Fisher? Marantz? Duh!)

Even so, *Audio Biographies* was the touchstone, the sole repository of audio lore beyond technical manuals and DIY books. But it was in desperate need of updating. Whole generations had come and gone. Who was chronicling the adventures of Mark Levinson, Sugano-san of Koetsu, Ivor Tiefenbrun, Dan D'Agostino? What about pioneering reviewers like J Gordon Holt and Harry Pearson? Quadraphony? Tweaking?

We once pitched the idea of a quarterly magazine about vintage hi-fi after we'd enjoyed great reader response to *Hi-Fi News*' 'Classic Hi-Fi' supplements, but new magazine titles, in the post-Internet era, are not exactly where one invests money. I also recall, when Mission briefly owned Wharfedale, suggesting to Farad Azima that he should revive the Wharfedale tradition of publishing hi-fi-related books, starting with a set of Briggs reprints. But that went no further, and Wharfedale ended up with IAG while Farad sailed off into the sunset.

Eventually, 'The Anachrophile' ended – not because of lack of interest nor because we ran out of vintage audio to write about, but because space constraints deemed it wiser to use every page in the magazine for current equipment. Let's be mature about this: aside from one or two vintage audio specialists, who buys advertising space to support pages on obsolete equipment?

Occasionally, Steve would have me write about something historical, usually because of an interesting reissue, such as the revived McIntosh tube amplifier of 1993, the anniversary Marantz valve amps or the appearance of the Garrard 501. But recently, we started noticing that nearly every other magazine on the stands – here, in America, in Japan, Greece, you name it – was running a classic audio series. Sometime you'd even see the term 'anachrophile' to denote those who worship the old stuff.

Time for a very British harrumph from a Yank: if any magazine was in a position to deal with vintage hi-fi, it was *Hi-Fi News*. For openers, it's the longest-surviving hi-fi magazine in the English language, probably in any language. For another, our archives and the collective experience of the writers made it a natural. For a third, our readers love the stuff. Or, at least, that's what they tell me at vintage hi-fi fairs.

A ticking clock reminded the publisher that *Hi-Fi News*' Golden Anniversary was soon to hit us. Steve, as one of his parting shots, had relaunched 'The Anachrophile' under the more contemporary heading of 'Classic Kit' and the reception was terrific. But something else happened which convinced *Hi-Fi News*' bosses that a nice way to mark our 50th anniversary would be a proper book covering the magazine's and high-end audio's past.

That 'something else' was a flurry of single-make books about hi-fi, all of which sold well enough to prove the existence of a literate audience with an historical bent, one that wanted authoritative texts on paper rather than downloads via cyberspace. The one-two punch consisted of Steven Spicer's *Firsts In High Fidelity: The Products and History of H J Leak & Co* and Barrett & Klementovich's *Paul Wilbur Klipsch: The Life... The Legend*. Shortly after these titles appeared, Marantz produced its history, via *Stereo Sound* in Japan, and Julian Alderton published *The Tannoy Story*. Clearly, something was afoot.

In the interim, with no small irony given that it was to Wharfedale we first suggested reviving the Briggs books, IAG approached me to write the history of Quad. At the risk of sounding immodest, I'm convinced that Steve and I got the green light for *Sound Bites* because one of *Hi-Fi News'* bosses saw 200 copies of *Quad: The Closest Approach* sold in 20 minutes at the book's launch at the Heathrow show in 2003.

The most overpowering concern was the sheer scale of the audio saga. We realised, from the outset, that if key companies like Leak, Quad and Marantz could justify their own histories, what hope did we have of telling the complete story in under 300 pages? Just listing all the brands that have come and gone since 1956 would fill that allocation. But a shelf-filling multi-volume masterwork was not possible.

Steve and I decided that hard data and dry text weren't what was needed anyway. There wasn't a brand you could name without some presence on the Internet. 'Google' any make you can name, and you'd find something. Besides the Internet, there were magazine back-issues if all you required was the contemporary review of the Denon DL103, or the dimensions of a Celestion Ditton 66. No, what we wanted to do was tell the story of high-end audio, preferably in the words of those who made that history. Above all, we wanted the behind-the-scenes stuff that you wouldn't find on the 'Net. We wanted it to be about people, not just hardware.

Although I had done my best to interview as many of the industry's pioneers as I could, time mitigated against it. In my relatively short tenure in audio, we'd lost pioneering giants such as Stan Kelly, Donald Aldous, Henry Kloss, Saul Marantz, Avery Fisher, Frank McIntosh, Gordon Gow, John Gilbert, Peter Walker, Jim Rogers, Raymond Cooke, Gerry Sharpe, Donald Chave, Peter Mitchell, Arthur Radford, David Hafler, Len Feldman, Julian Hirsch, Charles Trayhorn, Yasuo Nakanishi and many others. Tragically, we also lost a number of too-young, second- and third-generation figures including Jason Bloom, Sal DiMicco, Hy Kachalsky, Peter Snell, Hamish Robertson, Peter Merrick, Harvey Rosenberg, Richard Ross – again, far too many to name. We were overwhelmed before we began, because omissions would be glaringly obvious, as well as hurtful. So a format was needed.

Without hesitation, we restricted the book to what is arbitrarily called 'high-end audio' – you need to look elsewhere if you want the story of the ghetto-blaster, Amstrad, Pye's Black Box or Bose. Time frame? While a certain amount of pre-history was needed, and while *Hi-Fi News'* birth-year is the key starting point, we kept in mind throughout that the book should most be concerned with high-quality stereo reproduction, as instigated by FM radio and the LP. Which just so happens to correspond with *Hi-Fi News'* span. Less politically correct, but absolutely justifiable, was our decision to concentrate exclusively on UK and US contributions. It was justified because true high-fidelity audio was invented simultaneously in the UK and the US. These two countries easily account for 95% of all the important developments in high-end audio, the manufacture of the goods, the most important magazines, the records – you name it. With all due respect to the Japanese, the Germans, the Swiss and anyone else making high-end equipment, they're not even 'Avis' to the US' and UK's 'Hertz.' Sorry, but that's fact.

It was important to balance the contents between 'classic' reprints and newly-commissioned material, but the core was to be a series of anecdotes told in a 'you-are-there' manner. So, over two years, I personally solicited anecdotes from everyone I could. In true hi-fi form, I was greeted with near-total apathy. Out of 400 letters handed out, maybe 25 people replied. But, blessedly, among them were prolific and eloquent contributors like Howard Popeck, Richard Colburn, Bill Peugh, Karen Sumner and a few others. Their anecdotes are the glue that holds this together.

One poignant development of my importuning was the acquisition of Ralph West's final writings. I had struck up a friendship with Ralph when he agreed to contribute to *Quad: The Closest Approach*. His contribution was one of the most charming and eloquent elements of the book, so I asked if he had any other reminiscences he'd like to share. I received page after page, in longhand, of his personal recollections of long-departed audio giants. Although unplanned, *Sound Bites* now serves as a heartfelt memorial to Ralph, who was – fittingly – one of *Hi-Fi News'* earliest contributors.

Sound Bites is *Hi-Fi News'* pointillist history of hi-fi, a series of tiny moments, and some larger ones, that present an overview of a complex, multi-faceted hobby and industry that brought limitless hours of guilt-free, victimless pleasure to countless millions living outside of Taliban-run territories. And it just so happens to coincide with the life of *Hi-Fi News* up to the year 2005.

But we're hoping it doesn't end here. If Steve and I are not over-estimating the hunger for a hi-fi library, maybe this is the inaugural volume in the long-dreamed-about '*Hi-Fi News* Bookshelf'...

Ken Kessler
Canterbury, England, August 2005

1. Pre-history: the era of Paul Voigt

'What would we have done without Paul Voigt?' **Ralph West**

'It could be said that Percy Wilson was instrumental in causing this burgeoning industry to take a much more professional approach to design.' **Geoffrey Horn**

'Gilbert Briggs was a bit suspicious of science. Or, shall we say, of scientists. He once wrote of the folly of employing technical people at the head of things because they tend to go after brilliant technical solutions rather than the practical, commercial solution.' **Raymond Cooke**

'By 1956 the audio industry was expanding rapidly – stereo, magnetic tape recorders, good quality amplifiers and loudspeakers, and the possibility of FM were leading to a very effervescent and lucrative market. There was an urgent need for a specialist magazine.' **Stanley Kelly**

The life and achievements of P G A H Voigt. *By Geoffrey Horn*

It is now generally accepted that Marconi's genius, certainly initially, lay in the co-ordination and recognition of the commercial possibilities of the work of other pioneers, notably Heinrich Hertz and Oliver Lodge, whose findings he put together in a usable form. Voigt, on the other hand, was something of a polymath and a complete original in both thought and practice. Voigt's father had come to England in the previous century from the Cologne area of the Rhineland and had taken on British nationality before his marriage. Voigt had therefore always been English – the family home was in south-east London – although his German ancestry was reflected in those initials which stood for Paul, Gustavus, Adolphus, Helmuth. Names which were destined to appear on the many patents – over thirty – which he was to register in future years.

Little is known about his parents but they were sufficiently well-off to allow him an upstairs room in their house as a workshop and to later send him to school at Dulwich College, a couple of miles down the road. Boyish experiments were with model making, hydraulics and efforts at achieving perpetual motion. This all changed when he was twelve and his mother gave him a crystal set and the magic spell of wireless fell upon him, although there was little enough to listen to in those distant days.

Unfortunately, the First World War was soon to result in the impounding of all wireless apparatus by the General Post Office and in any case it was time for entry to Dulwich, where after the usual preliminaries he elected to join the engineering stream; there he remained, passing the intermediate BSc examination in 1919. He wished to progress to London University for his full BSc but returning members of the forces had priority and he was forced to take what we now call a gap year.

Wireless challenges

After the war, the ban on wireless was soon lifted and Paul, regarding this as an interesting subject with challenges which might call for his inventive abilities, entered into it wholeheartedly. His crystal set was returned but Paul had learned of valve practice and, although they were both rare and costly, he acquired one for experimental purposes. With adequate time whilst waiting for his university place he adapted his poor mother's treadle sewing machine as a coil winder and built a number of receivers with varying success; this judged by their ability to conjure forth the Sunday afternoon concerts from the Dutch transmitter PCGG.

In his first university year, he was sufficiently confident in a circuit he had invented to submit an article to *Wireless World* and this was published on the 10 December 1921, the day after his 20th birthday. However, before the piece was accepted the then editor of *Wireless World*, Philip Coursey and his assistant – later to become editor – Hugh Pocock, came to inspect the installation to make sure that the idea put forward, which was new to them, was not a hoax! The article was titled 'Simultaneous High and Low Frequency Amplification' and described what we would now call a 'Dual-Amplification' or 'Reflex' circuit. In those days when valves were very inefficient, costly and greedy on batteries, being bright emitters, his circuit soon became very popular.

Later it was found that in houses with AC mains installed – very rare in those times – hum was a problem and Voigt published re-designs to overcome this difficulty in the 27 May 1922 edition. F H Haines' 1924 book of *Wireless Circuits* (he was then a deputy editor of *WW* but later an early manufacturer of semi-kit sets) illustrates a number of such circuits. Paul thought that it was a new invention he would give to fellow experimenters rather than go for a patent; many years later it was found that there had been previous mention of such a possibility in a wartime patent although no practical circuit was proposed. Voigt was a popular member of the local wireless society because of his ability to explain complex technicalities in the simplest terms and this was to greatly affect his future. The south-east London firm of J E Hough Ltd had bought up the English Edison Bell company and was continuing their manufacture of gramophone records and machines. Fearing the impact of broadcasting on their future livelihood, as many in the record industry did – wrongly as it happened – they had looked to diversify. Moulding records led to moulding cabinet parts and components for the newly-named radio industry; younger management sought to extend this to the manufacture of complete radio sets.

The manager of Hough's machine shop was a member of the wireless society and one evening asked Voigt if he knew anyone who could set up radio manufacture at their premises. Voigt duly suggested someone but later thought that he might try himself. In the event, they were both taken on, Paul to do the R&D as we now call it and the other man to take charge of production. Voigt was fortunately sufficiently streetwise to arrange in his employment agreement that any patents resulting from his work would remain his property but that the firm would have preference in licensing.

He started work on 1 November 1922, a week before the BBC's official birth. It seems to me that this entry into the radio market only met with limited success; my early copy of *Radio Radio* lists only three Edison Bell products, a crystal set, a two-valver and a loudspeaker. This latter might be a significant indication of Voigt's leaning towards the audio side which was soon to become his major work.

Experiments in electrical recording
As a radio designer employed by a record company, Paul became increasingly aware of the superior sound quality which the BBC could offer when it was on form. Perhaps unwittingly, he had devoted much of his time to amplifiers and loudspeakers, applying for several patents. He studied the broadcasting chain, admiring the linearity of the huge Round/ Sykes moving-coil microphone then in common use and revelling in the evening dance music transmissions from the Savoy Hotel, adjacent to the BBC premises. He recounts in a memoir how on one day in February 1924, walking in the factory yard, he heard the sound of a military band through an open window of the upstairs studio and was immediately struck with the idea that it might be possible to put this on records electrically instead of the acoustic methods then employed. Of course other people in other places had similar thoughts but the excessive secrecy then endemic in the industry meant that neither Voigt nor Hough's knew anything about it. Paul put his rapidly forming ideas to Tom Hough, son of the founder, and was given an old cylinder phonograph with an

experimental electric motor drive to play with. He replaced the old hill-and-dale sound box with a Brown's headphone earpiece from which he had removed the diaphragm and attached a piece of hardened tinplate to the reed. That evening, 19 February 1924, he recorded a short section of the BBC programme and put the cylinder on Hough's desk for him to find in the morning. I quote Voigt, 'The old cylinder was very hard, the cut was terrible, scratch in consequence very, very bad, but on playing it back there was no question but that it was part of the BBC's programme'. Paul was immediately encouraged to go ahead with his experiments.

Of course, the eventual aim was not to record the BBC but music from their studio, so Voigt needed to install a microphone and it must not attract attention from any performers – secrecy again. He compromised initially by placing a Brown's horn loudspeaker on a convenient shelf and using it in reverse as a microphone, devising suitable correction circuits. He had already patented (231972, 29 January 1924) a circuit for improving the response of loudspeakers using what we now call motional feedback. In this resonances or dips in the loudspeaker's natural response unbalance a bridge and send a signal back to the amplifier input to correct the error.

This practical use of negative (and positive) feedback preceded by no less than ten years the accepted 1934 revelation of this valuable circuit device by U S Black of America's Bell Telephone Co. To Voigt this was just a natural approach and I don't think he attempted to pursue the patent.

The slack-diaphragm condenser microphone

Developments on the recording side now followed thick and fast as he concentrated on this, leaving radio to colleagues. His amplifiers were now reasonably close to perfection as improved valves came on to the market and he continued to use the benefits of negative feedback, often by including the loudspeaker winding of his output transformers in the filament return of the output valves. He developed a unique slack diaphragm condenser microphone (the word capacitor had not arrived), realising that ideally the diaphragm should be weightless and without resonance. His design initially consisted of an oval section ebonite bar which was copper plated and formed the 'hot' output; there followed a rubber insulator (actually a condom!), a layer of silk and the thin foil diaphragm wrapped around and sealed top and bottom with hard wax. This foil, at one time culled from cigarette packets, formed the earthed return (patent number 263300). It had to work into an extremely high impedance offered by a carefully selected valve and was polarised at 120 volts via a pair of 10 megohm resistors. Moisture was the enemy, producing pops as each molecule wandered across the gap and it was mitigated by keeping the polarising voltage present at all times; it took no current of course.

An interesting 'by the way' concerns the BBC's efforts to use these very superior microphones in the then-new Broadcasting House. Those with *BBC Year Books* on their shelves can see a photograph of one with its BBC design 'peardrop' amplifier on page 381 of the 1933 edition. Unfortunately it was BBC practice to switch off all power supplies for the night at the close of the day's broadcasting. That and the presence of moisture from newly-plastered walls meant that Voigt's microphones could only be used in the evening after they had dried out; his offer to supply HT batteries to maintain the polarising was not taken up.

Perhaps inspired by the Round/Sykes microphone, Voigt favoured the moving-coil principle for other applications. He designed several moving-coil cutter heads for recording on to the wax blanks then in use and also had several designs for loudspeakers. He had included his ideas when applying for a patent on the latter when the Rice/Kellogg disclosure was made in the US, preceding him by a mere 30 days. He therefore had to omit certain passages (238310, 20 May 1924).

A complete recording chain

By 1927 he had his microphone, a good disc cutter, feedback amplifiers and loudspeakers; all with excellent responses for their day. He had realised early on that if one held a cut record at a slant to a light bulb the width of the resulting reflection indicated the amplitude of the cut. He was about to patent this when Hough stopped him, saying it was too valuable to publicise when there could be no future advantage; later G Buchmann and Erwin Meyer got the credit (July 1930). His complete recording chain was complemented by a clever lossless microphone mixer which could take the signals from four of his mikes and adjust the gain by variable capacitors which were noiseless compared to the usual potentiometers and did not wear out (329747, 20 March 1929). The only other application of this invention that comes to mind is the swell pedal on a Hammond organ.

Edison Bell were losing out because the big record companies had a policy of signing up major artists to an exclusive contract. They sought to negate this by undertaking location recordings in untapped centres of musical excellence such as Bucharest, Budapest and Zagreb. In 1928/29, Voigt took his equipment to these destinations and produced some 600 masters for the company. On his return, he continued to perfect the system but, perhaps seeing the writing on the wall, began to turn his attention to other uses of sound amplification, particularly the cinema where 'Talkies' were emerging, Public Address, and improving the standard of sound in the home.

Rightly deciding that the loudspeaker was the weakest link, he went back to his 1924 work and developed a moving-coil drive unit with a very large and powerful energised magnet consuming 40 watts. This saturated the pole pieces and reduced the effective inductance of the moving-coil. He went for a lightweight diaphragm and coil assembly, winding the latter with layers both inside and outside the coil former. His aim was to thus improve the response at high frequencies; he later incorporated a small inner cone attached directly to the former extending the range to around 8kHz (413758, 26 July 1934). This was much copied, with and without license!

A final development in 1938 was 'The Light Coil Twin' which isolated this inner cone from the main and had a rising response to 12kHz compensating for the wide dispersion of his domestic loudspeaker, which we will come to shortly. Today amplifier powers of 100 watts are commonplace but in those times 4–6 watts was exceptional and 12 watts professional! Loudspeaker efficiency was therefore important. Back in the twenties, Voigt had investigated methods of loading the diaphragm to the air – including, incidentally, the so-called air suspension in a sealed box where the air acts as a spring. This was subsequently the subject of an American patent (2,775,309, December 1956) by Edgar Villchur whose AR company sold thousands, although MacMillan and West of the GPO had used the idea for an aborted pre-war relay scheme in Southampton.

Voigt's tractrix horn

Voigt concluded that a horn was the best solution, although to get a decent low frequency response would require something considerably larger than the 'loudspeaking telephones' of the 1920s. He therefore designed a bolt-together version with a 4 foot square mouth using a tractrix curve where the mouth finishes at a right angle to the source, unlike the more usual exponential which goes on for ever.

This was phenomenally successful and in a demonstration a pair comfortably filled the Albert Hall. And then in 1933 Edison Bell failed; Voigt was out of a job. Voigt Patents Ltd was formed and concentrated on promoting the loudspeaker for cinemas, dance halls and the like; he added a 2 foot square model for speech and a weatherproof version was made for outdoor use but major effort now went into seeking a domestic solution.

Paul had long had a 'hole in the wall' concept, born of recording rooms with opening windows on to the studio. He reasoned that if a loudspeaker could mimic this situation, great realism would result and when the orchestra paused a virtual announcer would appear in the 'window'. Standing one of his horns upright with a rough reflector above it proved the point, and taking two of the faces away and placing it against the wall suggested something domestically acceptable. A few of these 180° dispersion models were made but it was soon obvious that, stood in a corner, only a quarter of the horn plus the walls more than equalled the free-standing 4 foot original. A tidied-up design with a quarter-wave loaded bass extension below the horn, driven from the rear of the diaphragm, rapidly became accepted as the finest domestic speaker available and some are still in use to this day.

Voigt at Radiolympia, 1934

Boldly, Paul took a stand at the 1934 annual radio show at Olympia where, to avoid cacophony, each exhibitor was supplied with one watt of audio power from a central amplifier in the charge of the BBC. Makers of radio sets could couple this to their loudspeakers to give some idea of what they might sound like in the home. Now one watt into one of Voigt's 4 foot horns was a very loud sound indeed and he was immediately accused of using additional amplification.

Having carefully inspected the power supply used to energise the huge magnet, authority admitted there was no amplifier. They thereupon pulled the plug on him claiming that public address loudspeakers weren't radios! But Paul had an early version of his domestic corner horn on the stand and substituted that, which was almost as loud. There was an acrimonious debate during which he threatened to withdraw and asked for his money back – eventually, I gather he was allowed to demonstrate for five minutes on the hour. As a schoolboy not yet 13 I was there with my father who, in 1924, had opened what was I believe, the country's first wireless-only shop. I recall my excitement at what I had heard and my first meeting with Mr Voigt, who politely shook our hands as we left.

Thereafter, Voigt avoided Olympia and hired a room in a road adjacent. It was there that I had the biggest shock in my lifetime with audio. The Television Service from Alexandra Palace did not commence their evening transmission until 8.30, so some bright spark at the BBC decided to broadcast the first hour of the coincident Promenade Concerts, then from the Queens Hall, on VHF using television's sound channel. On the corner horn in a domestic setting this was a memorable experience indeed and when it was eventually faded for TV to begin, nobody in the room made a sound before, with absolutely shattering presence, the voice of Elizabeth Cowell, the announcer at AP, came on to introduce the evening's programmes. AP was equipped with the Holman/Blumlein EMI moving-coil microphones, the studio acoustic was open and free of colour. It was as if she had walked into the room; to this day I have never heard better reproduced speech.

Still a schoolboy, Paul happily sold me a light coil diaphragm offering hints on its use and I spent hours fitting it to the hefty magnet of an old Epoch Domino loudspeaker which I applied to a rudimentary horn. Saving hard, I later acquired a genuine Voigt unit, then £18: six weeks wages! Further frugality, and by 1940 I had the further £18 for a corner horn, but no luck, his supplies of wood had dried up and his cabinet maker called up to the army. By now I knew Paul quite well and had been to his rickety premises over a garage in Sydenham to collect my unit. I found I could still obtain the materials for a horn locally and was good with my hands, but details of construction were lacking.

A moving-coil pickup

By now, the ever-ingenious Paul Voigt had designed a clever moving-coil pick-up which used no scarce materials except sapphire styli which he could get from a contact in Switzerland. I went to hear one and placed an order, whereupon Paul invited me to take all the measurements and patterns of his horn that I needed to copy one. We were interrupted by an air raid but it was not close, and Paul showed me the model of an ingenious arrangement he had devised for accurately locating aircraft at night acoustically, complaining that officialdom had ignored it. Having signed the Official Secrets Act, I could not tell him that most night fighters and at least one searchlight in each group carried radar (Elsie) and they could aim it before striking the arc.

His long coil pick-up was easily copied, and was: Leak was one, but Voigt lacked the capital to take action. Later in the war, he had a serious breakdown and in poor health decided to move to Canada when hostilities ceased, hoping to find adequate materials there to resume production of the loudspeaker. I last saw him when he came into Peter Walker's Acoustical Manufacturing Co's room at the first post-war Radio Show and the three of us forecast the future popularity of music in the home.

He left for Canada in April 1950, but the task was too great and he eventually found employment with the Canadian Radio Authority. He died there in February 1981; he was 79. He almost completely neglected audio in his later years, becoming involved in the theory of electro-magnetic induction, some of Einstein's work and whether the speed of light was an invariable constant or slowed towards the extremes of the universe.

He was a remarkable man. I still have some of his rambling letters; happy memories.

Reminiscences: before *Hi-Fi News*. *By Ralph West*

When I left college with a Physics degree – 1935 – I was already fully immersed in what later was to be called hi-fi. I had started literally with 'phones in a basin' and developed gradually to moving-coil speakers in home-made cabinets, powered by home-made amplifiers and fed by magnetic pickups and BBC radio. My mentor was the old *Wireless World* and such grand originals as Paul Voigt. I still have an early electrostatic speaker, the Primustatic.

In 1936 I joined the staff of the Northern Polytechnic and found colleague John Gilbert an equal enthusiast and we soon found ourselves personal friends of Paul Voigt and a fair number of manufacturers who were really trying to produce better sound.

The war occupied us otherwise for a few years, but as soon as it finished developments raced ahead. Harold Leak produced the first commercial amplifier with only 0.1% distortion and it is interesting that he had to show the National Physical Laboratory how to measure it as they'd never had the need to measure below, say, 1–2%; and 5% on maximum output was the accepted norm!

By 1950 there were several magazines reviewing mainly recorded music and they started adding a little bit on high-fidelity apparatus. By 1956 Miles Henslow [who was publishing *Record News*] realised that, because new hi-fi material was appearing every month, this aspect was the more important.

There was so much new apparatus coming on to the market all calling itself 'hi-fi' that Miles decided to start *Hi-Fi News* to explain the problems and design of the various items and give a fair valuation of the performance of each. He already had four people writing for him in *Record News*: Cecil Watts on disc reproduction; Stan Kelly; and, just coming into the audio field and showing promise, George Tillett on tape recording; and myself on loudspeakers. In fact, the *Record News* of April 1954 divulged the design and action of the new full-range electrostatic speaker designed and demonstrated by Peter Walker for the first time on 20 March 1956 to the Acoustical Group of the Physical Society.

To this nucleus Miles Henslow added our colleague at the Poly, Bob Roberts, ex-RF-designer at Wearite and a radio ham withall. We were getting at last real high-fidelity signals from the new VHF transmissions, but only if the receiver was getting a good signal from the aerial system.

We all thoroughly enjoyed this writing as we were encouraging the various manufacturers – though we wrote without fear or favour. There were very few attempts to bribe us.

Contact with Paul Voigt

I first heard of Paul Voigt in the old *Wireless World* magazine. I met him briefly during a visit to the Radio Show in London. Voigt was demonstrating his 4 foot Tractrix horn in a private house close to the exhibition. The open mouth was 4 feet square and its length including the moving-coil driver was only 4 feet 10$^1/2$ inches. At the other end of this large living room was a grand piano and this is probably the origin of the remark, 'Well, it's no bigger than a grand piano'.

Voigt realised it was possible to cut this horn in half as long as the 'cut' was closed by a solid flat wall, as there was no lateral air movement across this plane. In fact, this could be cut again, so that the quarter that was left was used in a corner. This only took up 2 feet by 2 feet of floor space but needed a little cunning internal shaping to get the sound horizontally into the room. Hence the lovely Voigt Corner Horn.

While I was still a university student, he offered demonstrations in customers' own homes if they could accommodate his sales engineer and he could also invite a few other possible customers from the region. I managed to satisfy him that we could provide a suitable corner for the speaker and a date was agreed. I remember very well waiting for the sales engineer to come round the corner of the road. We lived in green country between Nottingham and Derby. At last, a long sleek black sports car (Standard Swallow) towing a trailer loaded with something the size of a coffin. So I met Gilbert Redgrave (of the well-known Redgrave family); we were soon close friends and remained so to the end of his life.

The demonstration was a success and I was thrilled with such a close contact to this remarkable loudspeaker, though I don't know whether that evening sold any. Gilbert was soon asleep as he'd had a busy day and we were at least 130 miles from Sydenham, though at least there had been no untoward incidents like the coupling coming undone and the trailer escaping. Quiet as a mouse, I filled sheets and sheets of paper with sketches in very precise measurements and I'm not the only enthusiast who has done the same.

Some time later I had the good fortune to find two large sheets of good birch plywood, half-inch thick and large enough to make the two sides of the Corner Horn. Bit by bit, over several years, I began to build it with the aid of my measurements and frequent peeps into Corner Horns I'd seen at exhibitions.

I often met Voigt and all the other audio folk at meetings. One day I asked Voigt if he minded my making one for myself. He did mind and 'I must say no', he said, as he'd had so many similar requests from people who had started and got into a mess. Anyway, it was too late, as it was nearly finished. I couldn't afford his delectable driving unit, only a spare cone. I'd picked up a hefty energised field coil from a local cinema fire and with a bit of lathe work it made quite a good unit. While this was being done, I ran it with an 8 inch Wharfedale speaker.

After the war, audio activities got going again, but Voigt's health and his business were in trouble and he decided to emigrate to Canada, so slowly closed down his English works. The driving unit part, especially the very high-flux magnet design, was taken over by Mr Chave of Lowther.

One day, Voigt rang me: 'had I got a Corner Horn?'. If so could he come one afternoon as there were some small experiments he'd like to do and 'would I mind if he slept for a couple of hours during the afternoon', as he had serious nervous problems, but could keep going with that much rest.

As he entered the room, he stopped at the door and said, 'You naughty boy!'. He knew it must be a copy as he'd never made one with that wood finish. I was able to assure him that every dimension was within 2mm of his production and he was very interested in the mould I'd made for the driving end and the 'horse' I'd made to shape the surface of the big reflector. He heard it going and said we need be the only people who know this is not a real Voigt production. I offered him the mould I'd made but his mould had already gone to Canada, but he would forgive me if I gave him the 'horse', a simple piece of plywood cut to the inverse of the reflector profile. He came next day with an original official Voigt Patents brass plate, with the number 0 if I remember, and fixed it himself.

When we emigrated to France in 1976, we gave it to Gilbert Redgrave so it could partner the one he had and he could enjoy stereo. Our 1763 farmhouse wall wasn't really big enough. We kept in touch with Gilbert and his wife Kit as long as they both lived but lost touch with their family: all grown up and dispersed. We just hope somebody is enjoying its music.

Voigt's brain never tired and he carried on working, teaching, thinking and pondering the whole working of nature. I have many of his typed letters that I ought to read again. They were typed on the thinnest paper

I've ever seen to save money, as postage was based on weight. High efficiency to the end! Over all of this time, Paul Voigt was ably sustained by his wife Ida. Though I had spoken to her over the phone many times and still exchanged Christmas cards after they moved to Canada, I never met her or even saw her. I suppose we were both too busy.

Jim Rogers and the Decca Corner Speaker

Voigt also designed a home constructors's horn, based on half the original Tractrix, and issued blueprints giving dimensions and instructions. When the wood was all assembled, one needed to lean it against a wall at exactly 45° and fill the narrow bottom end with a 1:1 sand cement mixture level with the lip. When set this made a hard smooth reflection surface to receive and re-direct the sound to the wide open end. It made an impressive improvement over the same driving unit in a cabinet or on a baffle.

Two years later, he issued a blueprint for making a bass chamber to fit the horn. This involved his quarter wave patent No 447749, so with this blueprint came a small numbered licence card to stick on to the finished loudspeaker. Once could buy further permits for 5 shillings each. This made it a real full-range speaker right down to organ pedal notes. These blueprints were issued in the years 1935–39 and most of us had to wait till after the war to make them.

I was so intrigued with Voigt's quarter wave bass chamber I decided to build one on my existing 3 foot square baffle with its 8 inch driving unit. This was done by adding a series of 10 inch wide panels edgewise around the driving unit and finally covering with another square of plywood. All joints had to be airtight. This transformed the sound and, demonstrated to the Organ Club loosely associated to our department in The Northern Polytechnic, created great excitement. It was compact enough to be portable and small enough for use indoors.

Another of Voigt's ideas was the need to make the sound come from an area much larger than a small hole in a box – his wide open window effect, which his corner horn did very well. By directing the speaker to a smooth solid wall and tilting it through a suitable angle so the reflected sound was not obstructed by the cabinet, I found it made the sound of an orchestra seem to be coming from a real three dimensional source. It has struck me since that some of the charm of Peter Walker's electrostatic speaker is the fact that the sound is launched into the room from several square feet of diaphragm. I even applied for a patent, No 673009.

I had by this time become very friendly with Jim Rogers and made him a 12 inch model, and I think he sold a few made by a good cabinet maker. He asked me if it could be scaled down to use a new 8 inch unit of outstanding performance that Wharfedale had just produced, so good in fact that I used one in a Voigt Corner Horn, until I'd saved enough to buy a real Voigt driving unit.

I sketched something out for Jim and he had a sample made by his cabinet maker and sent it to me to try out. It had to be the same height as the 12 inch model to get the correct quarter-wave frequency but by giving it a triangular shape, it tucked into its corner as a more acceptable domestic piece of furniture.

Paul Voigt was most interested in my efforts and in a letter he wrote during 1948 he introduced a Mr Mordaunt, who was looking for a new speaker design. Norman Mordaunt was working for Decca as their 'audio ear' and had a small private sideline making a very good speaker obviously inspired by Voigt's own Corner Horn. He was looking for something a bit cheaper, but wide range and better sound presentation than one hole in a box. He came to see me and found we had so many views in common so we were soon good friends.

He had come to see the 12 inch version, which is what would probably suit his requirements. The smaller one also interested him as, apart from power handling, it had a very similar performance. Then: may he take them home for assessment? Then: did I mind him taking them to the Decca laboratory as he was in the throes of changing his address and anyway the Decca lab would give them better surroundings.

Two days later, I had a phone call from Decca. Their chief engineer H F Schwarz wanted to see me urgently. It appeared that while Norman Mordaunt was trying out these speakers, he had happened to pass through that lab and was very struck by the sound, particularly the small design for Jim Rogers, so much so he wanted to buy it. So I had to explain it was a new model made by Rogers Developments to my design and I was giving it the finishing touches. Well, he persuaded Jim Rogers to give it up! Jim told me later it hadn't upset Rogers Developments as they had several other products in the pipeline.

Decca's financial people were very decent as I had no idea what it was worth. They offered me the choice of a lump sum or a royalty payment. My good friend Stan Kelly said take the offered lump sum. Though royalties may eventually give you a lot more, it will get frittered away as it arrives.

We'd just bought Colombie here in France with a large bank overdraft guaranteed by two very good friends. They took over and proceeded with my patent and I was able to reduce the overdraft and thank one of my good friends. I also insisted they paid Voigt a small royalty (although his master bass chamber patent was on the point of running out) as Paul was in dire straits with poor health and the difficulties of emigrating to Canada. I don't know how many they made, but we remained good friends and they went on to do very good work with gramophone records and pickups and also the Decca Navigator system.

Hi-Fi News went from strength to strength and home construction interest never flagged. Eventually Decca released the corner speaker design free to anyone making it for his own use, and *Hi-Fi News* produced the 'Five Speakers' booklet.

Every design described in that booklet is based on Voigt's acoustical work. What would we have done without Paul Voigt?

Percy Wilson: a gramophone man. *By Geoffrey Horn*

Percy Wilson's serious involvement with the gramophone began in his thirtieth year when he spent some £40, a considerable sum in the 1920s, on a handsome cabinet machine with internal horn. Born in Halifax on 8 March 1893, he remained the consummate Yorkshireman all his days, although he spent most of them in the south.

Leaving school, he went to Queen's College, Oxford to take his BA in 1915. The Great War was then raging and his mathematics and science degree earned him a job as a Naval Instructor and later Lecturer in Applied Mathematics at the Royal Naval College.

In 1919, now married, he became an Administrative Officer in The Board of Education where he remained until 1938 when, with another war imminent, he transferred to the Roads Department of The Ministry of Transport as Principal Assistant Secretary, his long career in the Civil Service ending in 1953. But, running in parallel with it, there was soon to be a second career with *The Gramophone*. He recounts in Gilbert Briggs's celebrated book of *Audio Biographies* (1961) how his early view of the inadequacies of the gramophone was completely upset by a record bought as a Christmas present for his mother-in-law in 1919. On it were Caruso, Galli-Curci, etc, singing extracts from *Lucia di Lammermoor* and *Rigoletto*. It 'just bowled me over'. He immediately started saving for that £40 machine.

The autumn of 1923 found him walking with his wife in Cheapside when he saw a copy of the third issue of *The Gramophone* in a music shop. Noting it was edited by Compton Mackenzie, he bought it, was greatly intrigued and wrote off for the first two issues. Sadly, issue number two was sold out, but in number three he had found that there was a continuing discussion about Needle Tracking Alignment and this intrigued Percy for, as he told me many years later, he had been over similar ground in his naval career. Apparently at some stage he had been required to produce formulae for the trajectory of the shells fired from the huge guns carried by our capital ships and this had proved to be an extremely daunting task pushing his considerable mathematical abilities to their limit. The similarities with needles working across non-radial transits of the disc immediately engaged his active brain.

His need to consult the missing second issue of the magazine took him one lunch hour to the editorial offices where he met Christopher Stone, the London Editor, who managed to find him a copy. It was the first of many visits and soon he was able to tell him that he had worked out mathematically the conditions for minimum tracking error. Stone immediately invited Percy to turn it into a form suitable for publishing and the result appeared in the issues for September and October 1924, running into six pages with a fair complement of mathematics which, although not difficult, would startle the modern reader. It also startled some of the readers of 1924 who had not experienced scientific theory applied to playing records before. It could be said that Percy was instrumental – with this and his subsequent writings on many allied subjects, and not least his remarkable ability to think in terms of the future – in causing this burgeoning industry to take a much more professional approach to design. Those two articles in particular, with their subsequent additions, are classics and as valid today in the dying years of pickup arms as they were then, a memorial which has far outlasted its author.

Those early day saw the creation of many gramophone societies whose members included a fair sprinkling of highly-placed professional people from all walks of life who found relaxation in music. The value of the tracking articles was not lost on them and resulted in invitations for Percy to talk at their meetings. In this way he made many influential friends who would help him progress the future of the gramophone over its growth years between the wars. A number of them persuaded him that his £40 gramophone had not been the wisest buy and he exchanged it for an HMV 'Schools' model with an external flared horn and four-spring motor. Together they experimented with tuning the 'Exhibition' sound-box and running melted wax down the joints in the 'flower petal' horn to prevent rattles. As he was to write, it became 'easily the best gramophone I heard in those days'. A rival was the machine later used by Compton Mackenzie, which had been built by another part-time enthusiast,

C L Balmain, then Deputy Controller of the Stationary Office; a note in the December 1924 issue invited interested readers to visit the Frith Street office to hear it. This ingenious model used a conical horn and sound-box which was arranged to float radially across the record on two open mercury baths – a material since known to be such a deadly poison that dire warnings are even packed with thermometers in case one is broken. How did we survive these dangers?

The alignment protractor and exponential horns

Percy became a regular contributor to the magazine and added the famous Alignment Protractor (March 1925) to his inventions; he was also aware of side pressure (or skating force) and suggested a simple remedy in the same issue. In November 1924, Christopher Stone proposed the setting up of an Expert Committee to advise on technical matters and this was easily formed from gramophone society friends, later joined in electrical recording days by more anonymous members from the National Physical Laboratory. Discussion had taken place about the shape of horns and George Webb, a member of the Committee and master builder with a huge collection of recording machinery, as well as a fine engineering workshop, had suggested 'exponential'. Percy was thus inspired to investigate the theory of horns, a neglected subject left to the ingenuity of the makers of megaphones, trumpets and trombones. By the end of 1925 he had derived formulae for the curve based on the assumption that the expanding wavefronts were spherical and should pass the horn contour at a right angle. The method was explained in *Modern Gramophones* written with G W Webb [Cassell, London, 1929].

Making one was a different matter but a visit to a pattern maker provided a wooden former some five feet long on which layer after layer of parcel tape was pasted, dried out and varnished. The resulting horn was then mounted on a Balmain carriage so that it could be floated on the mercury in place of the original. The Expert Committee decided it should be demonstrated to Mackenzie, then living on Jethou, one of the smaller Channel Islands. They took it down in the late summer of 1926 and, as Percy often gleefully narrated, completed the journey in a small boat with Percy in the stern holding all five feet of the precious horn between his knees. (Incidentally, Compton MacKenzie's wife Faith took a photograph of the team in the boat and captioned it 'Percy arrives with the horn'. It was not printed.)

It so happened that Mackenzie had just taken delivery of a new HMV machine fitted with the No. 4 sound-box which he had reluctantly found superior to his old Balmain. Choosing a Sousa march, one of the latest electrical recordings, they used the No. 4 on the new horn and floated it on Mackenzie's Balmain; the resulting sound was a revelation, a complete walkover and full justification of Percy's design. Back in England modifications were put in hand to make adaptors for the 'Schools' and other machines and a firm with expertise in papier mache (Scientific Supply Stores) engaged to market it as the Wilson Panharmonic Horn. He later told me that as his colleagues had been so involved his Yorkshire canniness deserted him and he asked for no share of the profits, even when competing firms such as EMG and Bond used the design.

However, in the gramophone world the arrival of electrical recording and reproduction was beginning to make its mark. Percy was well aware that if any attempt was to be made to cover a full range of sounds, down to the lowest notes, the horn would have to be large and he commissioned an eight-foot straight horn of square section which exactly fitted the upper half of his hall doorway; it could be raised and lowered by a system of pulleys and ropes. This apparently produced a superb sound for its day but we have no record of his wife's comments when she had to bend double to pass under it. Allowing for the fact that doorways in older houses were at least three feet wide we can calculate that it would have maintained full (high) efficiency down to at least 100 Hz.

The need for ever lower frequencies spelt the eventual death of the horn for domestic purposes but there were one or two ingenious variants by Paul Voigt in England and Klipsch in America.

Percy however was to have one last fling: early in the 1930s the Science Museum in London decided to install a state-of-the-art wireless receiver and invited him to design a huge horn loudspeaker which would be fixed to propagate through a seven-foot square hole cut in the partition wall between two sections of the museum. This 27-foot-long monster was hung from the ceiling and provided with a Western Electric type 555 driver, a new and very advanced moving-coil design with a two-inch aluminium dome diaphragm fed through a phase-aligned coupling to the one-inch horn throat. I recall as a boy hearing this magnificent effort which was fed from a receiver of considerable complexity and about the size of an old-fashioned telephone kiosk! It was switched on to the BBC London Regional programme, broadcasting from the new Brookmans Park transmitter at three o'clock every afternoon, and it was startling to hear the completely natural voice of the announcer sounding throughout the large hall.

The change to electrical reproduction made considerable organisational demands on the technical team and during the latter part of 1929 Christopher Stone decided to appoint Percy's younger brother Gilbert as Technical Editor. However, Percy continued as Technical Adviser and contributed a worthy series of articles which soon acquired the generic title 'Technical Talk'; they still make fascinating reading and contain many pointers to future developments which have since come to pass. Long-playing records and the possibility of stereophonic reproduction were among the subjects discussed. It was also the age of the radiogram and the annual autumn exhibitions at Radiolympia, but one common invention had really set the stage on which the whole industry performed and is still produced by the million today: the moving-coil cone loudspeaker.

Wartime and the LP record

War was declared in September 1939, in the middle of that year's Radiolympia. Much of the emphasis was on television, which had been inaugurated in November 1936 but was now to close down for the duration of the war – although not before the TV sound-channel had been used to broadcast the Promenade Concerts from London's Queen's Hall, giving a tantalising foretaste of the quality of sound to come. Percy and Gilbert ceased their activities for *The Gramophone* and technical comment in a much slimmed-down magazine was undertaken by Geoffrey Howard-Sorrell who held the reins until 1953, thus covering the important post-war years and the introduction of the long-playing record.

Percy, then with the Ministry of Transport, had a very busy time during the war but news of developments in audio and recording reached him from America via his friendship with David Sarnoff, later President of RCA. He learnt of the successful tests of FM broadcasting and of longer playing records – an early application of the latter took the form of the 'V Disc' which was issued to US forces and used a flexible base material to avoid breakage, and would later lead to the vinyl LP. Not much news emerged from the UK although progress in recording was being made, both to increase the frequency range for sound identification and in recording on acetate for broadcasting. However, informed listeners became aware that something novel was being used in Germany and at the end of hostilities the development of tape recording was revealed.

Retiring from the Civil Service in 1953 enabled Percy to relieve Geoffrey Howard-Sorrell of the burden he had carried so well and return as Technical Editor. Wartime pressures had resulted in developments in all fields of electronics and many people now found themselves immersed in and intrigued by the subject. Their wartime training, and the vast amount of surplus equipment sold off at ridiculous prices, encouraged an expansion of home electronics and as a result self-built amplifiers and other gear such as the emerging tape recorder proliferated. At the same time, pre-war manufacturers, now with enlarged wartime facilities, came back into the field and produced some excellent products, such as the famous Decola. Percy, although *au fait* with electrical matters following his university years, never had the same inclination to involve himself in electronics; to him it was a means to an end. Although very much a hands-on man and inveterate experimenter, it was the mechanical side which had the greatest appeal. Therefore he had the foresight to recruit a number of people to help with reviewing equipment. This was complicated because they could not be directly employed by any particular manufacturer but fortunately there were a few consultants such as the late John Gilbert of the Northern Polytechnic and Stanley Kelly.

In 1934 Percy had been involved with an early form of long-playing record required for Talking Books for the Blind: these had a duration of 24$\frac{1}{2}$ minutes per side at 24rpm. However, the stock held by the Royal National Institute for the Blind became unmanageable so in the early 1950s it was decided to change over to tape. Percy was again one of the team and helped to develop an early cassette player using half-inch tape travelling between two reels, one atop the other with 24 tracks giving 12 hours duration, later extended to 20 hours. This was probably the first cassette conception and offered an easily-handled and readily transported medium. (It was described in *Wireless World* for January 1954).

In the late 1950s Percy came to live in Oxford with his second wife and took a house in Headington. In 1949, on the other side of the city in Summertown, Philip Tandy and I had taken over a Radio and TV business which had been pioneered by my father. He had started up in the front room of his house in 1922 and two years later had been so successful that a shop front was put in and a proper business established, one of the first wireless-only shops in the country. We made an early decision to specialize in the growing field of high-fidelity reproduction; it had always been a major interest and hobby of mine since boyhood – Philip's was music and 'ham' radio. My pre-war education was as an electronics man, initially with what was then the Post Office Engineering Department. Together we were innocents in the world of retailing but enthusiasm won the day.

Eventually, we met Percy who was very pleased to discover a shared interest, and particularly to gain access to our workshop which was equipped with a good selection of test equipment. Entering with a carton containing some manufacturer's amplifier or whatever, he became a familiar sight, accompanied by his inevitable, 'Would you run your rule over this?'. Not infrequently in those days of hopeful cottage industries, and even large and established manufacturers trying to jump on this promising new bandwagon, the rule could not be made to fit and Percy, apprised by telephone, would come over in the evening to get the details which he would relay back to the manufacturer, often with suggestions for improvement. It was always his policy to do this and not publish a negative review. As he said, a bad review could put a small firm out of business when their next product might well have been a corker.

Percy became known to industry personnel on both sides of the Atlantic for he was a frequent visitor to the USA, where two of his academic sons held Professorships at State Colleges. Whilst visiting he joined the Audio Engineering Society, then a purely American group of which he was later to be a founder member of the British Section. He had the rare gift in this calling of being able to keep a secret so that he and I were often privy to developments months, sometimes years, before they became commercial. Typical examples were visits to Arthur Haddy at the Decca studios in West Hampstead where we heard early examples of stereo LPs, at first using a supersonic difference signal, a project later abandoned in favour of the Blumlein patent. Early work by Peter Walker on electrostatic loudspeakers was also fascinating.

Early in 1957 Percy passed me a book which he had been sent for review, and asked if I would like to read it and make a few notes for him as he was going away and was pressed for time. I have forgotten exactly what it was but I duly did as asked. When he eventually collected it he read my notes and proclaimed, 'You can write'. I replied, 'Yes I know, they taught me at school', but this did nothing for his Yorkshire sense of humour for he carried on, 'I shall publish it just as it is'. Thus began my totally unexpected but long and friendly association with *The Gramophone*.

Percy retired in 1966, but for some years had become engrossed with the problem of LP groove contamination by dust and airborne deposits of sticky particles from both domestic and outside sources. His development of an automatic washing and scrubbing arm with nylon bristles entering the groove, followed by suction drying, has since been incorporated in a number of commercial machines. However, none of them used his rather impractical but ingenious silent sucker, a suction pump in a wooden box buried in his front garden with a long length of tubing passing through a hole in the window frame. Unwary visitors could be seen nervously looking around for the source of the chugging noise.

But this was not quite the end of Percy's involvement with audio. He and his family were Spiritualists and indeed for many years he had been Managing Director of the Psychic Press Ltd. As a result of this connection he became involved as a consultant in a number of unique sound reinforcement projects – both in major hotels and also in Spiritualist churches – in all of which I was also associated.

At the end of this varied and distinguished career Percy finally did accept retirement, and went to live in a Red Cross home. He presented the Common Room with his record collection and, as you might guess, installed a high-fidelity gramophone. He died on 1 May, 1977, aged 84.

Raymond Cooke remembers Gilbert Briggs. *By Ken Kessler*

One of the first names mentioned when Gene Pitts suggested a series of interviews with British audio legends was Raymond Cooke, founder and Life President of KEF. In late 1994, I met with Raymond at the KEF factory in Maidstone, Kent, for what was to be a series of conversations about the history of KEF. We started with Raymond's own introduction to the industry, working for Gilbert Briggs at Wharfedale. Raymond, who had been ill, seemed fitter than when I saw him the year before; he was keen to tell me tales – many of which will never see print – and suggested we meet again. Sadly, Raymond Cooke passed away on the 19 March 1995, so it turned out to be the last interview he ever gave.

Ken Kessler: 'Before you created KEF, you worked with the great Gilbert Briggs of Wharfedale...'
Raymond Cooke: '...and he was great.'
KK: 'Was he your mentor at the beginning?'
RC: 'He was my mentor in the commercial sense but not in the technical sense; Briggs was not an engineer and he wasn't a scientist. We got together to complement each other. He had very clear ideas about business. That isn't to say he was the world's greatest businessman or a tower strength and expertise in the boardroom. But the things that he opined to me during the time that we worked together still come to mind and they're still true.

'For instance, he was not a marketing man. But he once said to me, "The public confused buys nothing". And of course he was absolutely right. But what was even more extraordinary was how many of the big companies in our industry failed to heed that simple rule. When, for instance, the Japanese went into four different four-channel systems in the 1970s, they all lost. And look at the number of completely false starts that people like Sony have made. You'd think that they'd have brighter people on their boards to prevent that. But he was always very clear. Every proposition and every move made by his company was examined from the point of view of how does it look from outside.'

KK: 'What kind of a company was Wharfedale when you worked there?

RC: 'Very solid. It had a high reputation, but it was quite small. When I joined, the turnover was less than half-a-million pounds a year, total. But the global reputation that he founded was so well done that in its restrictive way it was highly focused at the prime people. He very quickly made friends with C G McProud and it was through contacts like McProud that he came to take his books to the States. He eventually arranged the distribution through British Industries Corporation. And that's how we got started; I eventually joined him in editing the books, as technical editor.

'When I joined, he was running the firm himself – head boss, production boss, leaflet writer. He was doing all the things in that firm absolutely right. Anybody who's got anywhere in the hi-fi business since, be it in Japan or be it in the USA, they've always done it his way. I joined to take off his back the technical design. Subsequently I was able to take over other things. When he reached 65 and was getting rather tired of the whole thing, ultimately I was the one who'd go off and see distributors. I took over the advertising. We were already writing the books; then he gave me the leaflets to do. I had a remarkable, unintended apprenticeship. When I eventually decided to quit the Rank Organisation after its takeover [of Wharfedale] and come and start here, I already had far more experience than I could possibly have had in the ordinary way in another industry.

'How I came to leave Wharfedale...? I could see high fidelity wasn't going to get anywhere unless a lot more science was applied. Gilbert Briggs was a bit suspicious of science. Or, shall we say, of scientists. He once wrote of the folly of employing technical people at the head of things because they tend to go after brilliant technical solutions rather than the practical, commercial solution. He had seen many firms go down that way. It was great working with him because although he wasn't always right in all directions, he was right more than most.'

KK: 'So what was Wharfedale's technological state at the time?'

RC: 'When I joined them, extremely conventional. Gilbert Briggs had designed the drivers himself and they were all paper-coned. Big magnets and so forth. The things worked well, they had high efficiency. Their best system was the three-way, sand-filled corner enclosure. The thing really worked very well. But his claim to fame was that he embarked on a series of lecture-demonstrations all over the world in which the sound of live players was compared with recorded sound. The first one was in Canada, in a university hall, then St George's Hall in Bradford, and then in 1955 or '56 he hired the Festival Hall. You could hire it for a day for a £140, would you believe, complete with all the stuff.'

KK: 'Was Wharfedale one of the most important British makes then?'

RC: 'It was neck-and-neck with Goodmans.'

KK: 'You started to want to put your own stamp on a product early on?'

RC: 'Yes. It seemed to me, being a scientist, that when I looked into sound reproduction – which wasn't my subject; I was originally a chemist and then an electronics man – if only one could bring scientific procedures even to the experimental work, like listening tests, and then to the production work, we ought to be able to produce a better loudspeaker, smaller and cheaper. I think I was the first person to realise that you didn't have to have a 15in loudspeaker to get down to 20Hz.

'I wrote it up for Briggs on one occasion, that we ought to be able to get that response from a 10in loudspeaker provided that the resonant frequency of the 10in driver was sufficiently low. And he wrote back that while what I was saying might be theoretically correct, he wouldn't have anything to do with it practically because a 10in loudspeaker would very rapidly go out of alignment and get its voice coil rubbing. And I wrote back that that is true if you think of it in terms of today's suspensions. But if the suspension is redesigned and made in other materials like nylon it will be possible. This correspondence goes back to 1950-51, before Villchur.'

KK: 'Your remarks about the need for more science surprise me because certain of your contemporaries, ones who are leery of subjectivists, imply that all of the designing back then was pure science.'

RC: 'No. Very little science.'

KK: 'Wild'n'woolly, seat-of-the-pants...'

RC: 'The only people who were into science were Villchur when he came along and Klipsch before that. Most of the other people who were great names in hi-fi in the States, they were just fumblers, they worked on a cut-and-try basis.'

KK: 'But the BBC was so influential in the commercial sector, and the dominance of *Wireless World*...'

RC: 'That was later. Even in the 1940s when I started into it, all development work was done subjectively. One cut a hole, had a listen, cut a bigger hole, had another listen and so on. There were very few people around in the trade who understood how it worked.'

'We got to the point where I took out a number of patents on enclosure design as it was very clear that I wasn't going to get anywhere with drive unit design. The firm couldn't afford the cost of the tooling and every new design needed a diaphragm mould and die-casting plus the magnet. I then finally came up against it in 1959 [after Rank acquired Wharfedale]. It was staring me in the face that we needed to do something about diaphragms.

'Rank were trying to get into the record business and they also had some not well-defined ambitions in radio and TV. They could see a future in domestic entertainment. The notion was that, if they could buy a wholesaler, they'd have the whole thing down pat. Complete vertical integration. So they bought a wholesaler. Wharfedale had been a very successful, long established firm run by its founders but the whole thing was beginning to crumble.

'In 1960, I thought, "I don't know what I'm going to do here". I was a director of Wharfedale but one never got to talk to the people in London. I wasn't being introduced to Rank and couldn't speak to the new bosses. It became clear that Briggs wasn't anxious to leave; on the other hand, he had got to 70 so he wasn't scintillating or looking to the future. He was just trying to keep his little company together for the benefit of the people who worked the for a long time. There was no point in my talking about new ideas.'

KK: 'Was it hard creating a hi-fi company in 1961?'

RC: 'Because my relationships in the industry were so good, I had no problems starting up. At a meeting in Paris, at the Festival du Son, John Gilbert of *The Gramophone* said, 'I'll go on record for the British press if you decide to start on your own. Call a meeting to explain your product and we'll all be quite happy to take tea.' And I did just that the following November and everybody came. In droves. Percy Wilson [Technical Editor of *The Gramophone*] said, "We'll support you – glad to see a new face". They were getting a bit tired of some of the older faces when they didn't seem to be doing anything.

'We formed the company [KEF] legally in September, 1961. We finally managed to get assembly started at the end of October and managed to put together at least two of everything we intended to offer. A three-way system in a thin box, the same again in a four cubic foot cabinet which had much better bass, a line source speaker and another was a very thin, flat speaker to go against the wall.

'We organised the meeting for the whole day. In the morning we set up and in the afternoon everybody arrived, the press, wholesalers, that sort of thing. Ralph West actually took over the demonstration and we went on through the evening. By the end of that day I knew we had no market in the UK at all. One by one, the wholesalers said, "We need another loudspeaker line like a hole in the head".'

KK: 'Too many brands even in the early Sixties?'

RC: 'Too much product, too few sales. And so in the end I got on my bike and literally went off to Europe. And after a week in Europe I came back and I knew I'd got a business.'

The gestation of *Hi-Fi News*. By Stanley Kelly

The late 1940s, the War behind us and a brave new world to conquer. Technical development in electronics during the previous five years offered undreamed-of opportunities – Arthur Haddy's Decca *ffrr* system of very wide frequency range recording; the advent of vinyl records (remember, 33⅓ rpm records were used in the earliest 'talking films' *circa* 1926); very low playing weight (10gm) wide frequency range pickups; low distortion amplifiers, 0.1% THD designs from Walker, Williamson and Leak; and Tannoy and Wharfedale loudspeakers, to name a few pioneers.

The problem was dissemination of up-to-date relevant information; the IEE and Brit IRE were professional bodies with sound entertainment very low on their list of priorities. There was, however, one organisation, the British Sound Recording Association, always affectionately known as the BSRA, founded in 1936 by Donald Aldous, and revived after the War, which specialised in Audio.

We used to meet monthly at the Royal Society of Arts in London, and members gave lectures in their own specialist subject. These were written up in the monthly journal, which became the *sine qua non* for latest developments in audio, later translated to the euphemism high fidelity, reduced now (in substance as well as name) to hi-fi.

The highlight of the year was the second week in May when the Society held its Annual Convention at the Waldorf Hotel. Apart from the excellent dinner (and concomitantly, the speeches) we could sit and talk in the lounge until dawn. Selected manufacturers of high quality audio equipment were invited to demonstrate their wares on the platform in the Hall (15 minutes allocated to each demonstration).

It was all British, alfresco, and good clean fun; parallel was the Exhibition – trestle tables covered with green baize on which the latest technical delicacies were displayed. It did not meet with the approval of the large scale domestic radio manufacturers and importers (who were not invited). In the mid-1950s they mounted the opposition, the Audio Fair, held initially at the Russell Hotel, which by sheer financial muscle decimated the technically superior BSRA Show and led ultimately to the demise of the Association.

Where does *Hi-Fi News* come into all this? I believe it was at the 1952 Show when I met Miles Henslow – he came to my stand, placed a pile of magazines on the table and suggested that I would improve the tone of the exhibition by distributing them (free, of course) to any misguided individual who deigned to look at my wares.

At that time he was publisher, editor, and distributor of *Record News*. He occupied the top floor of 99 Mortimer Street, London, part office and part living accommodation which he shared with two Dalmatian bitches (a few years later he gave my wife one of Portia's pups, but that's another story). We became good friends, I contributed the odd article on sound reproduction, usually as the result of a phone call: 'Stan, I'm in urgent need of 500 words to fill a page!' and the equipment reviews.

By 1956, the audio industry was expanding rapidly – stereo, magnetic tape recorders, good quality amplifiers and loudspeakers, and the possibility of FM were leading to a very effervescent and lucrative market. There was an urgent need for a specialist magazine, and early in 1956, Miles came along to Enfield in his battered Bentley and told me of his ideas for *Hi-Fi News*. My wife and I were enthusiastic, and I agreed to act as technical adviser.

The next few years were hectic. Our basic idea was for a down-to-earth technical magazine which would reflect the state of the art in practical terms understandable by the lay public; we would produce technical articles describing in detail the design and use of audio equipment and components, and our reviews would be objective (rather than the present highly subjective) and capable of independent verification.

All the early contributions were written by practising engineers – James Moir, Ralph West, Rex Baldock, to name but three – and our aim was to educate the public to make rational choices when buying equipment and subsequently to obtain best performance by correct installation and operation. I know we made a coherent team.

Perhaps my most cogent memory of those early days was our thrice weekly management meeting (Monday, Wednesday, and Friday) at 11am. Miles had a small 'fridge filled with half-bottles of Taittinger, one of which was split between us to provide the sustenance for the battle ahead!

From little acorns...

2. The Henslow Era

'Miles Henslow was a born bluffer. When launching the magazine, he'd hired a chauffeur-driven Rolls in which to visit a printer, in order to establish his financial probity despite being broke at the time.' **John Crabbe**

My time at *Hi-Fi News*: February 1959 to February 1961 *by John Borwick*

Like many others, I welcomed Miles Henslow's brave decision to launch a hi-fi magazine in June 1956. The growth of high fidelity as a hobby, and as an industry, had begun around 1948 with many ex-servicemen, like myself, keen to combine their recently acquired knowledge of electronics with a love of music. But things took several years to hot up.

In the event, Miles' timing was excellent. The first London Audio Fair took place at the Washington Hotel just two months earlier. Visitors could examine and listen to a lot of exciting new products, and develop a deeper interest in high fidelity sound. Gilbert Briggs of Wharfedale had given the first of his lecture/demonstrations of live-versus-recorded sound in the Royal Festival Hall on November 1st, 1954. Since 1953, the record industry had gone over to stereo-tape master recording and the fruits of this were rumoured to be a new stereo LP format (major issues would begin in October 1958). The BBC had begun VHF/FM broadcasting in the previous year. All this produced a rush of designs for stereo tuners, then stereo pickup cartridges, amplifiers and speakers (in pairs).

My own first contact with *HFN* arose from a reader's letter in the October 1957 issue. This suggested that 'coloration' in bass reflex loudspeakers was the cause of a nuisance to neighbours. I submitted a reply (November 1957) pointing out that walls transmitted bass more easily than treble, room absorption soaked up treble and speakers radiated bass indiscriminately in all directions. Therefore, 'every extension of the reproduced sound down the scale increases the nuisance value to neighbours, even if the response characteristic is of unimpeachable flatness'. (Incidentally, that reader was A G Watling with whom I later struck up a friendship, persuading him to contribute a series of very funny cartoons to *HFN*).

Miles then asked me to come in to see him. This was easy for me to do, as I was working at the BBC as Programme Operations Instructor, with my training studio just across the road from Broadcasting House. The *HFN* office was a couple of hundred yards nearer Oxford Circus in Mortimer Street. Indeed Miles could often be seen striding past the Broadcasting House entrance with his two large dalmations.

Miles was all charm, and persuaded me to write a series of articles starting immediately. We fixed on a subject near to my heart, 'Microphone Balance'. I had started in the BBC as a programme/balance engineer but was later promoted to teach the techniques to others, first at the BBC Engineering Training School in Evesham, and then in London. In fact I had recently written the BBC's 240-page 'bible' on the subject, 'Programme Operations Manual', for issue to all programme engineers.

That first series of articles ran from February to May 1958, and was immediately followed by one-off pieces on 'Microphone Mixing' (June) and 'Can Television Sound Be Hi-Fi?' (August), Then came a series on 'Hi-Fi Physics' (September 1958 to May 1959) and at least one article in every issue for the next two years.

Around the middle of 1958, I was beginning to think of leaving the BBC. I had got the writing bug, I was Editor of the *Journal of the British Sound Recording Association* and had offers of numerous freelance jobs, occasionally as recording producer/engineer. Teaching studio techniques was less exciting than doing it and, worse still, it was rumoured that I would soon become Assistant Head of the Programme Operations Department – sitting behind a desk!

I dropped one of the aforementioned articles into Miles's office and, after some conversation about the BBC, he pushed open the door into an adjoining room and said, 'There you are, John. A job's waiting for you'. After a bit, I agreed to become 'Technical Editor', though the BBC insisted that I work out several months' notice. My name finally appeared on the *HFN* masthead in the February 1959 issue.

'Sound'

When word got round that I was leaving the BBC, all sorts of things began to happen. Most interesting was an invitation from Features Producer Marguerite Cutforth for me to present a new fortnightly programme on Network Three with a repeat a week later. (BBC policy discouraged studio staff from becoming presenters – but now that I was leaving…) The series was to be called 'Sound' and commence in January 1959.

This chimed in nicely with my move to *HFN*. The magazine brought me into contact with all the leading lights in the audio and recording world and I was soon calling them into the studio for interviews, talks and discussions. I had only been installed at *HFN* about a week when Miles returned from lunch with an amiable gentleman who seemed very interested to meet me. Miles made the introductions then said to me, 'John, this is the man who talked me into offering you a job'. They both chuckled and then explained that the stranger was a psychologist who could analyse a person's character by studying his handwriting. Miles had shown him something I had written, and he had given me a very positive report. I never did find out any more details.

Learning quickly

I was properly thrown in at the deep end and obliged to take on all aspects of the magazine's preparation. Tasks like handling news items, knocking out paragraphs on new products and dealing with readers' letters were easy enough – though not very exciting. Chasing up feature articles from existing contributors and seeking out new ones was more fun.

As a treat, and even before I moved into the *HFN* office, I was able to take on some key feature commissions myself. One early assignment meant travelling to the Brussels World Fair (April-October, 1958) in the company of the Chief Executive of Goodmans Loudspeakers, living in a posh hotel and having a free run of the Fair for three days. Goodmans had supplied hundreds of loudspeakers for public address and a unique high quality 'background music' system. Beautiful 'Gardens of the Four Seasons' had been laid out, with speakers in all the flower beds so that visitors could stroll to the sound of Vivaldi's 'The Four Seasons' (long before Nigel Kennedy made it popular) and other 'early music' pieces.

I had a pass to all the exhibits and happily jumped the long queues. I spent some time in the main control room having the whole system explained to me and this formed the basis for an *HFN* article (November 1958). Ironically, I had gone to the Fair for a day at my own expense some time before the Goodmans invitation and seen only a few of the exhibits.

Page make-up

A major monthly task was editing all the received 'copy' and sending it to the printer for typesetting and return. In contrast to today's slick desktop publishing techniques, our methods were primitive and time consuming. Once the optimum number of pages was decided for each issue, by means of a sliding scale relating the number of editorial pages that could be 'paid for' by the expected number of advertisements, we got the printer to supply a stapled 'dummy' of blank pages.

We would then cut up proof copies of the ads and editorial illustrations and texts. The latter were supplied as long galley proofs; the diagrams and photographs arrived as inch-thick blocks of wood carrying metal images.

These were all allocated to pages in the dummy and stuck into place using a grim jam-jar of wallpaper paste and an equally mucky paintbrush.

We were always in a mad rush, being held up by late supply of articles, illustrations or ads. Often I had to unpick pages if an extra ad turned up, which had to go in regardless, or change around articles, which were shorter or longer than planned. Last of all, Miles habitually delayed sitting down to write his editorial until the very last minute – with the printer's messenger already waiting downstairs. It was not unusual for some eleventh-hour crisis to develop which meant that I had to travel out to the printer and supervise changes on the production line itself.

The Tape Recorder

Only a few weeks after I started work at *HFN*, I arrived one morning to find Miles grinning from ear to ear and holding a tray with a bottle of champagne and two glasses. He poured, handed me one glass and raised the other high saying, 'Let's drink to the new magazine, *The Tape Recorder*. We've got about ten days to get it out.'

I knew that he had been infuriated by the recent launch of a magazine called *Tape Recording*. He hated the idea of a rival publication dealing with audio matters, which until then had been an *HFN* monopoly. What I didn't know at the time was that he'd consulted his solicitor to check that it was legally possible to bring out a magazine with a title so close to that of the other.

I became Technical Editor of both magazines, and our scramble to produce *HFN* was frantically redoubled. I wrote large slabs of the new mag, resorting to a number of pseudonyms – the funniest of which was 'Jack Forage'. Miles was finishing the page make-up and called to me next door, 'What shall we call you this time?' As a joke, I replied 'Jack Porridge', as a reference to my Scottish background. Miles either misheard me or deliberately translated 'porridge' into 'forage'.

We both chased up BBC colleagues and other recording personalities to get the first *Tape Recorder* into the shops for February 1959. Miles had also published a *Hi-Fi Yearbook* since 1956 and this added another ingredient to the workload.

Equipment Reviews

The team of superb equipment reviewers when I joined *HFN* were by then household names – at least in hi-fi households. They included great characters like Stanley Kelly, Ralph West and R S (Bob) Roberts, on the masthead as Technical Advisers. I became friendly with all of them, and with George Tillett, Alan Tutchings and B J (Bert) Webb. My duties were to approach manufacturers and importers for the loan of interesting new products and farm these out to the reviewers. Sometimes I would go along to see how the tests were carried out and contribute my own comments on the subjective sound quality. I also took products home with me for private listening. We reviewed many key designs that really raised hi-fi standards to new heights. I remember with affection and not a little awe the first SME 3009 and 3012 pickup arms, the Decca *ffss* pickup arm and cartridge, the Quad ELS electrostatic loudspeaker and Quad 22 stereo control unit, the Garrard 301 turntable and a unique, though short-lived, heart-shaped tape magazine deck, Tannoy Dual Concentric loudspeakers and the Cecil E Watts Dustbug.

I reviewed various accessories. One of these was called the Stereophoner. It was said to be based on an idea by the famous German conductor Hermann Scherchen and claimed to produce a stereo effect from mono sources (disc, tape or radio). Its advertisement modestly claimed, 'It's the greatest advance of all time in the realm of reproduced sound'. It consisted of an opaque plastic block containing a 'secret' circuit, with a single pair of terminals for the mono input and two pairs of 'stereo' terminals for connecting to spaced loudspeakers.

I didn't like the effect, which seemed merely to split high and low frequencies. The importer stormed into the *HFN* office and insisted that I go with him for a proper demonstration. I did this but was in no way persuaded on the device's effectiveness. Indeed the man weakened his case by playing a recording of a string quartet on which the device caused the cello to swim from left to right, making me feel ill.

My view was strongly corroborated a few days later when the stereo expert Bernard Shelley, accompanied by the actor Edmund Purdom, called at my house. They agreed that any stereo effect was spurious and took the Stereophoner away for tests. They diagnosed that the device was a simple bass/treble crossover filter and smashed it open to reveal a very basic combination of capacitors and resistors to send high frequencies to the left output (violins?) and low frequencies to the right (cellos?). Bernard Shelley then contributed an excellent article to *HFN* (July 1959) describing his technique using oscilloscope displays to examine phase variations in stereo signals.

'Belshazzar's Feast'

Miles and I often discussed ways to introduce musical topics to *HFN* and decided that I should arrange to 'sit in' on some record company sessions.

One prize example came when EMI agreed that I could attend the recording of William Walton's *Belshazzar's Feast* in its favourite recording venue for large-scale works, London's Kingsway Hall. The senior producer Walter Legge was in charge and his wife, the soprano Elisabeth Schwarzkopf, also attended. I was flattered when they remembered me from my BBC days. I had been the balance engineer for one of her recorded recitals with a small orchestra at the Edinburgh Festival. Walter Legge sat with me in the BBC control room, carefully watching my positioning of the microphones and listening to the balance. He was uncharacteristically reticent, but I suspect he secretly wanted to 'interfere'.

The composer conducted the Philharmonia Orchestra and Chorus, with soloist Donald Bell. Informality contrasted with the normal concert decorum. There was a profusion of shirtsleeves and braces, and a great deal of good-natured backchat on all sides. The recording occupied four evenings, with a series of short 'takes'. The score was not followed in sequence but with passages grouped together which demanded the Chorus, the soloist or special instruments. The recorded 'takes' were carefully monitored to ensure that tempi, tonal balance and acoustic balance were maintained.

Unusually, because stereo LPs were just beginning to become viable alongside their mono counterparts, the engineers were recording in both mono and stereo simultaneously. There were separate arrays of microphones and separate control rooms, between which I was able to walk freely.

Sir William and Walter Legge made a final selection of the best 'takes' on the stereo tapes at Abbey Road a few days later. I was allowed to attend this process and to follow the tapes and the marked-up score to the editing room. When a final version was completed, the mono tapes were similarly spliced together. I later watched the transfer-to-disc operation and my description of the whole sequence of events was published in the December 1959 *HFN*. The mono LP [33CX 1679] was released early in 1960 and the stereo equivalent [SAX 2319] a few months later; the CD number is EMI 5 65004-2.

Changes in fashion

During a nostalgic browse through these early *HFN* issues, I was struck by two important differences between the magazine then and now. First, there were numerous home construction articles with full circuit diagrams, layout sketches and detailed instructions. Notable examples were the Rex Baldock design for a unique 'numbers' VHF/FM tuner (May–July, 1959), sundry loudspeakers and amplifiers, as well as a condenser microphone (August 1959), multichannel electronic mixer (December 1959) and 20 watt amplifier (March 1961), all by Reginald Williamson – no relation to the famous D T N Williamson.

We even published articles on soldering and ran advertisements for solder, soldering irons and do-it-yourself hi-fi kits. Clearly, early hi-fi enthusiasts were keen to roll their sleeves up and build their own audio gear to obtain true high quality sound at a fraction of the price of off-the-shelf units. Sadly, the speedy advance of solid-state circuitry, miniaturisation and digital complexity has almost killed off this aspect of the hobby.

The other surprise was the extent to which tape recorders, tape and even microphones featured in the editorial and advertisement pages. Home recording, and outdoor recording of birdsong, etc, were very popular at that time. Clubs were formed all over the country and I produced for EMI a set of open-reel tapes with booklets explaining the basic techniques.

Record News
Miles Henslow had been publishing a handsome and very readable record review magazine called *Record News* for about six years before he launched *Hi-Fi News*. So the latter omitted this feature. However, he found it hard to keep *Record News* going. The record companies tended to favour the powerful *Gramophone*, which had enjoyed a virtual monopoly since its launch back in 1923, when placing advertisements or sending out records for review.

Therefore, in his Editorial in the July 1959 *HFN,* he announced an amalgamation of the two journals with effect from the August issue. The combined magazine drew favourable comments but just over a year later Miles had to 'admit defeat' and drop the Records section. (Later, in 1962, John Crabbe would persuade Miles to allow a few reviews of technically-excellent records. The subsequent history of music reviewing in *Hi-Fi News* is told in another chapter by Christopher Breunig.)

Signing off
Around January 1961, I began to think of leaving *HFN*. I had many attractive offers of alternative types of work, including books and recording, which I could run from the comfort of home. I couldn't decide how to tell Miles until one evening when we had decided to work through after hours on pasting up a new 100-page book that I had written based on some of my *HFN* articles. We worked on *Hi-Fi for Beginners* steadily for about two hours, then went for dinner to Miles's favourite restaurant

nearby. It was only as we climbed back upstairs to complete the book that I told him of my decision.

This got a cold reception, and my name disappeared from the magazine from the March 1961 issue. Miles said he could carry on perfectly well without a Technical Editor, but I doubted this. I discussed the matter with John Crabbe a few months later and, when he said he might be interested, I offered to telephone Miles to alert him that JC would be in touch. I'll leave JC to take up the story in another chapter.

Alan Lovell, who for a time edited both Hi-Fi News and The Tape Recorder, remembers:

'Working with Miles Henslow was an experience! From the very first time I met him there was never a dull moment. Not all of them were happy, some of them extremely sad, but somehow they were always different from the usual.

'Imagine a young chap who had just moved from Bristol to London three months earlier to work on a new *Tape Recording Magazine* in Fleet Street. Trying to come to terms with tube rides into the City during the rush hours and working in the hustle and bustle of that busy street, when all the National daily papers were published there. Then to learn after only three months that, due to lack of advertising, four members of staff had to go. I explain this merely to point out that this is how I came to meet Miles Henslow. A quick telephone call to John Borwick, the Technical Editor of *Hi-Fi News* and the newly formed *Tape Recorder* resulted in him having a word with MH who suggested that I contact him.

'An appointment was made and a few days later there was the five-floor trek up the stairs to meet Miles Henslow. There he sat in the largest chair, behind the biggest desk, with two (growling) Dalmatian dogs in a very large basket in a corner of the room. I was told to sit down on a chair with six-inch legs and asked what I could do and what did I know about electronics and high fidelity sound.

'Commencing my sales-patter, I suddenly found a ream of foolscap paper coming in my direction, thrown by Miles Henslow with the request to go into the next room where there was a typewriter and write 1500 words on any subject. I fed in the first sheet of paper, only to hear from the next room, "Don't worry about that now – can you come back to continue this appointment tonight at 8pm?" No, I said, I have another appointment. "Well, cancel that and come back at 8pm. Ring me to confirm that you can. Goodbye," said Miles, and closed the door. With that, I was off, at a quick rate of knots, down the five flights of stairs. Just as I reached the bottom, a voice roared from the top floor, "Don't worry about tonight, write me a letter asking for a job and get it on my desk within three days."

'Thinking to myself that I would never come anywhere near this man again, I left jobless. However, something about him was different, he was original and quite unique, although whether it was advisable to work with him created many doubts in my mind!

'Next morning, throwing caution to the wind, I wrote that letter and received a reply by return offering me a job. Years later, I asked MH about that interview and why he wanted a letter from me and I found out the facts. He had a handwriting expert, called Humphrey, a great friend, who read people's characters from handwriting and luckily mine must have been acceptable.

'Over the next six to nine months I thoroughly enjoyed my time working with John Borwick, who was a great character with a great sense of humour. He taught me many things about editing. Miles Henslow, I quickly found out, was rarely in the office; the only contribution he made to both magazines was the editorials, and these were always the last items to press. Sometimes the editorial had to be dropped into the forme on the press, as it was so late.

'After a time John left and I waited for a new editor to arrive. No such luck. On the first Monday on my own, I was told that I could edit both magazines, with Miles deciding future articles. It worked well and for my part I enjoyed it greatly although it was extremely difficult working to tight schedules.

'Miles would often visit Germany for three months at a time, and on one occasion he decided to publish in *Hi-Fi News* a feature of how to build an electronic organ. This would be a monthly article lasting for a period of nine months.

'He commissioned someone to write the articles and supply the illustrations but he quickly found out that the organ had serious problems for home constructors if they followed the plans and circuits! With that, he disappeared and spent the next six months building this organ and modifying the text and circuits. He would ring the office from time to time playing a tune over the phone and asking for comments. These he generally received – good or bad.

'During that time, I worked with most of the contributors – Ralph West, Stan Kelly, Graham Balmain, James Moir, John Crabbe, Gilbert Briggs, Rex Baldock. Others included George Tillett, Cecil Watts and all the owners of the companies manufacturing sound reproduction equipment, Quad, Leak, Lowther, SME, Ferrograph, Vortexion, Brenell, KEF, Radford and many others whose names I have forgotten over the last 40 years. Apologies to those omitted.

'Miles also published *The Hi-Fi Year Book*, which although being a bestseller caused havoc in the office due to the compilation of all the data submitted by manufacturers. There were also books backing up articles in the magazine. Then there were the vast Horn loudspeakers by John Crabbe, the Baldock Paraline speakers and many more.

'Later, Miles Henslow produced a subscription magazine on space travel to show what the Americans and Russians were doing during those early days in that field. He also ventured into printing himself, as he objected strongly to his printers' invoices increasing every year automatically.

'What owner of a magazine would call one of his staff (me) to his flat and spend the day going through the manuscript and pictures of a new book he wanted to publish, with the instructions that he was going to Germany again for three months and when he got back he wanted to see this new book out in the bookshop?

'Wondering how I was going to get all this paperwork back to Hampshire, he asked me if I could drive an automatic car, to which I said yes. He took me to his garage and pointed to his Bentley and said I could have that!'

Ralph West on comparing notes with Percy Wilson:

'Percy Wilson was 19 years my senior and had done very important work at the RN college, at the Board of Education and at the Ministry of Transport (the Highway Code) before I'd even heard of him! His great love, though, was acoustics and reproduction of recorded sound. He had already worked out dimensions for exponential horns and the head angles for gramophone pickups for minimum distortion.

'I first knew of him as Technical Editor of *The Gramophone* and by the time I was writing for *Hi-Fi News* we had become good friends. We bumped into each other from time to time and I particularly remember the series of March festivals at Blackpool where EMI and Decca vied with each other to provide interesting musical events.

'One day Percy did me the honour of asking me if I would like to write for *The Gramophone*. I declined and said I would prefer to remain faithful to Miles Henslow. Percy accepted that and we remained firm friends.

'A most amusing incident once involved us both. One day *Hi-Fi News* received a new loudspeaker for review of unusual design. It was a small, well-finished cabinet with a ball-bearing-mounted flap just fitting the rear port. The accompanying leaflet said that this was to relieve the internal pressure on large music signals! Not wishing to be rude, I tried it out, and keeping a "straight face" said that the sound was OK but lacking bass.

'Some time later I met Percy and he said he was a bit puzzled about my report on this unusual design as *The Gramophone* had also received one at the same time and he'd found it produced a balanced sound. When we looked into it a bit deeper, it seems the firm had made two different-sized models and they'd sent the larger one to Percy and *The Gramophone* as the senior magazine!'

Ralph West *on Jack Houlgate's work for Tannoy and his one-speaker stereo demonstration:*

'When Jack Houlgate left Voigt he did some very good work for Tannoy. In particular, he drilled the original series of radial holes in the centre pole-piece that conducted the acoustic pressure from the high-frequency cone to the beginning of the HF horn, nestling in the centre of the main cone – which also acted as the continuation of the HF horn. This co-axial design ran successfully for many years.

'When stereo came along we were all feted with rival demonstrations of trains and at one evening lecture to an enthusiastic group, he announced that he would demonstrate stereo from a single channel.

'From a disc recording of a small engine chuffing along very sedately, he had the sound coming from a small speaker on one side of the platform. Picking up the speaker and walking slowly to the other side, the little engine went "peep-peep" just as he reached the centre of the platform!

'Despite the humorous side, Jack was most astute engineer and did much good work verifying new apparatus for the BBC. We always said "If it will get past Jack Houlgate it is very good."

Jack had serious heart problems and eventually had to have one of the earliest mechanical replacements. Effective but noisy. He used to say he was like the crocodile that had swallowed the alarm clock in the Peter Pan story. While it lasted, Jack continued working.

Miles Henslow *writing on Stereo in his Editorial column for May 1959:*

'With this number we complete our Third Volume. Looking backwards over the past twelve months, it has been an important period in the world of Hi-Fi. The major event was, of course, Stereo. Mishandled shockingly on the one hand, it has caused many unnecessary headaches to the industry as a whole, and given the buying public an overdose of audio indigestion. Demonstrated intelligently on the other hand, it has proved itself to be an essential step forward in the direction of true high fidelity sound reproduction.

'Without chewing tediously upon this already well-gnawed bone, we feel we must "recap" on Hi-Fi as a whole, in the light of its stereo adjunct. For really good quality sound reproduction there are certain minima, in terms of essentials. A good quality transcription motor, plus a good quality pickup, for discs; an amplifier of adequate frequency response and negligible distortion; a good speaker drive unit, properly housed in an enclosure of adequate dimensions. These things cost money. Cut down on the £.s.d. and you inevitably cut quality. You do *not* make up for this lost quality by adding a second channel – stereo – with the money saved on the first channel. This, summed up, is the mirage which far too many people have been chasing.

'There are now no fewer than four approaches to so-called "hi-fi". (1) A really top-grade outfit for single-channel reproduction, from disc, tape and radio. (2) A "hi-fi" installation for single channel, chosen to fit the budget. (3) A twin-channel ditto, also bought to a price. (4) A really top-grade outfit for twin channel listening. Obviously, item 1 can be a starting point for item 4; likewise, item 2 can be a beginning for item 3. But the two groups do not mix.

'It is possible and reasonable to state – without lowering the standards of policy by one inch – that the quality of a great deal of the medium-priced equipment now available on the market will give the average listener a very high quality of sound reproduction. However grand one's dreams may be, realities have to be measured in terms of living standards, whether pounds-shillings-pence, or yards-feet-inches, or both. The size of the garage and the bank balance determine the size and luxuriance of the car to be used. The chosen vehicle gets one from A to B in the style that one has pre-selected.

'There are, we repeat no short cuts to true hi-fi reproduction of sound. For the best, the best is necessary. If the *whole* best is not immediately possible, good planning will make it ultimately possible; and this is where the motor-car-hi-fi simile ceases to operate, for the whole of the limousine is usually bought in one piece.

'We make these observations again, here, at the close of this volume because the number of potential hi-fi enthusiasts has increased by thousands, because the amount of available equipment has increased in direct proportion, and because it is important to us as it is to every reader of this magazine that the facts of Hi-Fi Life are properly understood, be they stereo or monaural.'

3. Stanley Kelly

'Full Name: Stanley Kelly. Date and place of birth: December 29, 1912 in Kirkstall near Leeds, Yorkshire. Education, training, etc: none – just an ignorant peasant. When and why started in audio? 1929, for money.' **Stanley Kelly**

In his own words. *By Stanley Kelly (from Audio Biographies, 1961)*

My interest in sound reproduction started, like that of most youngsters of my generation, with the building of ubiquitous crystal sets in the early 1920s. This interest was stimulated by the finding of large quantities of Galena in Esholt Woods, near my home, during excavations there. The Kelly genius for losing money was immediately sparked at the prospect of selling these crystals in competition with the well-known brands then offered on the market.

The plan was doomed to failure! Although the ore was undoubtedly Galena, the sensitive spots were few and far between, and my interest in 'wireless' would have died but for the acquisition in 1924 of an 'R' valve. With this priceless possession, an HT battery made from old flash lamp cells rebuilt into miniature jam jars, and a very second-hand accumulator, all manner of wonderful circuits described in *Wireless World*, *Popular Wireless*, *Amateur Wireless*, and a host of long-forgotten magazines, were tried and generally found wanting – presumably because of my inability to interpret correctly the designers' intentions. By careful swapping of stamps, bicycles, etc, I gradually built up a collection of wireless parts, most of them at least ninth-hand and originating from First World War surplus.

During 1929, in conjunction with Mr Johnson, a retired Post Office engineer, I commenced building 'real' amplifiers. Our first effort was three B.12s in parallel (400 volts, 30 milliamps per valve) driven by a pre-amplifier consisting of a PM.1 HF and two PM.1 LF valves with filaments in series connected in the negative HT line. This amplifier, with two moving-coil drive units and Kurz-Kash 15 foot horns, filled the local skating rink in opposition to the cinema organist.

At this time the indirectly heated valve was just coming into use and we produced smaller amplifiers using the Mazda 'Green Spot' and 'Red Spot' valves, giving about 1^1/2 watts output; and also some really large amplifiers, one series using two DO.60s and giving about 35 to 40 watts. Our *pièce de résistance* was a one kilowatt amplifier driving a Blatthaller; this had a range of about a mile and was hired to local aerodromes for their rallies, etc. Specification of the amplifiers, even then, was quite stringent, the limits being ±2dB, 5 to 10,000c/s, and a harmonic distortion of less than 5% at the rated output. And so on through the 1930s...

After a spell with Standard Telephones & Cables, I found myself at the outbreak of war in the Royal Air Force, and was posted to RAE Farnborough on AI Development (Airborne night fighter Radar). This particular equipment was 400Mc/s frequency modulated and during a hit-and-run raid on the Station the one aircraft destroyed was that which contained our only working model. The project was abandoned in favour of the AI Mark IV. At this juncture I met Blumlein, who had just developed his Pulse Modulator, using transmission line technique to give an extremely sharp pulse, which was then superior to anything available in RDF, the RAF's early name for Radar. (It may be noted in parenthesis that the Americans' fundamental contribution to Radar was its name, and I well remember at the US Naval Radar School in Boston the theme of the Principal's opening speech to the students in 1942 was that the British had developed the Cavity Magnetron, Centimetric crystal detector elements, TR cells, PPI, and all the operational techniques.)

From Farnborough to the RAF Delegation in Washington, the Pacific, and the Bahamas, thence home to TRE Malvern, eventually ending my Service career running the radar group of Transport Command Development Unit.

I joined Cosmocord in 1948 as Chief Engineer. My group was responsible for Medresco Hearing Aid microphones, the immediate post-war lightweight crystal pick-ups commencing with the GP.20 series, and various other electro-acoustic devices.

In 1956, my wife and I started Romagna Reproducers with the intention of producing specialised electro-acoustic equipment for domestic and industrial purposes, and this, except for a slight hiatus caused by my being involved in a car accident, followed two weeks later by a fire at the factory, has progressed more or less according to plan; and, who knows, we may even make a profit one day!

I resurrected the Blatthaller in miniature form in 1957, using printed circuit techniques on a Melanex diaphragm 5 x 4 inches. It gave a very good performance, but by this time I was committed production-wise to the ribbon high frequency unit and it seemed pointless to introduce a new model just because it was different. Current projects are concentrated on what my accountant euphemistically calls 'money spinners'. We have now developed an ultrasonic jig borer, which accurately drills holes exactly in the centre of pennies for the insertion of matchsticks!

Despite passing distractions, audio frequency and acoustic engineering has always been my first love, and given the chance of building another career I do not think I would change.

My hobbies are work, music, work, photography, work attempting (generally unsuccessfully) to lead my four children in the paths of rectitude their mother so ardently desires; and last but not least, penning random thoughts on acoustics and allied subjects. I hope one day to emulate Mr Briggs in this last venture, but have I fear a long and thorny path to traverse. (With exactly 22 years margin in time – GAB.)

An interview with Stanley Kelly. *By Ken Kessler (1994)*

When Gene Pitts of *Audio* magazine asked me if I'd like to oversee a series of conversations with the greats of British audio, I jumped at the opportunity. In my time as a hi-fi journalist in the UK, I'd been saddened by the passing of Donald Aldous, Arthur Radford, John Gilbert and other giants of audio lore; here was an opportunity to reminisce with the surviving founding fathers of the industry before it was too late.

For American readers, this should provide an intriguing view of the birth of the audio scene on the other side of the Atlantic. As I learned upon moving to England in the early 1970s, the US and the UK were – prior to the appearance of the Japanese manufacturers – responsible for the bulk of audio development and manufacture, with a few notable exceptions like Thorens, Studer/Revox and Dual. And yet Great Britain and the USA operated virtually in isolation from each other until the 1960s. Although numerous British brands exported products to the USA from the early 1950s onward – Quad, Tannoy, Leak and others had a presence in the States – a study of British hi-fi magazines and yearbooks from the 1950s reveals the presence of almost no US components whatsoever.

British designers were, however, familiar with American developments, even if the British public knew only of native hardware. For example, David Hafler, while at Dynaco, was an early audio ambassador to the UK and even sourced transformers from Radford, while Bud Fried was another Anglophile who imported Decca cartridges and other products into the USA.

To launch the series, we chose to speak with Stan Kelly. A lot of individuals have companies which bear their names; fewer are those whose name has come to stand for a specific product. British audiophiles still refer to Stan's horn-loaded ribbon tweeter as the Kelly Ribbon, not the Decca Ribbon, even though the latter took over manufacture from an early date. Stan also can take credit for inventing the 'flipover needle' for budget record players when 33⅓ rpm joined 78rpm. And he even helped Miles Henslow to establish *Hi-Fi News*, the first British hi-fi magazine; Betty Kelly guaranteed Miles's bank loans!

When he was a spry eighty-something, Stan still acted as a consultant and maintained a fully-functioning workshop where he makes his own prototype drive units for various manufacturers – including the magnet assemblies and speaker baskets. The workshop in his garden was an Aladdin's Cave, with some desk drawers full of ancient cartridges, others with what look like EMIT tweeters. 'Those? I made them myself in 1956.' And when his memory couldn't be jogged, his charming wife Betty was there to fill in names places and dates. The following interview is taken from conversations with Stan in November 1992 and September 1994, the latter inspired by the sudden appearance of a new source for Kelly replacement ribbons...

KK: 'How did you react when you learned that an independent individual had put the ribbon element back into production?'
SK: 'Frankly, I had no reaction. The thing is that I wasn't making it. Decca, or the people who have taken over Decca aren't interested in making it. If he wants to have a bash – good luck to him.'
KK: 'Did you not retain any rights to the ribbon at all?'
SK: 'I can't, you see. All patents lapse after 17 years. The only thing I have any individual title to is my name. If we'd have taken out a copyright on it, as distinct from or in addition to the patent, well, the copyright can last forever. But we didn't.'
KK: 'So what can people call this new ribbon, *without* your permission?'
SK: 'Well, they can't call it a "Kelly Ribbon" without my permission, and they can't call it a "Decca Ribbon" without Decca's permission.'
KK: 'What led you to produce a horn-loaded ribbon in the first place?'
SK: 'I wanted to make a wide range, high frequency transducer. At that time, I was making – here let me show you. [*Pulls out a scrapbook which itself would warrant facsimile reproduction.*] At Cosmocord, where I was technical director from 1947–1953, we were making tonearms, pick-ups and microphones. That included the first pick-up ever made to play at 8 grams, but I designed it to play at 5g. It became a standard. These [*pointing to the book*] were rather more ancient. And these featured the first cantilevers. Before that it was needles; I started making sapphire tipped rods to use in place of steel needles. They were fine for playing weights

of less that 20 grams. This pick-up, for example, had a playing weight of 120g.'

KK: (incredulous) '*How* much?'

SK: 'Four ounces. EMI and Decca produced their pick-ups at 'round about 40-50 grams. This was for the first LPs. I then produced the GP15 to play at 8g. And that meant that the vinyl now had a reasonable life. Then I produced this unit, the GP20, for 78 and $33^{1/3}$, with two styli, one on either side.'

KK: 'Had no-one else thought of that before? The Americans or the Germans?'

SK: 'No, no. This was a first.'

KK: 'So how did that idea hit you?'

SK: 'It was obvious. Look, if we started with a torsion crystal instead of a bending crystal it was quite obvious that if on the end of the crystal here you put a bar at the back end and pushed it that way it was twisting the crystal. If you pushed it the other way, it was also twisting the crystal. So you put two styli on it. We made a lot of 'em – this was around 1950; I left Cosmocord in 1953. And went on to start my own company, named Kelly. And the first thing I manufactured was that. [*Shows me the original ribbon.*] The RLS-1, 3k-20kHz.'

KK: 'Prior to introducing this drive unit, what ribbons were commercially available to audio enthusiasts?'

SK: 'There was the QUAD. In production quite early. It was a much larger ribbon. But the QUAD was extremely expensive, and you had to buy a complete full range system; you couldn't buy a single ribbon unit (tweeter). So when I made the ribbon I also produced a bass unit for it and a crossover network... but these were for the home constructor.'

KK: 'Was the home constructor market more important than the assembled-unit market in the mid-1950s?'

SK: 'In terms of real hi-fi, yes, because with the exception of QUAD and one or two others, you couldn't buy a complete system made up of separate components. You had to go to a specialist hi-fi dealer who had a range of amplifiers, a range of tuners, a range of speakers and hope that he'd got the right combination.'

KK: 'So how was the mass market being served?'

SK: 'There was no mass market hi-fi. Radios, radiograms and record players. If you went to a radio shop, you could buy a radiogram, which was a tuner, record player and speaker all in one box. And there was a whole range of those from bad-and-indifferent to quite good ones.'

KK: 'The enthusiast market to which you were addressing your products

– that was an immediate post-war phenomenon or did it not take off until well into the 1950s?'

SK: 'There was a hard core of 'hi-fi enthusiasts' from before the war, with Donald Aldous, who later worked for *Hi-Fi News & Record Review* handling the information side, from before the war. Percy Wilson was another one, the technical editor of *The Gramophone*. Gilbert Briggs [Wharfedale] pioneered the individual loudspeaker drivers, before the war, one of the first permanent magnet moving coil designs. They developed the hobby from the acoustic gramophones before the war to the very crude electronic gramophones immediately before the war. Then everything went into limbo for the next five years.

'Then, after the war with all the technical developments from military electronics and the mass-production of the equipment, it became possible for the man in the street to buy a good audio amplifier.'

KK: 'Military surplus?'

SK: 'No, not military surplus. Some of the manufacturers who were making the military equipment immediately went over [to civilian production], they'd got the technical know-how, the production facilities to make civilian equipment.'

KK: 'So when you decided to go into speaker manufacture in the early-to-mid 1950s, there was a ready market?'

SK: 'Oh, yes. You see, there were people like Celestion who'd been manufacturing pre-war, principally for the domestic radio market. They had played with better speakers before the war but after the war they then had the technical and commercial facilities to produce good quality loudspeakers. Of course, this was very much tied up with the cones.

'The normal tweeter purchase for the home constructor, before the ribbon was introduced, would have been a little three-inch or four-inch cone with a little dust cover – which was your dome, of course – and these were good for usually five watts. But you must realise that the sensitivity was about 85dB for one watt. Yet because of the limitation in broadcast frequency range – we're talking about AM, not FM, everything was on medium wave – you were limited on the frequency response and the signal-to-noise ratio. And you were limited in exactly the same way on 78rpm records. They [the speakers of the day] were consistent in quality with the records and broadcasts available at the time. And then LP and FM radio triggered each other.'

KK: 'So you came out with a tweeter good for 3kHz–20kHz.'

SK: 'Exactly.'

KK: 'Were you the first to put a ribbon in a horn?'

SK: 'As far as I know. It had a 3k–20kHz signal and I wanted at least a half an octave on each side; on the high end this immediately out-performed any voice-coil-cum-dome or what-have-you just because of mass and also because of the limitations on the magnet. The neodymium magnet was – well, you couldn't afford it. You had access to it but it was like buying gold. These are cobalt. [*Points to the Kelly speaker magnets.*] I had to keep an eye on price, even though I was going for the best performance.'

KK: 'The price of the original drive unit was 12 guineas in 1955 – that's roughly equivalent to...'

SK: 'Fifty pounds in today's money.'

KK: 'That's still not very expensive, even by Fifties standards.'

SK: 'Agreed.'

KK: 'How long had you worked on the ribbon before you produced the first production version?'

SK: 'Less than a year. The first problem was getting an efficient magnet. I didn't make many of the first type because, by re-designing the magnet I added another 6dB to the efficiency. It reduced the magnet's cost, too. The ribbon, the transformer and the horn remained constant ever since. The ribbon itself was an aluminium alloy which stayed constant, never altered it. The horn was cast.'

KK: 'Had you tried other topologies?'

SK: 'Not electrostatic. It had two things against it. It was high impedance. And high impedance transformers are very difficult to make because of self-capacitance and things like that. Then you've got to have polarising voltages on it and your high voltage production equipment was very, very costly compared to a magnet.'

KK: 'So cost ruled out electrostatics?'

SK: 'And simplicity. There's nothing to go wrong in this [the ribbon]. If you've got a high voltage thing with valves in it, something can go wrong. You need a power supply for it. Instead of two leads going to your loudspeaker, you had four.'

KK: 'And the existing dynamic tweeters of the day?'

SK: 'Well, they were domes and if you had them sufficiently large to give you the radiation, then you were severely limited on the high frequency side, and you had all the resonances of the dome and the suspension added to it. It worked well enough so that, during the peak of production, we were probably making about 500 drivers per month.'

KK: 'How was Decca involved?'

SK: 'Decca came along and said, "We want to use your speaker in our equipment".'

KK: 'They already had their own line of loudspeakers?'

SK: 'Oh, yes. So I said, "Yes", and they said, "Look, if we make 'em, we can make them for half the price you can because we can make four times as many. We'll take over the manufacture and give you a royalty". That was in the early 1960s. All the manufacturing moved up to their factory in the Midlands. I then played around with tape recorders, made microphones, and then moved onto complete loudspeaker systems. We closed down Kelly in the middle '60s, after I'd had my fill of it.'

KK: 'Did you keep an eye on Decca after they took over manufacture?'

SK: 'I was forbidden to. They didn't say so in so many words, but when I said I'll go up and see how they were getting on in the Midlands, they said you bloody well won't.'

KK: 'So you took their word on the royalties.'

SK: 'Look, I'm an engineer, not a businessman. That's the story of my life! But I was happy with Decca's drivers; they were exactly to spec. There was no way that you could complain about the quality.'

KK: 'But once they took over, the name changed to the Decca London?'

SK: 'Yes. It was Decca-Kelly originally. And then Decca London.'

Stanley Kelly *as parent: a tribute from Terry Kelly*

During the war, Dad was originally part of Coastal Command, working on radar and PPI systems. As a radar pioneer he was sent over to the United States to teach them how to build and deploy systems; during this time he accepted a commission in the US Navy and was stationed both in the Bahamas and Hawaii. He was present during the attack on Pearl Harbor, and still has many photographs that he took in the hours following the incident. Whilst in the USA he was also involved in the Manhattan Project (although he was reticent to divulge his exact role therein) and also in anti-submarine warfare.

The ASW work was mainly concerned with detection and prosecution, and he produced many different types of passive and active sonar systems to be deployed from aircraft, ships, and submarines. It was during one detection flight that his plane (a PBY5 I believe) was attacked by a Japanese Zero fighter. Unfortunately the plane was shot down, and my father was also shot in the neck; fortunately, because the bullets were at the end of their trajectory, they spent their remaining energy by removing four of his back teeth. Dad then spent some days in a dinghy in the Pacific awaiting rescue, during which time he was able to survive by drinking turtle blood.

This introduction to uncooked haemoglobin stood him in good stead, because some time later he unfortunately contracted Leukaemia and had to live on raw liver for a period of time. Neither of these incidents seems to have affected his enjoyment of offal as a foodstuff.

After the war Dad returned to Europe and seems to have spent most of his time in liberating fine wines and liqueurs from retreating Axis forces, and, of course, in verifying their suitability for human consumption. It was during this period that the beginnings of the legendary (at least amongst his audio conspirators were concerned) Kelly cellar were lain down. Many a fine evening was had during which Dad would demonstrate his largesse and comprehensive knowledge of everything. On one memorable occasion he was challenged that it was impossible to cook an egg in a toaster. Needless to say, he won the bet, and I was tasked with returning the toaster to the retailer as 'unfit for purpose'; nowhere in the instructions did it warn of unsuitability for cooking eggs.

In the 40 years that have elapsed since Dad wrote the brief synopsis above, the world of electroacoustics and high fidelity engineering has changed out of all recognition, yet Dad's principles of (to plagiarise a well-known advertisement) 'the closest approach to the original sound' ensured that he would be actively involved in many of the technological breakthroughs. I remember meetings with a young engineer named Ray Dolby, who approached my father for assistance in production engineering a device for reducing the 'hiss' that plagued tape recordings, and can, even now, lay my hands on the original prototypes and retail units for domestic and professional noise reduction using Dolby A and B, designed and built by my father. At around the same time, another young entrepreneur named Alan Sugar was a regular visitor, helping to swell the Kelly coffers with orders for coils and crossover networks, which were sometimes produced by all members of the family old enough to operate one of the domestic coil-winding machines.

The results of Dad's endeavours in audio engineering often led to unusual applications. Research into piezo-electric materials led to the production of accelerometers for NASA, which even now, are still on the moon having formed part of the luna-lander. Mum reminded me of a lorry we once saw on the North Circular Road, carrying a rocket or satellite to Woomera, which also contained some of these accelerometers. Some of Dad's miniature microphones were also used in the space helmets worn by the Apollo astronauts during the '60s and '70s. The accelerometers were actually a spin-off application for research done for the MOD into sonar transducers (both passive and active), that he started during the war in America, and I can still remember a dipping sonar case that had been converted into a lamp standard in his office, which I believe is now in the workshop at the bottom of the garden.

The family flirtation with wealth continued unabated: successful business ventures would result in wonderful jewellery for Mum, presents for us kids, and copious test and research equipment for the labs. In harder times the jewellery would be mysteriously converted back into lab equipment overnight, until Mum put her foot down.

My mother served triple duty as Dad's secretary, business manager, and financial conscience, doing additional regular duty as accountant, and delivery driver. In those days we had a big commercial van, the '60s version of a people carrier, into which Dad had made cunningly formed removable wooden boxes filling all available unused space. The roof was fully 'racked', with a ladder screwed to the rear doors for easy access and a number of 'octopi' – eight-legged bungee hooks, used to lash things into place, sometimes including itinerant or naughty offspring.

Holidays were an adventure for everyone, for the whole of the summer break, some six weeks in those days, Dad would close down the factory and we would all go abroad in the firm's van. Nowadays, these holidays will sound like a children's fairy tale, but Dad and Mum were both 'Europhiles' at heart and wanted to provide us with as broad an experience as they had enjoyed (albeit mainly in the wartime years as bomber pilot and WREN). We visited all of the usual tourist sites, and continued in the Kelly tradition of extracting as much fun from each event as possible, and then some more, by for example, insisting on circumnavigating the leaning tower of Pisa on the topmost floor, on the outside of the retaining pillars, whilst Dad filmed us on the Bolex and Mum was negotiating the purchase of industrial quantities of *gelato*.

As usual, money was in short supply on many of these holidays, so Dad had a French manufacturer construct the world's first (and probably only) six-bedroom frame tent – to a unique design of his own – so that we only had to pay for a single plot. We spent many a fraught evening in the garden in Romagna practice-erecting this monstrosity until each of us knew our respective roles backwards and were able to arrive at a camp site and erect and furnish the tent in under half an hour – ofttimes much to the astonishment of the other residents. Our holidays were so unusual and interesting that upon returning to school my youngest sister was often ribbed and disbelieved as she told of her experiences, which contrasted so dramatically with the two weeks at Skegness enjoyed by her classmates.

When Dad was developing miniature hearing aids (by miniature read those that were marginally smaller than a dictionary) we were all pressed into service as guinea-pigs. Not only did we have to wear the prototypes around the house, but we also were expected to complete performance sheets (at least those of us who were old enough to read and write). I have an everlasting memory of all of the kids sitting in the lounge, whilst Mum and Dad were playing a piano duet, wearing industrial pink earpieces shouting at each other; having a wonderful time.

Saturdays were usually reserved for the children, we often used to accompany Dad on explorations of the surplus shops in Lisle Street and Tottenham Court Road, and joy of joys to Buck and Ryan or Proops. We always used to return with some treasures, small parachutes to which we lashed Jennie's dolls, to be hurled from the top floor of the house, or on one memorable occasion a couple of almost working wartime RAF transmitters from Lancaster bombers.

We decided that we could get these working again, and with Dad's help (actually it was Dad who did all the work) succeeded in blacking out all communications within a two-mile radius for a short while. We eventually converted the power stage into a circuit to drive an RF heater coil, and created, possibly, the world's first microwave, capable of boiling a milk-bottle full of water in under a minute, as well as producing the most curious tingly feelings if you stood too close when it was turned on.

At that time Dad was working on the ribbon loudspeaker. Part of the design, and actually the whole secret of its success, were the crinkles that were put into the ribbon enabling it to flex. I remember many attempts at getting the crinkles 'just right', and in the end the solution turned out to be quite simple. I had, for my birthday, been given a Meccano set; and was continually adding to it by buying bits and pieces from the local toyshop. On one occasion I had saved my pocket money to buy some gears, and by chance they were just the right ratio for putting in the crinkles. The prototype crinkler worked so well that it, and many clones were soon to be found on the production line at the factory.

***

Brian Smith and John Wright *on the later Decca (London) cartridges:*

'The original Decca company was started in the 19th century, but its first musical product was with a portable record player used in the trenches during the 1914–18 World War. In the 1939–45 war the government asked Decca to produce a system to identify British submarines from German ones, which resulted in the *ffrr* (full frequency range recording) system. In 1944, Decca produced the first *ffrr* music discs. The first LP record (mono) came in 1951, followed by stereo in 1958. Engineers Bayliff and Cowie then designed the Decca *ffss* (full frequency stereo sound) tonearm and playback head which had Mk I, II and III versions.

'Meanwhile, the first item of consumer equipment was the Decola radiogram, with no fewer than five loudspeakers built in. In order that customers could use a Decca head with another manufacturer's tonearm, the company introduced the Mark IV cartridge with elliptical stylus in 1965 and soon after the unipivot International tonearm.

'To reduce cartridge mass, Decca in 1974 then designed the London Blue and its specially selected export version the Grey (both with a spherical stylus). Two years later came the improved Maroon (spherical) and Gold (elliptical). All these had a new mounting bracket for 1/2in centre mounting holes. A lighter tonearm, the London International, was also introduced.

Decca was also the first to produce a carbon fibre record-cleaning brush in the 1970s. This was further developed into the dual-fibre 2+2 which is still available. The next development came in 1985 with the Super Gold, featuring a modified body shape and a van den Hul I shaped stylus. A vdH II was also offered as an option.

'In 1989, Decca's owners, Racal, decided to close Decca Radio & TV and its Special Products (hi-fi) division. But they granted a licence to continue manufacturing the products under the London brand name (the Decca name was given to Tatung) to Decca engineer John Wright, and worldwide distribution and repair co-ordination to Brian Smith of Presence Audio. This license is still current. In 1989, London cartridges offered the Martin Bastin-designed Decapod aluminium mounting plate as a factory-fitted option. The first John Wright-designed new model was the Jubilee in 1992, with a two-piece aluminium body and extended line-contact stylus. The next, the Reference, came in 2003 with a revised two-piece body, designed with help from Conrad Mas of Avid turntables, and having an exclusive fine line stylus.

'For the spotters, the cartridges are:
Maroon, 1976: London body/mounting. Spherical stylus.
Gold, 1976: London body/mounting. Elliptical stylus.
Super Gold, 1985: London body/mounting (modified). VdH stylus to 1995, now XLC.
Decapod, 1991: solid aluminium mounting as an option.
Jubilee, 1992: new two-piece body plus extended line contact stylus.
Super-Gold, 2001: traditional crap body but stylus as per Jubilee.
Reference, 2003: new two-piece body plus exclusive fine-line stylus.'

4. Quad shows the way

'Some of them [liked the Quad Electrostatic] and some of them didn't. It was quite an oddball sort of thing. What's this funny-looking thing? They thought it looked like a room heater. In fact, we'd have people stand by them to feel the warmth.' **Peter Walker**

'One Radford amplifier in particular, the 2x25 watt STA25, became accepted as one of the best valve designs of the era and we sold quite a number to discriminating customers.' **Geoffrey Horn**

'It's only the concept which is old. The Tannoy Dual Concentric has gradually evolved to the work of engineering art it now is... The sheer transparency of the Kensington astonished. I've not before heard anything quite so coherent from a box speaker.' **Ivor Humphreys**

An interview with Peter J Walker of Quad. *By Ken Kessler (1994)*

Take a poll of British audiophiles (even those under 40) asking them to name the grandaddy of hi-fi in the UK and the majority will say 'Peter Walker' without hesitation. This quick, natural, almost instinctive response is the result of a legacy which includes a run of classic products and the creation of a company which is probably the oldest specialist hi-fi manufacturer still under the ownership of the original family.

Quad Electroacoustics Ltd – born as SP Fidelity Sound Systems in March 26, 1936, before changing its name that year to The Acoustical Manufacturing Company – has an uninterrupted history matched by no other producer of audio components, and Peter Walker controlled it for the first 50 years before handing over control to his son, Ross. Walker wrote, in G A Briggs's *Audio Biographies*, that: 'By 1952, my firm was of sufficient size to enable me to delegate nearly all management and departmental responsibilities; in fact, shed myself of all those aspects of business which did not appeal to me.' Luckily for us he immersed himself in research and design.

Any company would be proud to have created one milestone product; Quad can claim at least four with the Quad II tube pre-amp and power amp, the original electrostatic loudspeaker and the current electrostatic, the ESL 63. And it's as the seminal producer of electrostatic speakers that the company is known, but the company actually began with public address equipment and, eventually, a successful ribbon-hybrid, the horn-loaded Corner Ribbon Loudspeaker of 1949.

Ken Kessler: 'Why did you move from the original ribbon speaker to what became the original Quad electrostatic?'

Peter J Walker: 'From a theoretical point of view, an electrostatic is an ideal way to make a loudspeaker – it matches the air perfectly and it's all predictable, as ordinary loudspeakers are rather variable. It has some problems which are rather difficult, mainly due to the stretching of the diaphragm. It mustn't shrink and that sort of thing. Very high voltages, 10,000 volts, make it difficult but it's an ideal – I think most loudspeaker manufacturers have looked at it and said, "What a lovely way to make a speaker, but it's not very practical". And a lot of manufacturers have tried it, too, and most of them have said, "This is not profitable. Get back to putting loudspeakers in boxes and sell 'em, lad!" [Laughs.]

'I've always thought, right from, oh, 1945 I suppose or thereabouts, that an electrostatic would be a nice way of doing it. But it's in the back of your mind, how can you do it? And it had a lot of problems. But the ribbon was a very good way of getting very good high-frequency response – excellent.

'The ribbon was a hybrid. The ribbon itself was very good from 2000 cycles upwards and the bass unit was very good up to 500 cycles. Not very good in the middle, which I can admit now, but there you are.'

KK: 'Did working with the ribbon help you to learn techniques for later use in the electrostatic?'

PJW: 'Not at all. A ribbon is just a little bit of aluminium in a very large magnet array, a radar magnet in fact – and that would only go down to about 2000 cycles unless you had lots of magnets; you could make a long strip one but it would have been very expensive in those days.'

KK: 'At the time you introduced the ribbon [circa 1949–50], who was serving the hi-fi community in the UK?'

PJW: 'At that time the hi-fi industry hadn't really taken off. It never really took off until we had the LP record where you could play through a whole symphony without messing about, jumping up and down, and without having surface noise from the disc. It was a very small market. You perhaps remember the days of Voigt; I admire him greatly. He made an excellent speaker and he sold two a week. That was the sort of market. You made amplifiers and loudspeakers for yourself and your friends and a few fanatics, and that's as far as it went until the LP came along.

'During the ribbon speaker's life we sold less than a thousand units.

It wasn't pairs, it was all mono – there wasn't any stereo then. And they were £95 a time, which in present-day money is quite a lot. Around the same time that the LP was introduced, 1954, 1955, the electrostatic was introduced – I think we demonstrated it in 1955, about that time.'

KK: 'How many years had you been working on it?'

PJW: 'Well, you don't work on it for years and years. You have a little go and get rid of a few problems, and then you forget that and get on with other things that you can make, and it stays in the back of your mind and you think, "Oh, we could get over that – what about dust and these high voltages?". And you think of another idea and go on a little bit more. And then you forget it again for a long time; you're not working every day on the same thing. It's like the ESL 63 loudspeaker. It took us eighteen years to develop but it wasn't eighteen years every day. [Laughs.] Not at all.'

KK: 'Quad's roots, though, appear to be in amplification... or was there a speaker before the ribbon hybrid?'

PJW: 'Well, there was, but it wasn't very good. SL15 I think it was called, a quarter-wave resonant – don't forget we started off in 1936 making amplifiers for public address, dance bands and things and then started making high fidelity equipment because you were interested in it, for yourself, and your friends were interested. We made a jolly good amplifier before the war, triodes like PX4s – excellent, it would sell nowadays. Direct-coupled and all the rest of it, but there was no market for that in those days at all. Two PX25s driven by an MH4, an ML4 before that – and a bit of feedback on it, actually. Oh yes, feedback came out in 1936; wasn't used a lot, just a little bit. They were good amplifiers. 12 watts.'

KK: 'Were there any other, earlier electrostatics with which yours had to bear comparison?'

PJW: 'There was certainly the Janszen in the US. There was one before the war which was called the Primustatic, I think which was just a tweeter, several German electrostatics were made but they really didn't make a big market at all. Janszens came to England – unless you went over with a suitcase. The original ESL just competed against other loudspeakers, and it wasn't as loud, so people who wanted to shake the windows didn't buy a Quad electrostatic speaker.'

KK: 'Was it an immediate hit? Did the audio journalists of the time recognise it as revolutionary?'

PJW: 'Some of them did and some of them didn't. It was quite an oddball sort of thing. "What's this funny-looking thing?"

'They thought it looked like a room heater. In fact, we'd have people stand by them to feel the warmth.'

KK: 'Was it easier to launch in the USA?'

PJW: 'No. We had a very, very good review in America, a man came over and he said it was most wonderful but it's not loud, it doesn't shake the windows. But it gives the most natural reproduction by a wide margin more than we've ever heard before. And that got us some orders from America; some orders came in. But they weren't very good with American high-powered amplifiers, which would just bust 'em, spark 'em to bits.

'Americans had larger rooms, their whole basements given over to hi-fi, and it had to be pretty loud. And the poor old ESL wouldn't do that. But a number of people liked it very much. You either did that or you didn't like it at all.

'And when stereo came along, you had to have two of 'em. A bit big for that but it worked very well. In fact, after we made 400 of them we modified the directivity because of stereo. The directivity pattern was made for mono – not quite the same as stereo. Serial number 409 I think it was.'

KK: 'How did you change it? Driver shape?'

PJW: 'No, it was just the electrical distribution between the elements. No other modifications as far as I know.'

KK: 'At what point did you feel that transistors were acceptable?'

PJW: '1968. Prior to that you only had germanium transistors which didn't do high frequencies very well. They would blow up a bit and they weren't as good as valves. But in 1968 we could make a transistor amplifier as good as or better than valves – not everybody believes that, but there we are. That's what we thought.'

KK: 'But do you ever think that, while the solid-state equipment measured very well, maybe it didn't sound as good as the valve equipment?'

PJW: 'No. I think this going back to valves is partly fashion and partly the fact that you can make a valve amplifier fairly easily and it will always sound good. Transistor amplifiers are much more difficult to design and it's easy to make one that measures quite well but gives current overload, and things go wrong like that, secondary breakdowns and all sorts of things, so it's not so easy. But if you make it properly and do all the measurements properly, and do all the proper listening tests, oh, yes, then it's the right way to make an amplifier. It still is. The fashion for valves is, I think, *just* a fashion.'

KK: 'I won't challenge you on that one!'

PJW: 'But you don't believe it. [Laughs.]'

KK: 'If you were starting Quad all over again, what areas in the hi-fi chain would you feel still need to be addressed?'

PJW: 'The relationship between the loudspeakers and the room. And to somehow try to improve stereo – stereo comes out of two loudspeakers, whereas from an orchestra, for example, it comes out of a whole lot of little sources; and two loudspeakers – though extremely good – don't quite do that.

'Binaural could do it if you had special headphones designed to suit your own ears, pinnae, which is very difficult to do. Particularly taking into account the distance apart of your ears... but it's quite impractical from a commercial point of view. But if it is done, and the recording is made with little microphones in your own ears, then what you is hear is as perfect as it's going to get.'

KK: 'And if you were to produce a Quad ESL 95? How would it differ from the ESL 63?'

PJW: 'I don't know whether it would.'

KK: 'Bass response?'

PJW: 'Bass response on the 63 is quite good. It doesn't get the oomph-oomph-oomph like lots of cabinet speakers, but if you measure it then it's only 6dB down at 36 cycles which is not bad. Better than most, but not all. There are some which will go lower than that, but not many.'

KK: 'And maximum SPLs?'

PJW: 'We can get just over 100dB at two metres, which is adequate for me and 95% of our customers, but not all of them. With some sorts of music the louder you play it the better it sounds.'

KK: 'And what would you have changed about the original electrostatic?'

PJW: [Laughs.] 'Ooh, dreadful question. You take a silly old man of 78 and ask him what would he have done in 1950. Well, I couldn't have made it better at the time. If I had my present experience I'd have made something like the ESL63, which I made to improve over the first one in the first place. In a lot of respects, anyway.

'What was difficult about the first one? Well, it had what was in effect a woofer and a tweeter, and getting those two exactly level and matching in response, that wasn't easy because they'd vary slightly – variation in the gap, variation in the tension of the diaphragm would upset it a bit, you see. One wanted to avoid that. Can't think of anything else. Would I have made it bigger? Well, then it would have upset a whole lot of people who wanted a small speaker. Would I have made it smaller? No, because then you wouldn't have enough bass. It was roughly the right size.

'It cost £52 when it came out – what the price would be now goodness only knows. But there was always a waiting list for them. We allocated them to dealers, and the amplifiers at that time, and they were allowed six a month or three a month, what have you. You didn't ask a dealer how many he wanted. You told him what he could have. Didn't have any sales people; didn't need them. [Laughs.] Wonderful situation!'

Arthur Radford remembered. *By Geoffrey Horn*

Arthur Medley Radford was born in 1914, just at the start of the Great War. Few good things can be said in favour of wars but they certainly accelerate the advance of technology. Thus wireless as a means of communication grew apace and learnt the power of speech – as opposed to the primitive scratchy spark-generated Morse which had come to the aid of the *Titanic* in April 1912. Post-war thoughts turned to another use for wireless: entertainment. Hobbyists had long been able to buy components to build receivers and this trade now flourished, as numerous magazines showed how it could all be done on the kitchen table. Very soon ready-built sets came on to the market but were expensive by comparison with DIY! The young Arthur developed a major interest in components which lasted all his life and a particular interest in transformers. The second regrettable war saw Arthur in the army, somewhat involved in wireless and his beloved transformers. On leaving he found an opportunity to combine his interest with commerce. He bought and sold war surplus gear under the aptly named Cabot Radio in his native Bristol.

It was in those immediate post-war years that an enormous quantity of parts and equipment came on to the market at quite silly prices. Most were sold in London's Tottenham Court Road and Lisle Street, but a few enterprising provincials dealt in rather upmarket pieces. Thus it was that I first made contact with Arthur – though neither of us knew it. He had got hold of some rather swish ex-Admiralty mains transformers which were just the ticket for a small 2x 6V6 amplifier, and I must have made at least half-a-dozen for friends; a couple of years ago one of them died and I found he had still had one working every day!

I heard a possibly apocryphal story about the next move in Arthur's career. At one sale viewing he spied an interesting-looking transformer, still with its waxed paper wrapping, on top of some cartons. It was, he thought, a filament supply device with a lot of low voltage windings but of good make; his sale list quoted eight transformers and he pencilled in £16 as his limit, which was his normal practice at sales. As he had rightly guessed, other dealers were not interested as there was no HT winding and the auctioneer had few bids, so Arthur got them for a pittance. When he came to collect them, he found he had the eight cartons as well and each contained 10 transformers.

Shortly afterwards he had an enquiry from his local education people for some laboratory power supplies, so he rapidly found a firm to make steel cases, another to paint them and with a few switches and terminals plus his stock of bargain transformers made a large profit. Not long after this, he had an enquiry for school Physics Laboratory power packs from the Ministry. The Government thought we should grow more scientists and set up the Nuffield Physics Course; someone had seen his Bristol models, which were entirely satisfactory, and wondered if he could supply the whole country. He thought he could, acquired coil-winding machines to make the transformers, bought the firm that made the cases, set up his own paint shop, printed legends, found premises and took on staff. It was a wonderful foundation for his company. And it got better! Nuffield Physics was adopted widely overseas and Radford was the quoted supplier. He made thousands, well into the '60s, and many of them are still in use.

Whilst at Cabot Radio, around 1950, he had dabbled in electronics, producing a 25 watt public address amplifier. Now, following his success with power packs, he took on a modern factory on the Ashton Vale Industrial Estate and began to research high quality amplifiers. Studying the prolific literature on the subject he found himself at odds with much of the current thinking about the design of transformers to couple valve output stages to loudspeakers. This resulted in several prototypes which he thought might be superior to what was on the market, but he needed confirmation. And so it came about that one day, in 1959 I think, as I was completing a demonstration to a customer in the listening room at my shop, Horns of Oxford, a small man carrying a big brief case walked in. He gave his name as Arthur Radford, from Bristol (I could have guessed that) saying that a mutual friend, one Donald Aldous, had told him to come and have a chat with me. Eyeing the brief-case I asked, 'Is it serious?' and led him into my office.

After some preliminary discussion, he proceeded to demonstrate with numerous graphs and measurements how many current revered designs were compromised. He was particularly at odds with Baxandall's preference for separate feedback windings, and I remember thinking that anyone who could so readily dismiss the great Baxandall's work with a comment that went something like, 'It's a BBC idea that's fine for driving lines but flawed for use with practical loudspeakers', had to command attention. Delving into the large brief-case he produced a beautifully conceived mono power amp, compactly built on a milky white painted chassis with touches of chrome metal work; it became his model MA15. It was, he claimed, perfectly stable with 40dB of overall feedback and had only about 0.005% distortion – this at a time when the Leak company were making quite a fuss about its Point One!

Of course I asked how he could measure such low distortion, whereupon more literature appeared showing some very advanced test gear he had produced to do so. He said 'I'd like you to have a set Geoffrey,' and I've still got it. A whole range of amplifiers followed and one in particular, the 2 x 25 watt STA25, became accepted as one of the best valve designs of the era and we sold quite a number to discriminating customers. Inevitably we became friends, and as Arthur had bought a fine house on the hills above Weston-super-Mare the Horn family would visit on a Sunday and pile into jungle clearance of his overgrown garden. My science-oriented son was a favourite of Arthur's (he had daughters) and he helped him with an ambition to make his own STA25 from the chassis up, providing the transformers at cost and giving him the unique bits, such as the fascia plates and chrome work, that he couldn't make himself. He still has it.

Arthur was a man who readily acknowledged his own limitations and never hesitated to avail himself of expert guidance. He later went on to produce some fine loudspeakers with the help of A R Bailey and having no experience of transistors asked the late John Linsley Hood to provide circuit advice. He developed an interest in recording and bought several STC 4136 capacitor microphones, building his own amplifiers to feed his Revox recorder. I still have a few examples, notably the Avon Cities jazz band playing in the loudspeaker section of his factory, where the stored packaging helped the acoustic.

Sadly, his later years were marked by deteriorating mental powers – I suppose it was what we now call Alzheimer's disease – and went to a home where he died in November 1993. Little Arthur, as my family affectionately called him, was a kind and generous man whose contributions to audio will not easily be forgotten.

Tannoy: a brief history of a famous brand. *By Steve Harris*

As the company is always keen to point out, 'Tannoy' is the only hi-fi brand name that appears in the Oxford English Dictionary. It is there, of course, as a synonym for a public address system – used for barking out orders to troops rather than soothing the savage breast of the music-lover. But Tannoy does have an important hi-fi heritage, and a unique place in the history of the industry, thanks to the Dual Concentric speaker – first demonstrated in 1947 and still going strong today.

In the 1970s, when I first started learning anything about hi-fi, the Tannoy Dual Concentric had gone out of fashion. Valve amplifiers had given way to cheaper, more powerful transistor amps, so the Dual Concentric's high efficiency was no longer prized. Compared with contemporary multi-way speakers, the Dual Concentric principle seemed like an expensive and unnecessary technical luxury. On the other hand, those who'd been exposed to the Dual Concentric in its professional forms, which had their heyday in the 1950s and 1960s, were often fired with enthusiasm for it. Rock musicians would often tell you that no other speaker would do.

The Dual Concentric's fortunes may have dipped, but a revival came soon enough. Today traditional-style Dual Concentric speakers are still highly-prized by Japanese audiophiles, and Tannoy has cunningly applied the principle even to tiny home cinema satellite speakers. It's a story worth telling. So, with acknowledgements to Tannoy and to *The Tannoy Story* by Julian Alderton (2004), here's a potted history.

Tannoy beginnings

Back in 1926, the dry batteries used for wireless sets were expensive and had a short life. The alternative was to use lead-acid 'wet' batteries – which needed frequent recharging. Most commercial motor garages at the time had battery chargers, which could provide a profitable side-line. Guy R Fountain (whose father-in-law, incidentally, had founded the AC car company) owned one such garage, in Dulwich, south east London.

The commercial accumulator chargers then in use were based on expensive mercury-vapour rectifiers. This prompted Guy Fountain to turn to an electrolytic rectifier, using two different metals, tantalum and a lead alloy, and from this the name Tannoy was coined. Fountain set up a tiny factory at Dalton Road, West Norwood, in south west London, to manufacture these rectifiers and Tannoy the company was born.

Soon the company was making battery eliminators which would drive radio sets directly from the mains, and then amplifiers. This allowed a move into a new and booming field, public address systems. Large companies such as Marconi and Western Electric were already in the PA business, but their equipment was not flexible enough to cater for mobile and portable applications such as circuses and fairs. Early in 1930, Tannoy won a contract to supply the Bertram Mills Circus, the most famous circus in Europe, with sound reinforcement systems – and never looked back. At first all the PA loudspeakers were bought-in, but by 1934, Tannoy had developed its own range of microphones and loudspeakers, together with amplifiers of 10 to 200 watts, along with measuring equipment for precise evaluation of their performance. Even Gilbert Briggs of Wharfedale made use of Tannoy's measurement facilities. The company had also moved into a new factory in Canterbury Grove, Norwood.

During World War II, Tannoy developed and produced communication systems for airfields, crew communication for submarines and tanks and command systems for gun batteries. In 1945, Tannoy supplied the PA equipment for the Victory celebrations and received a letter of thanks from the King for its contribution to the success of VE Day in London.

Soon Tannoy would become one of the world's largest suppliers of translation and sound reinforcement equipment for international conferences, providing sound reinforcement systems for the House of Commons and translation equipment for the United Nations in New York. But in the immediate postwar period, Tannoy (like other similarly-placed companies) was in trouble. Income from its massive defence contracts dried up, while shortages of materials and other problems hampered peacetime production. Ironically, at the moment when Tannoy's most famous hi-fi product was born, Guy R Fountain Ltd was trading in receivership – a situation which lasted until 1950, when Fountain succeeded in buying back the business and restarting as Tannoy Ltd.

Birth of the Dual Concentric

By all accounts Guy R Fountain was a pretty difficult man to work for, but he knew how to hire brilliant engineers. The Dual Concentric driver, shown at the London Radiolympia show in September 1947, was Tannoy's state-of-the-art, with a very flat and extended frequency response, high efficiency and high power handling. It had origins in work carried out before the War by Jack Houlgate, but he had left Tannoy to work for the BBC, and the development was led by Ronald H Rackham. Julian Alderton quotes T B 'Stan' Livingstone (who was Guy Fountain's righthand man at the time) as stating categorically that: 'Ron Rackham was entirely responsible for this achievement. The detail design of the Dual Concentric loudspeaker, its development, its manufacturing specification, its excellent performance and its superb quality were entirely the achievements of Ron Rackham'.

For the first 15 inch Dual Concentric, a horn-loaded compression driver (basically an existing Tannoy type) was mounted concentrically at the rear of a direct-radiator bass unit, using a single magnet assembly with two gaps. Thus the rear gap was for the 2in voice-coil of the pressure-loaded treble unit. The treble diaphragm's concave (front) side faced a series of holes drilled radially through the convex block which formed the back end of the pole piece. This 'multiple throat' led forward and inward into the start of a horn bored through the centre pole piece itself. The flare of this horn was continued by the profile of the bass unit cone. Crossover frequency was 1kHz, and the claimed frequency response 25Hz–20kHz.

The idea of the reverse-throat pressure driver with the horn continued by a cone had been registered by Western Electric in America in 1936, the UK licensee being British Thompson-Houston. According to *The Tannoy Story*, BTH did make representations to Tannoy soon after the Dual Concentric was launched, but may have been persuaded by the receiver, Norman Wild, that Tannoy's application differed sufficiently in detail not to constitute an infringement.

Early Dual Concentric speakers were sold to AKG and to US microphone company Turner, and to the GPO, which adopted them as a standard sound source. At that time, Decca wanted a wide-response loudspeaker for its *ffrr* recording system, which went up to 14kHz. Decca was impressed by the original 15 inch models and asked for a 12in version for its high-quality Decola record player. After this, a Dual Concentric, housed in a suitable enclosure, soon became a standard studio monitor.

A brief report in *Wireless World*, September 1949 said:

'Against this type of concentric loudspeaker it has often been argued that relative movement between the two sections of the HF horn could give rise to intermodulation distortion between low and high frequencies. The makers have carried out two-tone tests to investigate this criticism and find that intermodulation products are less than 2%. We have heard the loudspeaker in operation and can confirm that, subjectively, intermodulation effects are negligible. There is, in fact, far less blurring in orchestral music than in many single-element loudspeakers with comparable amplitude/frequency characteristics. Attack is good and the transient response generally supports the makers' claim of aperiodicity. In a wide variety of test records, reproduction was of a very high standard, the only possible criticism being that in one case the high notes of a solo violin were incline to be metallic, though this might well have been a fault of this recording.

'The price of the unit, which weighs 30lb complete with crossover network and output transformer, is £26 5s. It is also available in a vented corner enclosure at £52 10s.'

To this day, well over half a century after its introduction, Dual Concentric speakers are revered in Japan. There they have won a string of 'Golden Sound' awards, the first in 1982 for the Westminster and a second in 1986 for the 60th anniversary RHR Special Limited Edition, while the GRF Memory model won the *Stereo Sound* State-of-the-Art Award.

So what is it about the Dual Concentric sound? The Dual Concentric provides a point source at all frequencies, with a uniform dispersion characteristic. This means that the loudspeaker simply fills the room in a way that conventional spaced-driver speakers don't, and this, along with the immediacy and impact which is helped by the horn-loaded tweeter, is really the key to its appeal.

Reviewing a recent model, the Kensington, which has a 10in Dual Concentric driver, Ivor Humphreys wrote (in *Hi-Fi News*, August 2004): 'It's only the concept which is old. The Tannoy Dual Concentric has gradually evolved to the work of engineering art it now is... The sheer transparency of the Kensington astonished. I've not before heard anything quite so coherent from a box speaker.'

In the early 1970s, when Tannoy was sold to the American Group, Harman International Industries, Guy R Fountain retired to live abroad (he died in 1977). Harman moved the operation to Coatbridge, Scotland, in 1976, then sold it (along with other audio businesses) to the Beatrice Foods company in 1977. Beatrice in turn decided to sell, and there was a management buyout by the directors, led by Norman Crocker, in 1981. In 1987, Tannoy merged with Goodmans Loudspeakers Ltd to form TGI plc, one of the world's largest manufacturers of quality loudspeakers.

Development of the Dual Concentric drive units was enthusiastically continued. The internal design has now been radically revised and refined in many iterations, but the principle remains the same. While the traditional 10, 12 and 15 inch Dual Concentrics continued, mainly for the Japanese market, smaller versions were developed. Tannoy also added its Wideband Technology – the first model to include a supertweeter was the Kingdom, which won yet another Japanese Golden Sound Award, in 1996.

In January 2002, TGI plc merged with the TC Group, forming a holding company of seven individual companies; Tannoy, Martin Audio, Lab Gruppen, TC Electronic, TC Helicon, TC Works and GLL, to which TC Applied Technologies has recently been added. In 2003, Tannoy was able to present the first fruits of the combined technological expertise within the TC Group – its Interactive Digital Programming technology, or iDP, described as the the digital solution to precision defined acoustics.

And the Dual Concentric lives on, not only in the top-of-the-line Prestige series, which wins all those awards in Japan, but in many other models including the Arena home cinema speakers – an application which, more than ever, shows the real benefits of a theoretical 'point source'.

5. AR and other American pioneers

'Acoustic Research's ads, the company literature, and the voluminous technical articles by Villchur set a standard for clarity and impact that was the envy of the industry.' **Roy Allison**

'I didn't invent the horn loudspeaker. I just folded it so you could get in the same room with it.' **Paul Klipsch**

'It is beyond doubt that David Hafler did as much for audiophiles and for the cause of spreading good sound to a wider audience as Alex Issigonis did to mobilise the British after World War II with the Morris Minor.' **Ken Kessler**

'I still use my Weathers FM pickup system today (mono only) and still consider it the best phono system available.' **Mel Schilling**

Acoustic Research Inc: The Golden Years. *By Roy Allison*

On rare occasions, a device is conceived that is needed and perfectly suited to the times, and then produced and marketed by the right kind of company. The acoustic suspension loudspeaker system was just such a device. The inventor was Edgar Villchur, and the company was AR Inc. (Acoustic Research). What they did resulted in an industry-wide revolution in loudspeaker system design.

Most readers will be familiar with the product and its design principle, so I won't go into great detail. Briefly, woofer suspensions (spider and outer surround) until that time had been made stiff enough so that the woofer could be used in so-called infinite baffles, or other large enclosures, without being torn apart by large low-frequency power inputs. This mechanical restoring force, unfortunately, was unavoidably nonlinear, and generated large amounts of distortion when the woofers were driven hard. Also, when these woofers were put in small boxes, the resonance frequency and Qtc rose unacceptably, with limited output below resonance and high-Q boom at and above the resonance frequency.

An acoustic-suspension woofer has very compliant suspension elements, just strong enough to keep the voice coil from rubbing and centered in the VC gap with no signal input. If used in a large enclosure or an infinite baffle, strong low-frequency signal inputs would destroy it. In a small enclosure of the optimal size for the design, the stiffness of the enclosed air replaces the missing mechanical stiffness and raises the resonance frequency to the proper value. Not only is the system desirably small, but the controlling air suspension, which is much more linear than a mechanical one, enables the system to produce large amounts of fundamental low-frequency output with negligible distortion.

This represents a simple solution to a big problem. Like many other 'simple' ideas, however, no one before the inventor had thought of it. No one before Villchur had realised the full scope of important benefits this system provided. The boxes are of reasonable size. Stereo then was still fairly new and exciting, but not many listeners were willing to put two big boxes in a domestic living room. The time had indeed come for small systems that were capable of really full-range high-fidelity sound. Recording media were improving in faithfulness to the original music sources, and acoustic-suspension systems – relatively inexpensive – were needed to take advantage of these improvements.

An 'impossible' solution

Edgar Villchur earned his MS degree from City College of New York in 1939. He had been devoted to formal music for many years and built his phonograph from parts purchased at electronics hobbyist stores. During World War II, he served as a communications officer in an Army Air Corps fighter group, maintaining electronics equipment in fighter planes, and attained the rank of Captain. As Group Communications Officer, he headed the group's maintenance personnel.

From 1951 to 1956 he taught a course called The Reproduction of Sound, at NYU. Materials from these lectures were published in a series of articles in *Audio* magazine and, years later, in two books, one published by Audio and the other by Acoustic Research, later taken up by Dover Publications. AR also published my book *High Fidelity Systems: A Users' Guide*. Both were favorably reviewed as authoritative and completely non-commercial.

During the early 1950s, Villchur pondered the problem of woofer distortion, tinkering with suspension elements in attempts to make them more linear. Finally the solution presented itself: eliminate the mechanical suspension as much as safety allowed, and replace it with a cushion of air stiff enough to take the place of the mechanical stiffness. In late 1953, he altered a conventional 12in speaker by cutting away most of the spider and all of the outer surround.

Villchur's wife Rosemary, who had been a draughtsman during the war years, laid out a pattern for the first half-roll surround on a sheet of mattress ticking. This was cut out and glued to the cone and the speaker basket flange. The resonance frequency was reduced to about 10Hz. A sturdy, well-braced cabinet of 1.7 cu ft in volume raised the resonance to 45Hz, the calculated optimal frequency, which provided full response to below 40Hz.

Its performance was all that had been predicted: powerful, audibly pure bass that astonished listeners. Villchur applied for a patent in March 1954, and it was granted in December 1956. Villchur's disclosure article, with full details of the prototype design, was published in the October 1954 issue of *Audio*.

It seemed obvious that this was an important enough breakthrough to warrant the attention of large and well-established loudspeaker companies, and Villchur approached two of the ones he thought most likely to be receptive. An executive at one of them explained that the company had a big and experienced engineering staff, and if any system had been worth developing, the staff would have done it. The other company's representative told him flatly, 'What you describe is impossible.'

The first products

At that time, Henry Kloss had a loft operation in Cambridge, Mass., making Baruch-Lang speaker systems (compact vented systems using multiple small holes as a distributed port). He was doing his tour in the Army, stationed at Fort Monmouth, NJ, which was close enough for him to become a night student of Villchur's at NYU. The two had obvious mutual interests. Kloss immediately understood the principle and potential of the acoustic suspension system, expressing later that it was a mind-expanding revelation to him.

The two pooled resources and found a few small investors, and incorporated AR Inc. with an operating capital of $6,000. Kloss did the production engineering of the woofer; Villchur selected the mid-range/tweeter (a Western Electric 755A 8in unit that had full-range applications), designed the crossover, and determined the system's resonance frequency and Q_{tc}. Kloss had ordered the cabinets without a removable back panel. Rather than alter the cabinets in order to mount the speakers and other components from the back (in the conventional way), Villchur decided to install the crossover and acoustic stuffing through the woofer hole and mount the speakers on the outside of the front panel. The cabinet thus became less expensive and more rigid.

The first AR model, the AR-1, was shipped in March 1955, with the AR-1W (woofer only) shipping at about the same time. The choices were soon expanded. Both models could be had in mahogany, birch, walnut, or cherry finishes, as well as in unfinished pine. The AR-1 suggested retail prices ranged from $172 to $194 each, depending on finish; and from $132 to $145, depending on finish, for the AR-1W. These prices were simply astounding for speaker systems that could, according to a rave review from *The Audio League*, produce more output at 25Hz and below than the huge and hugely expensive Klipschorn. A direct quote:

'At first listening, one may conclude that the AR-1 is deficient in bass, since absolutely no bass will be heard if none is in the program material. It is startling to be listening to music which suggests that the woofer is inoperative, and suddenly to feel the fundamentals of a bass viol, piano, or organ, or the solid impact of a bass drum. Everything sounds a bit "different" on an AR-1, since it adds to or subtracts from the program material to a far lesser extent than any other system we have tested.'

Other reviews followed along the same vein. As they came in, Villchur (who wrote all of AR's ads during the entire time he was with the company) incorporated them in catalogs and in the ads. He knew that readers would believe what others said about the products far more than what the manufacturer would say, and he quoted the reviewers faithfully. AR's ads, the company literature, and the voluminous technical articles by Villchur set a standard for clarity and impact that was the envy of the industry.

Arthur Janszen's electrostatic tweeters were properly considered at that time to set the standard for mid- and high-frequency performance. He had been demonstrating them with a large four-woofer Bozak system. (*Author's note*: My own stereo system then consisted of four Bozak 12in woofers in a fibreglass-filled enclosure that stretched 10 feet along one wall, with a four-panel Janszen sitting on top of it at each end.) When Janszen heard an AR-1W, however, he switched, and he and Villchur gave a joint presentation at a meeting of the Harvard Electronics Club.

A parting

Sales increased rapidly, and AR actually made a small profit in the first year on sales of $57,000. In 1956, sales were $383,000, and in 1957, $973,000. Both sales and profits increased every year thereafter through 1972, which is the last year for which I have figures. Although the financial fortunes of the company were reason for celebration, personal differences in policy objectives arose between the co-founders. As Villchur, who was president, put it afterward, 'Henry was presidential material, and you can't have two presidents in one company.' It was obvious that one or the other had to leave.

After much discussion, it was decided that Villchur would stay with AR and that Kloss's interest would be bought out. Villchur put together another group of investors including Abe Hoffman, a CPA, who became vice-president and treasurer. Harry Rubinstein became plant manager, Maurice Rotstein, sales manager, and Emmanuel Maier, materials manager. All were long-time friends or acquaintances, and although only Hoffman had had any business experience, all were successful in their previous careers, and quick to adapt. Moreover, all were known to be completely trustworthy.

The interests of Tony Hoffman and Malcolm Lowe were bought out as well as that of Henry Kloss. Together they went on to found KLH, which took a license under the Villchur patent, and had a long and initially successful run under the presidency of Kloss. He developed many visionary projects along the way at KLH and later at another of his companies, Advent, culminating in large-screen projection television systems. Unfortunately, that product proved to be his financial undoing, even though it is fair to say that it initiated a chain reaction among major manufacturers that has resulted in the wealth of giant-screen systems we have available today.

Just before leaving AR, Kloss had been working on a smaller speaker system that became the AR-2. It was to have a 10in woofer and a pair of cross-firing 5in tweeters – the tweeters just garden-variety OEM units, modified by AR with small pads of fibreglass stuffed between the back of the cone and the metal basket. This clever trick smoothed the response significantly. However, the system couldn't be put into production because the woofer coil wouldn't stay centered longitudinally; with application of signal it gradually crept toward the end of its excursion capability.

Villchur was able to correct that, and AR-2 systems were shipped beginning in 1958. But later, another problem arose: many AR-2s arrived at dealers with woofer cones crumpled near the cone/voice coil junction. That was a puzzler, because it was positively known that there was no damage before shipment.

The reason finally determined was that the packing cartons were too airtight, and any hard blow to a carton surface (almost inevitable during shipment) forced the woofer cone inward until the voice coil bottomed hard against the metal back plate.

The problem was solved by adding a sheet of corrugated cardboard covering the entire front surface of the grille panel. Such were the unanticipated side effects of the acoustic-suspension woofer system. The AR-2, selling for well under $100 each, was enthusiastically received by both reviewers and customers.

'Fried egg' speakers

Meanwhile, Villchur had been working diligently on the design of improved mid- and high-frequency units to replace the weakest link, the AR-1 tweeter. His efforts bore fruit with the introduction of the dome speakers in the AR-3 system. These were shaped as sections of rigid spheres 2in and 1.375in in diameter, driven by a voice coil at the outer edge in each case. Affectionately termed 'fried eggs' for their yellow colour, they were, in their own way, as significant an invention as the woofer. Nearly every serious loudspeaker system now being made uses a dome speaker at least as the HF unit. The disclosure article was published in 1958.

AR-3s were first shown at the New York High Fidelity show in October 1958, and shipped to dealers in the first half of 1959. Priced in furniture finishes at $225 each, sales soon exceeded those of the AR-1. It is no exaggeration to say that AR-3s became the quality standard for many years. They were used in many prestigious applications, including the listening rooms at the Lincoln Center Library in New York City. An AR-3 is on permanent exhibition at the Smithsonian Institution.

In 1959, the AR executive team added a second-echelon set of managers, with several of the first echelon looking toward their return to academia. I joined the company in early 1959 as assistant to the president, but was soon made chief engineer, working for plant manager Harry Rubinstein. George Benedetti helped Rubinstein in manufacturing. We were joined by Jerry Landau in sales, under Maurice Rotstein, and Ray Block in accounting under Abe Hoffman. Manny Maier in materials added an assistant. In due course, after we had become conversant with company policies and outside contacts, we moved up as Rubinstein, Rotstein, and Maier left.

From the very beginning, AR had an unwavering policy of treating consumers with complete support. Letters were answered promptly and fully. Problems were fixed at no cost and with the goal of complete satisfaction of any reasonable request. In fact, AR implemented a full five-year (and beyond) warranty long before the term was defined by government fiat.

Employee satisfaction was another policy goal. Promotions were made from within whenever feasible, and there was a firm non-discrimination policy. The company instituted a year-end profit-sharing bonus program that was beyond generous, in addition to wage rates that were kept above area averages. Another benefit available to everyone was tuition reimbursement for those who wanted to further their education. The result was unparalleled employee loyalty with very low turnover. It was a very good company to work for.

A different spin

For a year and a half, while Villchur was working on the AR-3, he had an outside engineer designing a turntable. It had always been his intention for AR to offer a complete high-fidelity system. That turntable project had come to nothing, and as soon as the AR-3 was launched, he turned his attention to a turntable design done in-house.

Again he reduced the problem to basic principles. It was obvious, on reflection, that relative motion between the tonearm spindle and the turntable platter had to be minimised to prevent rumble – both horizontal and vertical motion, since the new stereo pickup cartridges were sensitive to vertical motion as well as lateral. Solution: do what Stromberg-Carlson had done in its turntable, mounting both arm and platter spindle on a rigid bearing plate isolated from the base, and do it better if possible.

Stability and isolation were accomplished by using a three-point damped spring-mount system for the bearing plate, with a very low resonance frequency and with the springs located at equal load points. Isolation from the drive motor was to be accomplished by a rubber belt between the drive pulley and the platter. The pickup arm had to be lightweight, with a damped descent, an offset and overhung pickup head for minimum tracking-angle error, and balanced completely except for an adjustment to achieve the proper stylus force. It also needed geometry that placed the stylus in the same horizontal plane as the arm's vertical pivot, to minimise warp-wow.

It was far easier to state these requirements than to implement them. Along the way, finding a satisfactory belt manufacturing process proved to be a major headache. To achieve nearly perfect dimensional uniformity in a simple cast rubber belt was impossible – until an extra-thick belt was put on a machining mandrel and frozen to rigidity while being ground to spec. It was also discovered, after some frustration in achieving adequate isolation, that the rubber in production belts had to be completely free of acoustic resistance from additives, as the prototype belts had been.

The arm and platter spindle bearings were originally bored to specified ID in cast Delrin – a new plastic at the time, claimed to have all the properties you could desire for use in bearings, including dimensional stability. The stability claim was somewhat exaggerated, to put it mildly. After a month or so, the ID would close in and seize the spindle.

Along came Mitchell Cotter, who said that the supplier had not properly annealed the castings and that he had a facility to anneal and re-bore them. He was given the go-ahead to do a fairly large quantity. And what do you know: after a month or so the reworked bearings contracted and seized the spindles. That problem was fixed by putting steel-jacketed Babbitt-metal inserts into the Delrin, but it took time.

The first turntables were shipped to dealers in 1961. They were a completely assembled package except for the pickup cartridge: the drive/platter system mounted on a finished wooden base, tonearm, power and amplifier cables, foam turntable mat, overhang template, stylus force gauge, and transparent dust cover. The initial price was $58, on which the company lost money. It was subsequently raised in steps, but in 1972 it was still only $90.

The turntable quickly gained profitability, and AR sold many hundreds of thousands of them. Although it was the least expensive quality turntable on the market, many reviewers and consumer organizations rated it the best—with one exception. *Stereophile* thought it was pretty good, but said that the record spindle was too big. In fact that was an incorrect call; the spindle diameter was precisely what the industry standard specified.

Other ventures

In the years following, AR produced three series of live-versus-recorded concerts, in which the performers (the Fine Arts Quartet, Gustavo Lopez's classical guitar, and finally a nickelodeon) were recorded in an open field at Villchur's home in Woodstock, New York, and those recordings – played through a pair of AR-3s – were compared directly with the live performers. The venues were various halls throughout the country (beginning at Carnegie Recital Hall), and at high-fidelity music shows. Reviewers and the public were invited. The vast majority were unable to tell the difference, according to their own reports.

The company also set up two music listening rooms, one on a balcony above Grand Central Station in New York, the other on Brattle Street in Cambridge, Mass. They were open to all-comers free of charge, who could listen to loudspeakers of their choice with no accompanying sales pitch. The speakers were simply not for sale there. A demonstration room was also located in the Better Living Building at the 1964 New York World's Fair. All these customer-friendly policies, the superb products at relative bargain prices, the innovative promotions, the genuinely persuasive ads, and the many published articles and papers, produced phenomenal growth for AR. In 1967, sales were more than 7.5 million dollars. *Stereo Review* magazine began collecting market share figures for the industry in 1960, and AR had 16.3% then. By 1966, it had risen steadily to 32.2%, its maximum value ever, and higher than any other company ever achieved.

Edgar Villchur left AR in 1967, when the company was sold to Teledyne, Inc. He had wished to make his next project an investigation into speech processing toward better hearing aids for hearing-impaired people, and had wished to do it while at AR, but had met with resistance from his management team. By consensus, it was decided to pursue the Teledyne offer. Typically, Villchur, the majority stockholder, insisted that the deal could not go through unless Teledyne agreed to give all first- and second-echelon employees five-year contracts with the same salaries and bonus provisions. This was granted. Abe Hoffman became president of the new regime. Jerry Landau (sales) and I (manufacturing and engineering) became vice-presidents. All other management personnel stayed.

Villchur repaired to his Woodstock home and established his Foundation for Hearing Aid Research, entirely funded by himself. In the years following, he first developed an improved version of the standard audiometer earphone that gave better consistency in measurements than the existing model. Then he proceeded with his accustomed attack at a problem, to analyse why conventional approaches had not worked well and what could be done to improve intelligibility for the hearing-impaired.

His research once again proved fruitful. Using dual-channel compression followed by equalisation, both tailored to the client's needs, he achieved substantial improvement over existing speech processing methods. Instead of patenting his method, he simply published several papers describing his innovation, thereby granting to the world the freedom to exploit it without royalties. The great majority of current hearing aids now use some version of this processing system.

In the next five years, Villchur's management group adhered to the policies that had made it successful previously, developing a succession of new or improved loudspeakers and a line of electronics, completing the goal of complete music-playing systems. By 1972, when the management contracts expired, both sales and profits had doubled from the figures of 1967. However, the industry as a whole had expanded dramatically, and AR's share-of-market according to *Stereo Review*'s annual survey had fallen to 12.2%.

This performance did not make Teledyne happy. The corporate entity asked for and received Hoffman's resignation and installed a marketing whiz from a record-changer company as president. Seeing the handwriting on the wall, many of us resigned soon afterward. What happened to AR after that is not cause for celebration.

[*Editor's note:* Roy Allison sent the draft of this article to Edgar Villchur, asking if there were any inaccuracies. Villchur's answer was: 'My only criticism is that the article understates your role at AR. You were certainly the single most important person in AR's production design, and you designed AR's later models.']

This article is reprinted with the permission of Audio Amateur Press, from Multi-Media Manufacturer, Vol 1, issue 1, Jan/Feb 2004, by Roy Allison, p18. Copyright 2004, Audio Amateur Corporation, PO Box 876, Peterborough, NH 03458, USA.

An interview with Edgar Villchur. *By Laura Dearborn (from Hi-Fi News, February 1989)*

The acoustic suspension system, the dome tweeter, and the three-point suspended subchassis turntable were all designed by Edgar Villchur: three breakthroughs that became, and still remain some 30 years later, the standards in audio design worldwide. One alone would be a significant accomplishment; all three together is extraordinary.

Villchur's basic training came from five years of electronics while serving in the Army Air Corps during World War II – before that, Villchur had been a music-lover, an art student living in Greenwich village, and only a dabbler in building audio equipment. When he got out of the army, he opened a radio repair shop and started custom-building hi-fi. He also gained a Masters in Education and developed and taught a course in acoustics and electronics.

But what he really wanted to do was basic research in sound reproduction. So he decided to 'make his living out of the mail-box' (after moving to the country, to Woodstock) – he wrote three articles a month on audio (for *Audio*, *Saturday Review*, and *Service*) and continued to teach his electronics course, commuting each week to New York. For two weeks of each month he earned money, and for the other two weeks pottered. Out of this 'pottering' came the acoustic suspension system and, soon after, in 1954, the formation of Acoustic Research.

During his years with AR, he kept on with his 'pottering', including designing the dome tweeter in 1958 and the venerable suspended subchassis turntable in 1962. In addition, he set a certain 'quality of life' at AR that helped attract good people, a number of whom went on to form companies of their own, including KLH, Allison and Advent. Villchur was even criticised by some of his colleagues for telling too much, not playing everything close to the chest. 'My best defence,' he says, 'was that we must be doing something right because at the time I left AR (1967), in a field of perhaps 35 speaker companies, we had some 32% of the business.'

Although Villchur never wanted to go into business, once in that position, he was innovative in his commercial practices, not only in his attitudes towards employees (most uncommon for the time, he paid their major medical and life assurance, offered profit sharing and top salaries) but also towards his prospective customers. His clear, informative articles promoted audio without pitching for AR: they are still well worth reading today. (Articles written for *Audio* magazine are collected into a book: *Reproduction of Sound in High-Fidelity and Stereo Phonographs*, Dover Publications, New York.)

Believing that sales are made by wooing the hearts and minds of the consumers, not dealers, he set up 'listening rooms' in Boston and in New York's Grand Central station – 100,000 visitors came through here each year. No equipment was for sale, but the curious could listen to AR equipment and have their questions answered by expert staff. He also set up a rental plan for a short while in the early '60s: for a small fee, a prospective customer could take home a pair of AR speakers for two weeks. The dealers baulked and it had to be stopped. Villchur also set a policy of lifetime availability of parts and repair for all AR equipment.

The importance of Villchur's three milestone designs goes beyond their engineering contribution. They did more than change the way equipment is designed; at least as important, these excellent and affordable components offered a large number of people the opportunity, not otherwise available, to actually hear high fidelity for themselves and therefore realize how much they enjoyed it. One can therefore argue that he brought the desire for high fidelity to the surface in many people's lives.

He lived with his wife in Woodstock where they moved in 1952 to a house overlooking a steep valley and rolling hills. I drove up from New York as the leaves on the hillsides were turning their autumn reds and golds. We had the last raspberries of the season, sweet, heavily scented and somehow fittingly unique, not the expected raspberry-red, but white with a delicate peach 'blush'.

'Did you realise,' I asked him, 'at the time you developed the acoustic suspension system, the significance of what you had done?'

'When I designed the acoustic suspension system I felt – and modesty has nothing to do with it, I'm just trying to be accurate – I felt that what I was doing was correcting an error that had been made for the past 25 years. That was really what it was – there was something there and instead of using it, speaker designers fought it.

'A lot of people played around with speakers, but few actually built the entire speaker system; most bought the drive units and built the cabinet. So people had accepted, as frozen, the way we made the driver itself. And when you have a standard loudspeaker with a stiff suspension, this creates certain problems. designers just kept working at different ways of fighting this stiff suspension and the air in the cabinet, which makes it even stiffer. We had these two things fighting each other, when they should be helping one another.

'I went to a couple of different speaker companies to try to sell them my design – one of them, I guess, was at that time the biggest company, and they said to me, "Ed, you know, we have a pretty good staff of engineers and if there was something around such as you describe, I think they would have found it." A friend of mine approached the owner of another company, whom he knew, and described my speaker and the organ sounds he'd heard coming out of it, and the owner said that he wasn't interested because what he'd just heard described was impossible.

'So with this kind of reaction – the NIH (Not Invented Here) factor – I thought there was indeed a possibility that the acoustic suspension system would be ignored but, by and large, I thought that sooner or later this would be the way speakers were made. I didn't have any idea of whether I would participate in this myself and I was all set to sell the design outright. I planned to ask $10,000 and was prepared to accept $5,000. But, as I said, I couldn't find any company that was interested.

'Henry Kloss, who later became the K of KLH, was a student of mine, and he said, "listen, I have this loft in Cambridge" – a small production shop which made speakers for mail order – "why don't we get together?" I had a working model and had sent in the patent application. One day after class, we drove up to my house together. On the way up I explained the principle of it, which took a little time, as it was a little out of the ordinary in its thinking. And then he listened to the speaker, and after 15 minutes, he said "That's it, there's no question about it."

'And so we started to form the company; he was vice-president, I was president. We had between us $6000 – $2000 was mine, $4000 came together from various people – and we couldn't afford to hire a loudspeaker designer so Henry became one. Our first model was the AR-1. Henry was responsible for 75% of the production model of the AR-1, in the sense that he worked out the specific materials and production processes necessary to convert a theory and one hand built prototype into a production model. That changed later.'

Was anybody else working on the idea of the acoustic suspension system at the time you were?

'No, not to my knowledge, but ten years earlier, that's 1944, RCA had filed for, and had received, a patent for a unit which had a very loose suspension and which was meant to be used in a very large infinite baffle at a very low resonance frequency. After they had finished reciting all their claims, patent lawyers like to throw in the kitchen sink, so they threw in a couple of extra claims which said, in effect, that if you put this kind of a speaker in a small cabinet, it'll still be pretty good. They didn't say this is the way to make a speaker, they said it will still be pretty good. And that was the problem that ultimately made me lose the patent, after about five years, when Electro infringed the patent.

'We had licensees, so we had to object. We lost the case (because of the reference in the RCA patent) and I decided not to contest it, though I think I could have because I had a very strong case. But Armstrong, the man who invented FM and the super-heterodyne receiver, had recently thrown himself out of a window. He was in a life-long patent suit with RCA. He finally threw himself out of a window and, three months later, he won his patent suit. Modern electronics wouldn't have been possible without his work, but RCA infringed, said no, it's not you at all. So I said to hell with that, I'm not going to waste my time in court. If he hadn't wasted his time in court, who knows what else he would have done.

'The problem that I was trying to solve was how to radically reduce bass distortion in loudspeakers – in the very early 1950s, this was of the order of tens of times greater than the distortion tolerated in amplifiers. I concluded that most of this distortion came from the non-linearity of the drivers' mechanical suspensions. If you push them too far, they begin to bind, which flattens out the tops of the waveforms. People had been making attempts to design newer and fancier suspensions for the last 25 years and so, instead of trying to improve the suspensions, instead of trying to unravel the Gordian knot, I cut it. I got rid of the suspension almost entirely, designing instead a simple half-roll surround with very little stiffness. Then, I put this very floppy speaker with insufficient restoring force into a cabinet with the proper volume of air to substitute for the elastic stiffness that I had decimated in the mechanical suspension.

'That is the principle of the acoustic suspension system – the substitution of the acoustic stiffness of the air in the speaker enclosure for the mechanical stiffness of a cone suspension, hence the term "acoustic suspension". This design ends up with the same amount of elastic stiffness but with a much more linear restoring force (air is inherently more linear in this application than a mechnical device). That's its most important element but, as it turned out, most important commercially was that it also ends up with a much smaller enclosure.

'The conventional wisdom had been that you designed your loudspeaker [driver] so that all by itself, sitting out on a table, it would have the resonance frequency – which determines the low frequency roll-off – that you planned for it when it was in the enclosure. Then you made the enclosure large enough so that its acoustic stiffness did not raise that frequency appreciably. So you made the enclosure as large as you could. As you increase the enclosure size, the resonance frequency becomes lower and lower, towards its original value. As a matter of fact, the ideal was considered to be to mount the speaker in the wall between two rooms so that the entire room behind the speaker became the enclosure. There was a minimum required cabinet size, and anything beyond that was so much to the good, but then people had to settle for a practical size.

'In the case of the acoustic suspension system, there is a specific *optimum* enclosure size and you have to build the enclosure with this optimum, correct volume, not just a minimum volume. If you make the enclosure too small, the resonance frequency will be too high; if you make it too large, the resonance frequency is too low. Remember, in this design the values of the air stiffness and the mechanical stiffness are interchanged. The very compliant mechanical suspensions – creating a very low or subsonic unmounted resonance frequency – no longer provide the bulk for the necessary restoring force and only serve the function of keeping the voice-coil centered, while the final resonance frequency is determined by the stiffness – *ie*, the volume – of the air in the enclosure.

'When stereo came in, some five or so years later, all we had to do at AR was to sell twice as many speakers without changing anything. Two of our small speaker cabinets were a lot more acceptable in the home than two huge ones. Stereo was a great boon for us, but if we hadn't come up with a smaller speaker, someone else would have done it, it was an historical necessity.

'And the idea stares you in the face. You know, why build a speaker with a resonance frequency of 50Hz and then fight like hell to keep the resonance that low by building this giant cabinet which is expensive and heavy and takes up room? Why fight it when you can easily build a speaker with a much lower resonance frequency and then bring it back up to 50Hz with a small cabinet? People just get used to thinking in a certain way.'

The dome tweeter

'When I designed the dome tweeter, in 1958, there was no question in my mind what it was. I believed then that it was the best – by which I mean the most natural – high frequency sound, with the most extended high end, that existed. I felt very confident that the AR-3s, which were the first speaker to use it, would be a great success.

'Now, if you think about the problem, it's the logical way to design a tweeter. If there's any approach that can be said to characterise my work, I go for the obvious. You look at the problem, and you figure out not what is the cleverest way to solve it, or the most original way, but what's the *obvious* way to solve it, which very often has been ignored, and also what's the simplest way to solve it.

'The dome tweeter is a very simple device. The standard cone speaker is suspended at two points: at the apex of the cone, and at the periphery, what's called the surround. So then you have to take care of both points and treat them differently – one has a spider and the other a surround. With the dome tweeter, there's only a gap and a single voice coil, and it's suspended – in my case, it's suspended right in the gap, and then there's no second point of suspension. And by using the dome shape, you get a very strong, rigid diaphragm.

'The real secret of the dome tweeter is the fact that it's small, an inch or less in diameter. You can't make a cone speaker that small. Well, you can make it, and they do make them that small for earphones, but it will have very little power handling capability.

'With the dome tweeter design. you have a voice coil as large as in many larger speakers, so it has all the power capability and yet it's a small diaphragm that vibrates rigidly. Also. its dispersion comes from its small size, not from its shape.'

The AR turntable

When you designed the turntable, what were some of the problems you identified?

'I started to design the turntable for, quote, "less important" reasons: the acoustic suspension system and the dome tweeter were meant to make things better; the turntable was designed because I wanted to have a complete AR reproduction system of turntable, amplifier and speakers. I thought, well, what do I know about turntables, so I gave the job to an outside consultant. Several years and $25,000 later, I realised that that wasn't going anywhere so I took it over myself and I then came to the realisation that indeed there were things in 'table design that needed to be improved.

'I originally thought we'd just make a good turntable, as good as the others on the market. But by the time I got through, our turntable – well, I don't know that it had any truly unique features but it combined things that hadn't been combined before.

'It was a three-point suspended subchassis unit where the pivot of the tonearm and the platter bearing were held together with maximum rigidity. All adverse effects come out of relative motion between those two things, so you hold them together with steel one-inch beams, which is what we used, and then suspend it from the plinth. The three points of suspension were equidistant, making an equilateral triangle, and the centre of that triangle was also the centre of mass of the whole shebang, when there was a record.

'You see what that means? The centre of gravity, of mass, and the centre of the three points of suspension are the same. So the platform will go straight up and down, instead of rocking sideways, because it's balanced. Also, in this way, it's self-levelling. I can tilt the entire turntable, but the platter and tonearm will still remain level. The springs will just stretch more on one side to compensate but it will seek its level in relation to the earth, not in relation to the turntable's base. By the time I got through with the turntable, I realised the things that turntables ought to have.

'For example, what the suspension had to do more than anything else is reduce the rumble; but that's not the main thing, the main thing is that it reduces feedback. And the feedback that I'm talking about is the insidious kind, where you don't really hear any howl, there's nothing overt, but it comes through as a slight smearing of the music; it comes through as a slight lack of clarity. One of the write-ups of the turntable at the time said it had an unusually clear, clean quality in playing. That was the first time, to my knowledge, that anyone had ever written up a turntable by talking about the quality of sound you get out of it.

'The other thing I did in designing the turntable was that I realised the extreme importance of flutter: which is *any* variation of speed at all. Minimising flutter gives the signal a solidity, a musical strength, a stability.

'This was not an expensive turntable. I lavished all the expense on only the things that count. For example, our pulleys were individually machined. And the belt was machined. It took me a year to discover that you could not buy a cast belt that was adequate to the task, and so, finally, we froze the belt and machined it, and then individually tested every belt. So when it was all through, I thought OK, now I've got a good turntable, and one of the cheapest ones too, at $70, which was about half the typical price of the others on the market. I thought we'd just be another good turntable but it turned out not to be that way – I think on the manual turntable market, we took over the major part. That was something I had not anticipated.'

You are a vigorous proponent of live-versus-recorded demonstrations, even though these have historically (and inaccurately) engendered an audience reaction of 'Wow, I can't tell the difference.'

'Well, you're right that live-versus-recorded demos have been done forever. The earliest that I know of was referred to in an old Victor ad, in 1910 or 1912. Now, obviously, the difference between the original and the reproduction was gross, but they said you can't tell the difference.

'There are any number of tricks that can be used in a live-versus-recorded demonstration, if it's a snow job, if you're doing it the way they run the political campaigns. We did it in a way that was calculated to provide what we felt would be a fair comparison. Perhaps one of the most important things we [at AR] were trying to do with our demonstrations was to define what our standards were. We were saying: "We're not trying to make dramatic sound, we're not trying to make sound that knocks your socks off, we're just trying to make sound that is as dramatic as, neither more nor less than, the original. If the original is quiet and staid and not exciting, that's what our reproduction will be, too".'

'We would make a demo recording with the quartet or the guitarist or whatever playing certain sections of full volume and other sections at very low volume. Then at the demo, the performers would begin playing – over a low volume section on the tape that the audience could not hear – until, at a pre-determined moment that the performers all knew about, the recorded music would come up full, the performers stopped playing and the audience would be listening to the recording. So without missing a beat, you heard parts that were live and parts that were recorded. The trick is, can you hear the difference, and one way to test yourself is to look away and say, "Oh they've changed." Few people could do that.

'Of course, one thing the live-versus-recorded demo does not touch is transferring the acoustical environment of the concert hall to the playback room. We made our recordings outside – in effect, in an anechoic chamber, to avoid having a double set of room reverberations to contend with during playback. When the recording was played back through speakers during a demonstration, the only reverberation was that of the demo room, not of the recording venue. This way, the comparisons of live and recorded performances for the purpose of demonstrating the equipment were more alike because both the live and the recorded performances had the same set of reverberation.'

For the past 20 years, since AR was sold in 1967, Ed Villchur has been engaged in pure research on hearing degradation and hearing aid design. True to form, he has been able to see the problems, and therefore the solutions, uniquely, and has developed a completely different hearing correction system, which is about to be manufactured. When I asked him whether this again was another milestone, his response was: 'Possibly, but only if it works! It hasn't been proved yet.' Bell Labs, however, has confirmed his research. He has chosen to hold no patents on this, publishing his research as he develops it, and has no role, other than as adviser, in the manufacturer of his design. His Foundation for Hearing Aid Research is a non-profit organisation, its only products Villchur's articles.

First encounter with the Klipschorn. *By David A Wilson*

Yellowstone Avenue, in my hometown of suburban Sacramento, California, gently curves before intersecting Carlsbad Avenue. It was this fortuitous serendipity of road engineering that allowed me to hear the Klipschorn for the first time.

It was the night before Christmas, 1958, and, as it was our family's tradition to exchange gifts on the morning of Christmas Day, I was suffering from youthful anticipation insomnia! That year my heart's desire was a chemistry set… and if my numerous hints had succeeded, it would be the brand that contained potassium chloride.

I just wanted to doze off, so morning would arrive sooner, but sleep eluded me. There were Christmas carollers singing up the street, and it was enough to keep me tossing and turning. Finally, I looked out my window, and singers were nowhere to be seen! What I didn't know at the time was that a Mr Bob Wills, up on Yellowstone Avenue, had put his Klipschorn on his front porch to play Christmas music for his neighbours.

Because of the curve of the road and the cold outside temperature, that sound had a very direct acoustical path to my bedroom window. It fooled me! It sounded *real*. Mr Wills was an early high-end audiophile, decades before Harry Pearson coined the term. I wish I had known him better.

His son, Randy, was a friend and fellow perpetrator of noxious pre-teen pranks, so I was often in their home.

I do remember this huge thing – the Klipschorn – which resided in the corner just to the right of the front door. To the left of that door was the equipment console. I would later learn that the treasures contained in that piece of furniture included Fisher and McIntosh electronics, and (be still my heart!) a Weathers FM cartridge, arm and turntable. This was great stuff in 1958 and would serve to create a 'vision of the ultimate' for me once I was finally and thoroughly infected with the hi-fi bug.

My friend, Don Alley, who had been a protégé of Mr Wills, was in turn the one who introduced me to the joys of hi-fi. Don would intrigue me with stories of Mr Wills' visit to Arkansas to meet Paul Klipsch and get plans to build his own Klipschorn.

This was no simple box. Paul Klipsch patented, among many other original inventions, the utility design of his Klipschorn in 1945. The Klipschorn's great strength is its electro-acoustical conversion efficiency. While the best ported speaker designs exhibit a little more than 5% efficiency, and acoustic suspension designs as low as 1.5%, the Klipschorn (depending upon driver selection) was over 35% efficient! This was a huge advantage in system dynamics when 12W amps were normal and 50W units were 'monsters'. 'Quality,' said Paul Klipsch, 'is directly proportional to efficiency.'

To achieve this efficiency, Klipsch mounted either a Stephens or ElectroVoice 15in woofer in a small sealed enclosure, deep within the maze-like structure of the corner folded low frequency horn. The driver could be removed, if desired, via a panel on the side of its relatively small internal enclosure. Output from the front of the driver was directed through a folded horn, which, because of its corner placement, could (and had to) utilise the walls of the room to extend LF response. Deep bass (below about 40Hz) was never the forte of the big Klipsch. Don Alley's 15in Jensen Flexair woofer, in a large ported box, could probably go almost an octave lower. But when it came to fortissimo dynamics, the Klipschorn was in a league of its own.

I literally had dreams about this speaker. My own pitiful early projects, inspired by the delightful writings of Gilbert A Briggs, founder of Wharfedale Wireless Works, could never measure up (effectively or imaginarily) to the mighty Klipsch.

And then, one day, Mr Wills was moving and he offered to sell it to me! In retrospect, I think he could have gotten more money, but he saw how smitten I was by this legendary machine. A deal was struck, and there it was in my bedroom... The Klipsch had to lower her standard of living when she moved in with my system. Rather than feasting on harmonically rich McIntosh amplification, she had to endure lean and buzzy Heathkit. The Weathers FM cartridge's little, and much lesser brother, the C-501D, got the signal path going in the Klipschorn's new low budget system.

Living with her, I got to know her a lot better. She wasn't a totally complete Klipschorn. Two Philips Norelco 8in Coax drivers had been substituted for the original compression M-R and HF horns. This 'home-made' unit was thus dynamically hobbled compared to a standard Klipschorn. It turns out that Bob Wills was not really that fond of horn mid-range. Based on future purchases, I suspect mid-range dynamics were not the highest listening priority for Mr Wills. His replacement for the Klipsch was a pair of KLH acoustic suspension speakers. The Norelco's never really quite matched the bass, but they were very sweet-sounding.

The story behind another oddity of this particular Klipschorn reveals another facet of Mr Wills's personality. The Wills family had a large (fat) longhaired cat. It was an impressive, if lazy, beast. I can recall one of its favourite haunts was atop the Klipschorn, where it could sleepily survey the state of its realm.

One day, upon observing this scene of tranquil feline indolence, a devilish notion crossed Mr Wills's mind. Quietly he turned on the electronics. He put the preamp's input selector into an unused position and turned the still quiet volume control all the way up. The very slight hiss was not enough to disturb a snoozing Lord Puss so on to the Weather's low mass platter went one of Mr Wills's favourite LPs, Audio Fidelity's *Brave Bulls*. Into the lead-in grooves went the FM cartridge, and when the barely audible needle talk harkened the beginning of the heroic opening theme, the input selector was switched to 'Phono'. Over 30W erupted into a 104dB sensitive Klipschorn!

The cerebral cortex, or thinking centre, of a cat's brain is noted neither for its size nor its intellectual capabilities. However, the (startled) cat's cerebellum is very capable, so its skeletal muscle strength, response time and co-ordination easily (and instantly) make up for its lack of genius. The sequence must have gone something like this, under the caption 'Brave Bulls meets Ballistic Butterball':

0 seconds: leading edge wavefront of sound begins to be abruptly launched by Klipschorn drivers.

0+ 3 milliseconds: wavefront strikes (still) sleeping cat's tympanic membrane.

0+ 6 milliseconds: bioelectric nerve impulse signal transferred along eighth cranial nerve to brain of (still) sleeping cat.

0+ 10 milliseconds: fully aroused cat is beginning rapid vertical acceleration with all hairs, tail, claws and legs maximally erect. The cat's pupils are fully dilated.

0+ 24 milliseconds: position of ceiling interrupts and slightly deflects vertical trajectory of cat. Musk gland empties.

0+ 35 milliseconds: in vain attempt to halt rapid descent, cat's claw digs into soft mahogany front of woofer cabinet.

0+ 500 milliseconds: confused cat is in Randy's bedroom.

0+ 625 milliseconds: Mr Wills's allegedly superior intellectual facilities begin to react.

That little mid-life crisis episode would explain the 5 inch vertical scratch on the front of the cabinet, the stain on the top, and the low price. 'I guess I deserved it,' Mr Wills would later confess.

Playing with speakers as much as I did meant that I was always magnetising my Wittnauer watch. It didn't help the fate of my watch that I was trying to be cool and wore it with its face 'looking down' under my wrist. This fashion statement positioned the watch deeper into the magnetic field of the speakers I handled. Happily, though, I was always able to de-magnetise my temporarily paralysed timepiece using a Thompson apparatus I made in high school electronics shop, while sitting next to Mark Overmeyer who, for his assignment made an 'electron emitter'... but that's another (frightening) story! All I will tell you is that his 'emitter' consisted of one high voltage AC power cord and one small rectangular piece of galvanized sheet metal with a hole drilled on each end. The school's circuit breakers were never the same! My heart goes out to all high school shop teachers.

One day, I read how much Gilbert Briggs had lowered the free air cone resonance of woofers by replacing their paper accordion type surrounds by cloth (I believe it was flannel). I sacrificed an old set of pyjamas to get the cloth, hefted the Klipschorn out of its corner, and opened the access door. There it was, the metallic blue hammer tone finish of a Stephens 150W! That was some beautiful driver, and with almost 20 pounds of magnet structure, it was a bear to lift out. Soon I had it resting, cone facing up, on my bed. With Exacto knife, scissors, glue and Vaseline all lined up, the surgery was about to begin.

With my left hand, I reached across the face of the driver to pull it closer. I heard a tiny 'tic' sound. I looked at the cone to see if something small had fallen on it, but nothing had. I discovered the source when I looked at my wristwatch. The second sweep hand was lying loose against the crystal of the watch: a victim of the massive magnetic field of the Stephens woofer!

Large speakers have always been a tough sell at the mass consumer level. A limit to market growth of hi-fi existed because deep bass was not available from (relatively) small speakers. This all changed after Edgar Villchur introduced the acoustic suspension speaker. The AR speakers with 12in woofers actually got bass extension down to 20Hz out of a 1.7 cubic foot enclosure. Julian Hirsch's microphone approved, thus naturally, so did he. By the mid-1960s, everyone, it seemed, sold low bass-producing bookshelves.

Unfortunately, they all demonstrated severe dynamic constriction, which was especially disappointing to those accustomed to the dynamic swagger of a big system. But all the systems of those days were very primitive compared to the better systems of today in the areas of resonance control, diffraction reduction, group delay correction and passive component performance.

In 1963, I sold the Klipschorn through Darrel Handels' Stereo Shop in Sacramento, California. The passion to design and build my own speakers was just too strong to resist. It was (at that time) only a hobby: I knew I could never make a livelihood of it, but I had limitless curiosity and energy in it. After the Klipschorn, my experience over the next 18 years would include modular reflex designs (which would extend the bandwidth relative to the Klipsch, but not approach its dynamics), commercial acoustic suspensions from AR and Advent (which would be smoother than the Klipsch, but which would also be dark, dynamically compressed and uninvolving), Quads (I didn't appreciate their considerate resolution at the expense of scale, bandwidth and dynamics), and Dahlquists (a better balance for me than the early Quads). Then, from 1978–1981, I designed the WAMM and finally began to get the balance of sonic values I desired.

While the WAMM embodied what I had learned from all these earlier designs, it was really the Klipschorn and the Dahlquist DQ-10 that were, for me, defining foundation designs, the former for dynamics and the latter for coherence. It was my good fortune to have had a very friendly personal relationship with Jon Dahlquist. Sheryl [Mrs Wilson] and I used to enjoy visiting him on Sundays at CES shows. Jon was a great creative mind whose design career in loudspeakers was sadly very short.

It was only through the thoughtful invitation of Ken Kessler that Sheryl and I finally met Paul Klipsch in his suite at Caesar's Palace at Las Vegas CES in 1999. Although he seemed a little uncomfortable with all the attention he was receiving, he was nevertheless very gracious with Sheryl and me; taking great care to explain concepts of acoustical energy transfer. After the show he had his secretary send me copies of all his patents and technical papers.

In the world of audio, poor or mediocre products are as numerous as fleas on a junkyard dog. They go along with a larger system designed to protect and promote trash. Standing apart from these are many 'good' products... which serve us well, but can be quickly forgotten as is any worn-out appliance when its service to us is over. Finally, there are those very few great products, truly realisations on inspiration, which, however obsolete, and though they may have passed from our lives, cannot be removed from our hearts. They are industrial art. They enrich our lives. The Klipschorn is one of them.

David Hafler 1919-2003. *By Ken Kessler*

Among the many friendships I've made over the years are a handful involving heroes of mine from the time before I became a part of the industry. Despite meeting these giants of audio and sharing their company, I remain in awe of them, and will always appreciate the genuine privilege I've enjoyed in making their acquaintances. I cherish three in particular, because I was invited to the homes of these legends on a regular basis, purely for social purposes with no agendas regarding reviews, especially as two were well into retirement: Alastair Robertson-Aikman, still actively of SME, Stan Kelly and David Hafler. Even their wives tolerated me.

Writing from the eastern side of 'the Pond' but growing up on the western, I was aware that UK-based enthusiasts have a full appreciation of Messrs Robertson-Aikman, Kelly, Peter Walker, Raymond Cooke, Gilbert Briggs and myriad other British pioneers, but – due in no small part to the precious few imports sold in Great Britain before the mid-to-late 1960s, and the scarcity of American magazines – there was shocking ignorance of the American contribution, bordering on the xenophobic. (If proof is needed, consider the ratio of British-to-American industry figures in Gilbert Briggs' *Audio Biographies*.)

Among the precious few to enter the UK consciousness was David Hafler, and even this was more for one of his lesser achievements than for the reason why we should worship at his feet. British audiophiles 'of a certain age' remember Hafler for the Dynaco Quadaptor, a clever

INCORPORATING **TAPE RECORDERS**

Hi-Fi News

JUNE 1956   Vol. I   No. I   Price 1/6

★ TRANSISTORISED, BATTERY-DRIVEN PLAYER. Page 20 ★

The first issue, June 1956. The picture dates from 1902 and shows an Edison-Bell phonograph, which recorded and replayed wax cylinders: 'Beside it sits Ernest Watts, father of Cecil Watts, our contributor, whose photomicrographs of grooves and styli are known the world over.' Cecil Watts was later best known as the originator of the Dust Bug tracking record cleaner. Colour cover pictures were introduced in October 1967, but a yellow border was retained until the end of 1981

i

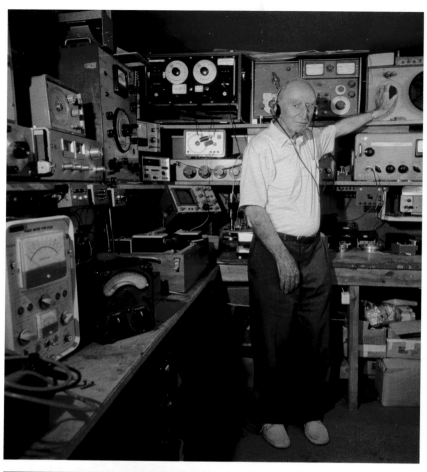

While Stanley Kelly was the major founding contributor to Hi-Fi News, his wife Betty helped to finance the magazine at its launch in 1956

Miles Henslow (right), the founder of Hi-Fi News and (far right) Ralph West, another of the original contributors. Living in retirement in France, Ralph continued to wind the local church clock well into his 90s

Thomas Heinitz, doyen of audio consultancy and classical record retailing in London from the 1950s on. He was an influential record reviewer for Records & Recording until its demise, and then briefly for Hi-Fi News

Brilliant hi-fi pioneer Paul Voigt (above), and Donald Chave (above right), whose Lowther company took up Voigt's loudspeaker design

A trendy graphic cover for Gramophone Record Review, June 1957. Re-titled Audio Record Review, and finally Record Review, it was absorbed by Hi-Fi News in 1970

Arthur Radford in 1968 (top); and Peter Walker of Quad (above) with ESL63, 1982

Paris, 1969 (left to right), Cyril Rex-Hassan, organiser of the Audio Fair; Donald Aldous of Audio Record Review; Raymond Cooke of KEF; and HFN editor John Crabbe

Paul Voigt's corner horn, the outstanding high-quality speaker of the pre-war period

*Tannoy's Dual Concentric driver was launched in
1964; this 1964 ad shows the GRF corner enclosure,
named after company founder Guy R Fountain*

v

*Peter Walker as a young
man and (above left)
Harold Leak advertising
his new transistor
amplifier in 1964*

*Edgar Villchur, inventor of the acoustic suspension speaker
and the dome tweeter and (right) the AR3a loudspeaker*

Recording for Hi-Fi News: John Crabbe looks on while the Fidelio Quartet perform at the Conway Hall, February 1972, during the making of 'What Is Good Recorded Sound'

From 1972 to 1982, Hi-Fi News honoured leading musicians with the annual Audio Award: here André Previn is seen receiving the Award from Joyce Grenfell in 1978

'Can you tell the difference?' Clearly not here to enjoy themselves at a 1978 amplifier listening test set up by James Moir and Quad are: (front) John Borwick of The Gramophone, Jim Rogers, Mike Ballance of Popular Hi-Fi, and (behind) Laurie Fincham of KEF, John Crabbe of HFN and David Stripp of the BBC

Harry Pearson of The Absolute Sound (below) received the Hi-Fi News Award in 1985

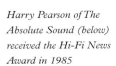

In 1984 'PJW' was one of the first six recipients of the Hi-Fi News Awards. The guest presenter was cellist Julian Lloyd-Webber (left)

Alastair Robertson-Aikman of SME and (above) one of the famous china cabinets (see Chapter 6). He received the Hi-Fi News Award in 1988

*Steve Harris (right),
Editor from 1986 to
2005, seen here with the
first 'new look' issue in
October 2000*

John Atkinson with former HFN colleague Ivor Humphreys and (right) Angus McKenzie, MBE

*January 1977: a youthful,
long-haired JA with viols*

*February 1987: Oracle
turntable, AirTangent arm*

*May 1990: an exclusive test
on the Finial laser LP player*

Music Editor Christopher Breunig (left) seen with Barry Millington of The Times (second left), writer and broadcaster Rob Cowan and (far right) an unidentified colleague

November 1990: SME 30, more high end, Which CD

October 1993: well, at least this speaker was a nice colour

August 2004: you still can't beat a big Tannoy 'Dual'...

The finest UK valve amplifier? This (left) is the stunning Radford STA-25 stereo power amp, beautifully built, as were all Radford's products

Amusing anti-marketing from Glasgow (above): of course, if you were a Linn follower, you'd know which reviews to dispose of

Class A: Sugden's A21 amplifier of 1969 sounded more exciting than it looked. The Goldmund Reference (right) was indeed the reference turntable for many US reviewers

CD arrives: Akio Morita of Sony (right) demonstrates the new medium to Herbert von Karajan

UK classics: Linn Sondek LP12 turntable (with original rubber mat!) fitted with Grace arm and Supex cartridge and (right) the immortal BBC LS3/5A loudspeaker

US personalities of the 1980s-90s high end scene: (clockwise from top left) Harvey Rosenberg; Arnie Nudell of Infinity with Chrissie Yuin of The Absolute Sound; Herb Belkin of Mobile Fidelity; Jason Bloom and Leo Spiegel of Apogee Acoustics; and John Bicht of Versa

Ken Kessler in Hunter S Thompson mode: this shot illustrated his 1984 report from the USA, visiting high-end hi-fi makers coast-to-coast (Chapter 12)

Krell heatsink fins, superbly photographed by Tony Petch, adorned an HFN high-end special in 1988. Tony also shot the 1997 Show Guide cover

Clockwise from top left: David and Sheryl Lee Wilson meet Dave's early hi-fi hero, Paul Klipsch, in 1999; Ivor Tiefenbrun of Linn; Julian Vereker of Naim; Bob Stuart with the first Meridian CD player; Tim de Paravicini

Left: HFN's first foray into 'Home Theatre', December 1992, and a recent high-end exclusive. The scoops keep coming!

device for extracting ambient information from stereo recordings, and in retrospect a cornerstone in the foundation multi-channel sound.

American enthusiasts, on the other hand, know Hafler because of what Dynaco did for music lovers of limited means. Dynaco amplifiers, whether in kit form or factory-assembled, gave true high-end performance to the people who would appreciate but could not afford Fisher, Harman-Kardon, Marantz, McIntosh nor the other luxury brands of the era.

It is beyond doubt that David Hafler did as much for audiophiles and for the cause of spreading good sound to a wider audience as Alex Issigonis did to mobilise the British after WWII with the Morris Minor and then the Mini. Rest assured, in David Hafler we find a designer and entrepreneur to rank with Edgar Villchur, Henry Kloss, Saul Marantz, Avery Fisher or any of his other contemporaries. His peers acknowledged this in 1984, when David Hafler was inducted into the Audio Hall of Fame. That he was an absolute gentleman only adds to his stature.

In the USA during the decade after the Second World War, when music lovers were driven to own something more sophisticated than a radio, they were able to indulge in the newly-born passion for hi-fi in one of two ways: they either bought expensive, factory-assembled components from then-new companies such as Marantz or McIntosh, or they saved money by building kits. Because of the strong DIY element of the period, numerous companies were founded to supply parts and actual components (as opposed to the later usage of the term, when 'component' meant an entire, assembled amplifier or tuner).

A graduate in mathematics from the University of Pennsylvania, David Hafler's experience in World War II – like many of the other audio pioneers of his generation – served him well during peace-time: he was a communications specialist in the Coast Guard. In 1950, David Hafler and his friend Herb Keroes, financed by Keroes' mother, started Acrosound in Philadelphia, Pennsylvania, designing and producing audio-quality output transformers. Both were early champions of Blumlein's 'Ultralinear' circuit, which used taps from the output transformer to feed the signal back into the output stage screen grid circuitry. Acrosound quickly became one of the most popular sources of transformers, and their products could be found in a number of early audio amplifiers, whether purchased in kit- or assembled form, or completely home-made.

Although Acrosound commenced business by serving both the DIY enthusiast and what we now call the 'OEM' market, Hafler wanted to sell whole amplifiers and complete kits, the latter within the grasp of those who could read and solder. (Even I built a couple.) His kits would be a direct and revelatory alternative to the hair-shirt path of choosing a circuit diagram or schematic from one of the numerous sources, primarily electronics magazines or publications from the valve manufacturers, gathering the parts – especially output transformer and tubes – and making one's own chassis from scratch, hoping the final result would work.

Hafler supplied what would be the heart of every Dynakit and its original, main attraction over contemporary competitors, including the well-established and highly-respected Heathkits: in a Dynakit, the customer found pre-assembled, fully-tested circuit boards, thus relieving the builder of the most time-consuming and possibly problem-prone stage of assembly. This main PCB was then connected to the transformers, the controls and the power supply to create a working unit.

Keroes, however, didn't share Hafler's passion for producing kits, so they parted company in 1954. Hafler found a new partner in Ed Laurent, whom he met while visiting Brociner Electronics in New York. Laurent had designed a single-tube driver circuit for a power amplifier, Hafler had expertise in transformer design – the two put their talents together to create the Dyna Company, incorporated in October, 1955, in Philadelphia. From the outset, the company produced what are now recognised as classics, including the Mk II 50W amplifier, sold in assembled and kit forms until replaced by the legendary Mk III 60W unit in the 1960s.

Hafler's reputation was strengthened by his clarity of thought and articulacy, exemplified by an article for *Radio-Electronics Magazine* in 1955 describing his design for a high-power version of the famed Williamson amplifier using Ultralinear circuitry and the new output transformers, which differed slightly from Dyna's own Mk II and Mk III models. Moreover, Hafler's personal generosity led him to foster great talents under his aegis.

Creating a legend

Demand for the PAM-1 pre-amp, the Mk II and the Mk III was sufficient for Dyna to develop new offerings. Chief Engineer Laurent and Bob Tucker created the legendary Stereo 70 (ST-70) while – famously – Hafler was on a business trip. Considered by many to be one of the five most important stereo power amplifiers of all time, the 2x35W ST-70 was consciously or unconsciously the basis for countless rivals' designs, and its core elements can be found in amplifiers introduced as recently as 2005.

By the early 1960s, Dynaco could boast a fairly comprehensive catalogue, including pre-amplifiers and power amplifiers, mono and stereo, and it didn't take long for them to add a tuner. Designed by the great Stewart

Hegeman and tweaked by Laurent, the FM-1 was launched in 1961. Sid Lidz developed a very cost-effective stereo adapter that slotted into an aperture inside the FM-1. A stereo tuner soon followed.

Solid-state equipment from Dynaco appeared in the mid-1960s, commencing with the PAT-4 pre-amp and Stereo 120 power amp, which were deservedly instant successes. (This author recently heard that exact combination, nearly 40 years after they were first produced, and found them to be noticeably unlike first-generation solid-state equipment.) It was also in the late-1960s/early-1970s that David Hafler began experimenting with what would later be called 'surround sound', starting with his seemingly-humble Quadaptor.

A very inexpensive and compact item, the QD-1 Quadaptor was a passive matrix device that recovered of ambient signals from conventional stereo recordings. It managed this elegantly and simply by exploiting the difference signal between two channels of sound, accessed by wiring a third speaker across the positive leads. Canny users didn't even need to buy a Quadaptor to do this, but it was cheap at, I believe, $35 and provided the user with a nice switch and level control in a well-finished box. This 'Dynaquad' system was also fitted to the SCA-80Q '4-dimensional' integrated amplifier.

Yet more masterpieces followed: in the late 1960s, when the USA was already rife with magnificent and affordable two-way box-type speakers such as the Advent and the EPI 100, Dynaco released the A-25 bookshelf loudspeaker, designed by SEAS in Denmark. It sold over one million units and was followed by both smaller and larger models. Naturally, they mated perfectly to Dyna electronics and probably provided more legal pleasure to a greater number of university students during that era than anything else.

Dynaco cannily kept the valve models in its catalogue, and was indirectly responsible for 'birthing' the Audio Research Corporation: ARC's Bill Johnson was an early tweaker of Dynaco amps and the company once offered modification kits, as did many others, such as Van Alstine.

In 1969, Dynaco was purchased by Tyco, and David Hafler stayed on for a few years, leaving in 1974 to join Ortofon. But in 1977, Hafler formed yet another company, this time eponymous, and it would prove to be equally successful in accessing the still-viable kit market as well as the middle-price market for assembled hardware. With former employees from Dynaco, Hafler released a series of exceptional budget pre-amps, including the DH-101 and DH-110 – I managed to build one in an evening! – and a series of MOSFET power amps. Among these, the DH-200 is fondly remembered as an absolute bargain and a genuine powerhouse.

David himself, by now nearing retirement, continued to experiment, coming up with the straight-wire differential test (SWDT) for assessing amplifiers in the mid-1980s; this magazine ran features on it, and it showed that David's acuity was still peerless. But in 1987, the Hafler Company was sold to the Rockford Corporation and David retired.

In the intervening years, the Dynaco name has emerged, disappeared, and re-emerged. Stereo Cost Cutters released products in kit form, as well as spares and modification kits, and the line itself was reintroduced with updated versions of the valve originals, under the aegis of the Panor Corporation. As for David, he enjoyed retirement, and it was his regular visits to his apartment in Green Park that enabled me to see him on numerous occasions. He never stopped surprising me: one day, I picked up an in-flight magazine to see an article on David, in his role as one of the world's leading collectors of chess sets.

On Sunday, 25 May, 2003, David Hafler died of complications of Parkinson's disease, at St Agnes Hospice in Philadelphia. No words can describe the sense of loss, the passing of another of the giants, like Peter Walker and Stan Kelly, to whom we owe so much. And for those of you too young to recall Dynaco, but who adore small but feisty, classic tube amps, well, if it has an Ultralinear circuit, a quartet of EL34s, a power output of 2x35W and sound so good that you think you've died and gone to heaven, it was probably based on an unassuming power amp manufactured by someone who surely must already be there.

Mel Schilling *remembering the Weathers phono system:*

'In the very early days of hi-fi, the 1950s, several of my friends and I all used the Weathers FM capacitance pickup system for phono playback. In those days, most audiophiles were using the GE variable reluctance cartridge tracking at over 6 grams. Along comes this new *wunderkind* with its 1g tracking, balsa wood tonearm and power supply oscillator which sold complete for $37.50!

'The issue with the Weathers system was 'drift'; the oscillator needed to be re-tuned literally after every record played. What stuck with me was my friends and I would gather together on a Saturday and drive out to Barrington, New Jersey (home of Weathers Industries) and march ourselves into the building, all carrying our Weathers FM phono systems for 'tweaking'. None other than Paul Weathers himself would greet and welcome us, and then he would go about re-doing everyone's phono system. This included replacing, if required, the pickup cable (it almost always needed replacement), the stylus or anything else necessary to get each system 'up and running' to its maximum. This would last for a week or two or maybe more and then the same problems would rear their heads again. We would then all go back to Barrington on the next Saturday and the process would renew itself all over again. Let it be noted that Paul Weathers never charged us for his service!

'I still use my Weathers FM pickup system today (mono only) and still consider it the best phono system available.'

Roger Walker *former Sales Director of Acoustic Research, on loyalty:*

'When I was Sales Director for Acoustic Research UK in the 1980s, I was negotiating with a sizeable Korean company who wanted to manufacture AR drive units and speakers in Korea, under licence. At the time, we were nervous that if we gave them a licence, Korean-made AR speakers would leak out into the Asia-Pacific basin and beyond and devastate our carefully managed global distribution chain.

'I duly delivered my lecture in the board room, ending with something like, "Gentlemen, in the end, it all comes down to mutual commitment and loyalty."

'There was a hushed silence for a few seconds, then the president's face broke into a huge grin and he shouted, "We *pay* you loyalty! Five per cent on serring plice!"

'We never did sign that licence agreement.'

Allan Markoff *on selling hi-fi to The Beatles:*

'We sold McIntosh to all of the Beatles individually. One night I got a call from a friend of mine who was with Apple. He called me one night at 10 o'clock, at my house.

'George Harrison was staying at the Plaza Hotel and he wanted a massive sound system there. In the hotel. He had like half-a-floor, George Harrison and his friends.

'We delivered it at 1 o'clock or 2 o'clock in the morning – four JBL S8Rs, which were the equivalent of two Paragons, and a rack mount of McIntosh power amplifiers and pre-amplifiers, and a turntable, tuner, things like that. We set it up in his room and he played it so loud you could hear it four or five blocks away, let alone throughout the hotel.

'And it got him thrown out of the hotel.'

6. The John Crabbe Era

'I remember winding 50swg enamelled wire on to minute celluloid formers into which were cemented some of the earliest properly polished sapphire styli. It was fiddly, but enormously satisfying especially as it was then possible to equal or exceed the performance of any commercially made pickup.' **John Crabbe**

Forty-five years with Hi-Fi News. *By John Crabbe*

Having been involved with *Hi-Fi News* for 45 of its first 50 years, first as a freelance contributor on DIY loudspeakers (1961/62), then as a Technical Editor (1962–64), then Editor (1965–82), and latterly as a monthly columnist, I've been granted a free hand to offer a medley of magazine events, autobiography, opinion, and hi-fi-*cum*-recording history. Much of the following was put together originally in response to previous commemorative occasions. so a few readers might therefore find themselves in familiar territory, for which I apologise – but reminiscences are, after all, usually most effective when offered in their original guise.

The above 1961/62 DIY project involved an 8-month series of articles entitled 'Horn-Type Speakers', the last three of which gave constructional details of a massive concrete system built into a house wall. A little later, and largely on the strength of those articles, the magazines's owner/editor Miles Henslow took me on as his Technical Editor. Prior to that I'd spent three years with the retail magazine *Electrical & Radio Trading*, where I'd been deemed acceptable by virtue of various writings in *Wireless World*, which had in turn been put together during five years as a research technician in a university phonetics laboratory, following an industrial lead-in via inspection and testing work in the radar field.

At *ERT* I covered everything from TV circuitry to washing machines, tape recorders to refrigerators, house wiring to oscilloscopes, and also produced a column called 'Sound & About' devoted to audio matters, plus an occasional 'Gems for Dems' item detailing recordings suitable for demonstrating hi-fi. The latter was in effect a trial-run for *HFN*'s more musically-oriented 'Recommended Recordings', which Miles Henslow had agreed I could introduce on my arrival at the end of 1962. The feature was gradually expanded, and had become a regular three or four pages of signed reviews by the time *HFN* merged with the magazine *Record Review* in October 1970, a conjunction that brought a huge expansion of musical content; reversion to plain *HFN* occurred in October, 2000.

Moving back now to 1956, the galaxy of experts gathered together by Miles Henslow to help fill the pages of his pioneering magazine still has a ring of authentic hi-fi quality as it shines across a half-century of progress and expansion. Cecil Watts, Ralph West, Gilbert Briggs, Stanley Kelly, James Moir, R S Roberts and H Lewis York; then, during subsequent years, G F Dutton, John Borwick, Rex Baldock, George Tillett, Angus McKenzie, Gordon J King, Reg Williamson, J Somerset-Murray, E J Jordan and P J Guy plus (still with us) Barry Fox, who in those early days wrote as 'Adrian Hope'.

All played a part in creating an image of accuracy and reliability. In his Editorial of June 1956 (Vol 1, No 1), Miles explained and justified his use of the hi-fi tag in a magazine title:

'We feel strongly that the term "Hi-Fi" should be held in respect. It does not matter much, in itself, if the tag is misused, but it matters a great deal if people are misled by its misuse. Since Hi-Fi or High Fidelity is the term which thousands of people, the world over, have accepted in their minds as a guarantee of quality, in terms of sound recording and reproduction, a High Quality label tied on to the wrong piece of baggage can very easily do a lot of harm. It is inevitable that more parcels will be incorrectly labelled; but it is our aim to see that this does not happen in the sorting office of *Hi-Fi News* ...by purposely using the tag Hi-Fi in our title, we shall have before us a constant reminder that we ourselves have a standard to maintain.'

Miles casually assumed in that first Editorial that the term hi-fi was accepted as an assurance of quality by 'thousands of people the world over'. Whether or not the assurance is still as clear now as it might have seemed then, the number of people owning and using hi-fi equipment around the world has now rocketed up into the millions or tens of millions, while those simply aware of the term must run into hundreds of millions or even billions: a revolution in scale, if not performance.

Hi-fi phases

One way of looking at the transition of hi-fi from evolution to revolution is to divide it into five phases. There have always been the technical enthusiasts, and insofar as a hi-fi hobby could be said to have existed before the 1939–45 war, it was the tinkerers and dabblers who kept it going: Phase One. Then, in the immediate post-war period a huge growth in the numbers of men with experience of electronic circuitry was joined by considerable improvements in recorded quality on the 78rpm disc (largely by virtue of Decca's *ffrr*) to make the home-built amplifier or loudspeaker a more worthwhile project than ever before. This was Phase Two: an exciting time aptly symbolised by the first edition of Gilbert Briggs' *Sound Reproduction*, published in 1949 and the bible of thousands for a decade or more. And the name of that great pioneer Paul Voigt spanned the pre-and-post-war phases by courtesy of Lowther.

This period also saw the birth of domestic hi-fi as a viable business activity, with the more enterprising among those post-war technicians using their audio wits to make money as well as reproduce music.

Of those who remained hobbyists, some went beyond radios, amplifiers and speakers to tackle pickups. I remember doing this, winding 50swg enamelled wire onto minute celluloid formers into which were cemented some of the earliest properly polished sapphire styli. It was a very fiddly business, but enormously satisfying especially as at that time it was possible to equal or exceed the performance of any commercially made pickup.

Phase Three began with the long-playing microgroove record around 1950. Decca were again pioneers (in the UK) in providing the software signals to stimulate hardware experiments and production of equipment. As FM radio was not yet known in Britain and tape recording was still a rather awesome new idea, those LP records offered quite the best source of musical sound to be had. Once pickups and/or their associated circuitry had been adjusted to allow for the effect of compliance in the vinyl record material (which lowered the HF resonant frequency and made some pickups sound very toppy in early LP days), it rapidly became clear that here was a great new source of sonic pleasure. An ever-growing body of enthusiasts built amplifiers based on *Wireless World* circuits or loudspeakers using the latest combination of Wharfedale or Goodmans drive units, while the annual London exhibition of equipment organized by the British Sound Recording Association was fast changing from a trade display to a public show.

Then, in 1956, the BSRA dropped out and we had the first Audio Fair under that great impresario Cyril Rex-Hassan and *Hi-Fi News* was born. The scene was now set for Phase Four, primed by the introduction of EMI's superb Stereosonic music tapes in 1955, oiled by a now-expanding interest in tape recording and a nascent FM broadcasting system, and launched with the stereo disc in 1958. Stereo on disc had its birth-pangs, of course, and once again it fell to Decca to achieve the first cleanly cut two-channel records. But within a year or so the better issues from all the major companies were very impressive, a growing number of stereo pickups and stereo amplifiers of good quality became available, loudspeaker manufacturers started looking seriously at the possibility of exchanging electro-acoustic efficiency for reductions in size, and we were on the verge of Phase Five.

But first came a process of conversion, for while the wider public was at last beginning to show an interest in hi-fi, it had to be moved away from the one-piece player to an acceptance of two loudspeakers separated from the 'works'. Resistance was as much commercial as domestic in those crucial years, as although the pioneering specialist hi-fi manufacturers were serving a lively and fast-growing market, the big traditional radio/record-player/TV manufacturers weren't convinced that hi-fi could ever bite very deeply over a wide area.

But they were wrong. Phase Five saw the 'big boys' move in during the mid-1960s: the low-distortion transistor amplifier started to look viable, what we cheekily on the magazine called 'chopped up radiograms' proliferated under respectable names like 'unit-audio', separate bits and pieces became acceptable in previously non-hi-fi homes, and we were away! The age of mass-production hi-fi had come, and small pioneers were in some cases absorbed by giants who knew all about selling to the big general public. The old-style Audio Fair at the Hotel Russell came to an end (1968), the Japanese started taking an interest, and the present-day international hi-fi scene was born.

An expanding readership

When I joined *Hi-Fi News* in 1962 the subject was hovering near the middle of Phase Four, and it was perhaps symptomatic of hi-fi's oncoming 'big business' epoch that in 1964 Miles Henslow sold the magazine and its partner *Tape Recorder* to Link House (with JC in tow as potential Editor and David Kirk, who would become editor of *Tape Recorder* and hence of *Studio Sound*, as his assistant.) Not that the Link organization was massive enough or faceless enough to be compared with Rank or Thorn, but I do remember being cornered by apprehensive people in various corridors of the Hotel Russell during that year's Audio Fair to be asked whether it was true that we were being taken over by *Exchange & Mart*! My replies were necessarily evasive during a period of confidential negotiations, but, unlike *E & M*, we managed to carry on printing some editorial material to balance the great explosion of advertising support that accrued in the following years.

In fact, during 1962/63 an issue with 25 pages of editorial was enormous and represented an almost unmanageable amount of work for the occupants of Henslow's tiny Mortimer Street offices, whereas today the editorial page allocation is typically around 75. And such was the expansion of both the magazine and the supporting industry between June 1956 and November 1973 that the total number of pages (Ed + Ad) was 40 in one and 310 in the other. Indeed, so grotesquely massive was the latter that a visitor to the Audio Fair famously suffered a broken instep as the result of a copy falling on his foot!

And physically big magazines were paralleled in the early 1970s by a dramatically expanded circulation, with *HFN/RR* even snapping at the heels of *Gramophone*, which with our large classical music coverage, it seemed for a while we might actually overtake. But by then other hi-fi titles were starting to compete for readers, causing that epoch to be regarded eventually as *HFN*'s golden age.

Editorial milestones

But I must get back to earlier times, and answer the inevitable question: Which items stand out particularly in my mind? April 1963 was notable for Rex Baldock's 'Paraline' article, which set the tone for a seemingly endless stream of constructional loudspeaker features. We usually published full working drawings for these, but in the case of Peter Atkinson's 'State of the Art Loudspeaker' (April 1976) we felt that the design was so elaborate that only a small number of readers would actually build it. So, assuming that the article's main function would be to educate, we simply offered to provide full details by post for an extra fee of 50p. But by June 1977 we had sent out 2500 sets of drawings and notes so there must still have been a lot of very keen DIY people around on the magazine's 21st birthday!

In 1965, I was greatly angered by some chamber concerts given in London for audiences in 'evening dress only'. This struck me not only as a sartorial anachronism, but also as a betrayal of the universality of music, an attempt to equate a great art with narrowly restrictive social elitism. In my view the *raison d'être* of hi-fi and of much other communicative technology is its capacity to bring otherwise inaccessible experiences to a widening audience, and it therefore seemed to me appropriate to comment adversely on the evening dress episode in an Editorial. Goodness me, what a response! We had more letters on the topic than on any other single matter ever touched upon in *Hi-Fi News*. To my relief the balance of comment was overwhelmingly in favour of the Editor, but it dragged up an astonishing amount of ire, not a few blimpish *non sequiturs*, the cost of hiring a dress suit and preparing a hamper of food for an evening at Glyndebourne, and much else besides.

In December of that same year we tried our hand at the art of parable, using the Leader column to chide the British Radio Corporation over a particularly foolish series of advertisements for a one-piece stereogram, a sort of last-ditch stand before succumbing to the 'separates' philosophy. At around the same time we also launched (for 1966) a pocket diary full of audio and musical data, which was published for four consecutive years and also an *Annual* which appeared from then on until 1982. Then in July 1966 we carried what I believe remains the biggest ever magazine report on the making of a classical recording 'Project Mahler 8', a multi-part article by seven authors on every aspect of Leonard Bernstein's recording of Mahler's 'Symphony of a Thousand', from public performances in the Albert Hall to detailed balancing at Walthamstow.

Moving on from Mahler but still underlining the magazine's commitment to music that can be taken seriously, in February 1967 I wrote an Editorial attacking the (then active) offshore pirate radio stations. This was prompted in particular by a pirate ship owner who stated in response to a TV interviewer's suggestion that his transmitted material was moronic, that his audience was made up of morons anyway. The piece naturally said much more than that, being critical of the whole ethos of down-market, commercially motivated pop. But it was taken by many as an attack on popular music in general, and produced a storm of protest. The post wasn't so massive as that sent in my defence over the evening dress issue, but letters on the topic were persistent enough to find their way onto the correspondence pages until October.

More *HFN* milestones

It was with that issue, October 1967, that *HFN* proudly flourished its very first colour cover picture. Still at that time framed by the traditional yellow border, it nevertheless seemed like a big breakthrough.

A rather different sort of breakthrough for me personally came a year later with the publication of *Hi-Fi in the Home*. This drew deeply on knowledge and experience gained in the six years I'd spent with the magazine, and eventually went through four British and one Dutch edition, selling a total of over 30,000 copies and even appearing for a while in Foyles' best-seller window in Charing Cross Road.

Now, of course, there are plenty of second-hand copies around, but it I have to admit that it has been gratifying to find several which had been presented as school prizes to pupils for good work in science subjects.

Frank Jones joined the in-house staff in October 1967 as the first in a line of editorial assistants who came and went across the years, and had it not been for his able support I doubt whether the book could have appeared without another year or so to mature. Which reminds that his successors also deserve a mention, as *HFN* could never have managed to handle so much material without them. After Frank, in order of arrival they were: Gareth Jefferson, Gary Bellamy, Geoff Jeanes, Mike Thorne, Ray Carter, Paul Messenger, John Atkinson (who succeeded me at the end of 1982), and Ivor Humphreys.

In April 1969, Frank and I attempted a sort of bird's-eye view of domestic audio, with him looking ruminatively to the past and me daring to predict the hi-fi future, and failing miserably even to mention digital possibilities. 'Daring' was also the word for some of the entries in our limerick competition in October 1971, an altogether hilarious episode, some unused bits from which found their way into the magazine across quite a long period. And 1972 saw the making of an LP by an *HFN* team in collaboration with Discourses, issued on that label as *What Is Good Recorded Sound?* It featured examples of good and bad techniques as applied to various ensembles, supported by an instructive booklet.

Various excursions into the vexed business of retail trading crossed our pages over the years, especially as the Resale Prices Act gradually came into force. This certainly changed the character of much retailing, with a great upsurge of 'sealed carton' sales to customers who were/are happy to rely on audio show impressions or magazine reviews (or simply the manufacturer's literature?) and don't want to be bothered with demonstrations or detailed advice. The magazine's 'line' was to accept in principle the argument for greater retail competition and the resulting reduced profit margins, which should benefit the consumer; but we had reservations about the more pernicious by-products of the change, which led Raymond Cooke of KEF – acting as a spokesman for the industry – to accuse *HFN* of conveniently backing all the horses (Letters, May 1970).

We had perhaps sailed too close to the political wind on that occasion, but mention of politics reminds me that for some years in the 1970s, hi-fi had a sympathetic mole tucked away in high places. This was when Bernard (now Lord) Donoughue was head of the policy unit at No 10. He used to write to the magazine from time to time and on one memorable occasion he invited Gisela Berg and me (representing in effect producers and consumers) to Downing Street to discuss the industry's problems and consider what it might be possible for the Government to do about the then-serious problem of under-capitalization. Goodness knows if this ever gave rise to a memo on Prime Minister Callaghan's desk, but it did make me realise how personal enthusiasms might sometimes get near to influencing those in power.

Well away from those seats (at least in the political sense), two other subjects which popped up fairly regularly over the years were omnidirectional loudspeakers and multi-mike recording techniques. My own animadvertions on the former in April 1971 ('In All Directions') caused something of a stir by suggesting that the Sonab advertising of that time made claims regarding stereo reproduction which were, and could only be, the exact opposite of what actually happened. The Trade Descriptions Act eventually came into force to curtail such things, although even today I sometimes feel that it's only timidity which prevents serious challenges being made under the Act regarding claims that certain components can affect aspects of sound over which their properties could have no possible influence. But even reviewers who should know better are sometimes misled or misleading on such matters, perhaps exhibiting symptoms of what I've called CSD (Capacity for Self Deception).

The Audio Awards

As mentioned by Christopher Breunig in Chapter 8, one upshot of the 1970 *HFN/RR* merger was that we took on the Audio Award scheme, and here are some details to fill out CB's note.

The first year under *HFN/RR*'s tutelage was 1971, when the recipient was Neville Marriner, who joined Peter Gammond and me for lunch with Harley Usill of Argo Records. On that occasion it fell to me to hand over the statuette, when there was a moment of shock/horror as Neville remarked that our engraving was at fault regarding the number of Rs in his name! But he was pulling our legs and subsequently expressed huge gratitude, so from then on we became more ambitious, hiring a suite at the Royal Festival Hall, inviting anyone and everyone of possible relevance, and engaging public figures with musical connections to make the presentations. I chaired most of these events, with Peter recounting the background for the benefit of guests and media, all set against displays of record sleeves.

In 1972 we honoured the 83 year old Sir Adrian Boult, with special reference to his Vaughan Williams recordings. The splendid McFall sculpture of RVW was on display and we were delighted to have the composer's widow Ursula to present the Award. Raymond Leppard was the choice for 1973, when we cheekily brought in fellow-awardee Marriner for a surprise conductor-to-conductor presentation, while in 1974 there were two recipients, Peter Pears and the record producer Kinloch Anderson, with John Culshaw as presenter. Colin Davis came next, with the Liberal leader Jeremy Thorpe as presenter, followed in 1976 by Janet Baker, with her namesake Richard Baker doing the presentational honours. In 1977,

John Williams and Julian Bream were our twinned recipients, served by Robin Ray, and 1978 saw André Previn honoured by the inimitable Joyce Grenfell. In 1979 Decca's Arthur Haddy and EMI's Anthony Griffith were chosen to represent the recording industry's boffins with Master of the Queen's Music Malcolm Williamson as presenter, and in 1980 Norman del Mar was joined by Richard Itter of Lyrita, when the humorist Paul Jennings made his presentation speech in verse.

Sir Charles Groves and veteran recording engineer Kenneth Wilkinson were our choices in 1981, with pianist and TV personality Joseph Cooper doing the honours; and in 1982 that renowned talker-about-music Anthony Hopkins presented the Awards to Vernon Handley for his music and to Quad's Peter Walker for a lifetime's devotion to sonic excellence. They were great days but that was the last presentation, as I vacated the Editorial Chair later that year and the Audio Award was then dropped.

More on recording techniques

The debate about recording techniques was given a lively fillip in November 1967 by 'Fizzed Up Music', an article from conductor Bernard Keeffe, who, a little later and wearing his broadcasting hat, included in a TV programme some shots of a concert of recorded music being given before a small audience in the home of *HFN*'s Editor. This was to make a point about the role played by domestic listening in appreciation of the classics, which was fine by me, especially as it gave the magazine some free publicity in the process.

In his article, though, BK's thesis was that it is all too easy to enliven music by artificial means: in fact to add a touch of 'fizz' for extra impact, a process to which multiple close-miking can contribute. My sympathies were very much with him, being as I was at that time still something of a purist and always rather inclined to dismiss pleas for compromise and practicality from people working against time with diverse ensembles in a variety of venues.

But as the years pass I've come to realise that multi-miking doesn't necessarily produce false-sounding results particularly if tastefully blended with something like a crossed-pair 'scene-setter'. Indeed, I now accept that many impressive and seemingly natural recordings were made using numerous microphones with their outputs manipulated on mixing desks. I don't like having to admit this, and it may simply be that my judgement is now suspect due to declining aural acuity with advancing years.

Indeed, this could also be the explanation of my failure to hear most of the dreadful faults attributed by today's would-be gurus to digital recording, or to appreciate the superiority of vacuum-tube amplifiers and anything analogue. It's a real curiosity that when I and others of my generation were young turks, we welcomed the LP and wide-ranging orchestral sound set against a near-silent background, and dismissed old fogeys who preferred their hissy 78s and even (in some cases) hankered for a purely acoustic past in the conviction that electrical waveforms couldn't be true analogues of mechanical vibrations. But now, while one can understand people having an interest in audio antiques, there's a craze in some hi-fi quarters for reproductions thereof, coupled with an unquestioning faith in their performing superiority *vis-à-vis* anything digital (plus acceptance of ludicrously high pricing), which many of us 'oldies' see as echoing the reactionary attitudes we met from the old-guard in our youth.

What, I wonder, would Miles Henslow have made of all this if faced with something comparable in 1956? On the verge of the stereo age, would he have launched a magazine defending single-channel sound or campaigned for a reversion to expensively prettified radiograms? Of course not! In his London flat he housed a vast professional EMI open-spool tape recorder, a device symbolising a path to the future, and there's little doubt that today he'd have the best digital gear at hand. As for valve amplifiers or even the most prestigious LP disc players, he'd probably have been contemptuous.

When Miles launched *Hi-Fi News*, he did it for fun and interest, not to make a fortune. But the publishing business has shifted somewhat since those happy amateur days in Mortimer Street, so all we can do now is hope that his progeny at least remains prosperous enough to survive for a few more decades.

Alastair Robertson-Aikman *of SME recalls a loudspeaker story*

'This is the story of two china cabinets situated one at each end of a high-level landing in my music room, such that they are passed by anyone entering or leaving. They originated circa 1963 when my quest for loudspeakers lighted on the studio monitors designed by Dr Dutton at EMI. The Dutton Columns, as they were known, stood about 4ft high, with a 13x8in EMI elliptical woofer, two GEC metal cone tweeters and an integrated amplifier in the column base which could be tweaked on site. By the standards of the day, they offered remarkable stereo placement, particularly and not altogether surprisingly, with EMI recordings.

'The late John Bowers, then a partner in Bowers & Wilkins Ltd, a firm of Worthing hi-fi dealers, was one of the first of my visitors. He left in thoughtful mood. A week or two later, he told me he had obtained a pair of columns for himself, so, for the next six months, we enjoyed good listening until, in the nature of true enthusiasts, we began to wonder what we could do next. John said that Mullard had just marketed some new Ferroxcube inductors ideal for crossovers. I was to make a pair of heavily-constructed corner enclosures in ply and concrete. Other parts came from the Duttons and the results were very good but, of course, never for a moment could we realise the portent of our work.

'To improve the appearance of my corner units Tichmarsh & Goodwin of Ipswich, who made the furniture for my house, were asked to solve the problem. They did so with two carved oak aprons with tygan front panels, which did wonders for the domestic situation.

'John now had the interest of one of his customers, a lady who commissioned similar speakers for herself. Possibly she had a listening peculiarity but insisted that the tweeters be mounted side by side! It is what she was reluctantly given and they were built in a lock-up garage behind the shop. Soon the word went round and with the aid of one or two more lock-up garages Worthing saw some small scale production.

'On a visit to the USA, I came back with two DuKane Ionovac tweeters, which soon replaced the metal cones in my corner units. In the UK, an almost identical unit by Fane appeared in some of John's speakers.

'The sequel to this story? I eventually fell in love with the Quad electrostatic and so back to Tichmarsh & Goodwin with the aprons to be squared off and re-built as... you've guessed it: china cabinets! John, of course, went on to make loudspeakers on an ever-increasing scale. I sometimes tell my visitors the story of the china cabinets and the small part they played in the founding days of a business now reputed to turn over something in the region of $300 million a year.'

Christopher Breunig on going in search of the Worden Articulated Arm:

'In 1961 William Worden launched an articulated stereo tonearm comprising an inverted U-section in maple wood with a gloss black finish, and removable matching headshell. Arm geometry was optimised by a rod action which increased the offset angle of the headshell as the stylus traversed the record.

'For one of his advertisements Worden had a fanciful drawing of a hand poised over the headshell, with the promise of perfect tracking. I remember at the time taking this to the posh Cheltenham store Cavendish House – which not only had a classical record department where you could listen to LPs in closed booths equipped with Pye Black Boxes, but a hi-fi section (of sorts). Showing the illustration to an assistant I asked if they stocked the Worden Arm. The assistant studied the drawing and helpfully observed, "No. But it would be tiring having to hold the cartridge over the record like that".'

Colin Walker remembers Yorkshire hi-fi makers Richard Allan and J E Sugden

'In 1966 I joined Richard Allan as its Technical Sales Representative. Prior to that, I had been an engineering draughtsman living in Chester with my wife Janet, and three young sons. During this time books by A B Cohen, B Babani, and of course, Gilbert Briggs, were essential reading, and many loudspeakers of various designs were built. So, by 1966, a reasonable, if amateurish technical knowledge had been acquired – enough at least, to persuade Richard Allan to take me on (albeit at a not-insubstantial drop in salary), and a move to Cleckheaton in West Yorkshire.

'Richard Allan Radio Ltd (later, Audio Ltd) was founded in 1947 by three men, Eric Worley, Ken Sykes, and Denis Newbold. They began making speaker drive units working from an old Nissen hut, supplying them to radio and TV manufacturers. The name Richard Allan came from the forenames of two of the founders' young sons. A move to an old chapel premises in Batley followed as the business expanded.

'Dennis Newbold left the company, and together with Arthur Falkus, founded Fane Audio, the name derived from the first two letters of their names. Falkus did a great deal of work on the Ionophone speaker principle resulting in a high-frequency horn, and which was used by B&W in its large P3 loudspeaker. It was however, very unreliable, although without peer when it did work. (Unreliability was also a feature of its dynamic drive units, Jim Rogers told me; he used to return about 50% of the 5in units he used in his Wafer loudspeaker, in contrast to none at all from Richard Allan.)

'In 1965, Richard Allan moved again to another modern premises in Gomersal, Cleckheaton. They were then in the process of trying to become established in the hi-fi world, and were working on three new slimline models which were in vogue (short-lived) at the time – these were the SC8 (8in plus HF unit), SC10 (10in plus HF unit) and SC12 (12in bass, 8in mid and HF unit). But the speaker which captured the imagination most was the small Minette, following the pattern begun by Goodmans with its Maxi. Memory tells me that the Minette, housing a 5in long-throw, high-flux magnet – 14,000 lines – with 4in tweeter, sold at that time for £15. It was however, the module which really caught attention. This, in essence was the front (aluminium) panel of the Minette, with the surround of the 5in unit being bonded to, and forming an integral part of the panel, together with tweeter and crossover network, which was unique in its day. It came complete with drawings for cabinet construction, at I think around £9–£10.

'Now becoming well established, the next model was the Sarabande, a large, 6cu ft loudspeaker using a 15in bass unit and a modified version of the module for midrange and high frequency, selling for £39 17s 6d. The next two models were the Pavane, a three-unit system, based on a 12in bass unit (£32), and the Chaconne (about £17), which sold well.

'It is worth remembering the curious Purchase Tax anomaly that applied before the days of VAT. Loudspeakers containing one or two units were subject to Purchase Tax, but those housing three units weren't, as they were considered to be for professional use. This led to some manufacturers designing two-unit systems, but adding a third, often unconnected, or dummy, tweeter to surmount this problem. Purchase Tax was also not levied on drive units of 12in or over, and the only ones to escape were the Lowthers, who managed to persuade the Revenue to zero-rate them.

'The man behind the designs of these loudspeakers was Alan Thompson, the Chief Engineer. He has never been accorded his rightful place in the annals of hi-fi history, perhaps because he was a very quiet, deep-thinking, even introvert, character, and also because Richard Allan was not a fashionable company in the manner of KEF and other competitors. His name is more than worthy to be placed alongside his more famous contemporaries, and he should be remembered for his contribution to the world of sound reproduction.

'It was, I think, in 1967 that Jim Sugden wrote an article in *Hi-Fi News* describing a Class A transistorised amplifier of his design, which caused some controversy (not least from Clive Sinclair) in the correspondence columns following the article, and also from Roberts Radio, which claimed it had been the first user of transistorised Class A, although its table-model radios would hardly have been described as hi-fi.

'Sugden, who was a manufacturer of scientific instruments, was unknown in the hi-fi business at the time, and, following discussions, manufactured the amplifiers under the Richard Allan name for marketing purposes. There were two models, the integrated A21, and the power and pre-amp A41 and C41, providing 8 watts and 15 watts respectively (later upgraded to around 12 and 20 watts).

'These new additions further enhanced the Richard Allan name, and aroused much interest when exhibited at the Russell Hotel Audio Fair. It is true that their appearance, in particular the A21, looked a little amateurish in comparison with other amplifiers of the day, but sonically it was quite superior, and it was not difficult to demonstrate this superiority.

'In 1969 Jim Sugden decided to market the amplifiers himself, under his own name, and persuaded me to join his company as sales manager. Although it was a good move in many ways, Jim was not the easiest of people to work with, and after a year I decided to leave and form my own company. Sugden later sold the business to Andrew Clokie who, I gather, was not too successful, and the company was then acquired by Tony Miller, who continues to run it to this day.'

Howard Popeck *of Subjective Audio recalls the early days of Meridian*

'I started Subjective Audio in 1976. The first amplifier agency that took me on (it certainly wasn't the other way in those days) was Lecson. Due to unique and very serendipitous circumstances, I rapidly became its largest worldwide dealer. My amazement at the aesthetic design and sound quality was almost evangelical. By then, though, Bob Stuart and Allan Boothroyd had left Lecson and via Orpheus had started Meridian.

'Meridian was announced to the world in *Hi-Fi News* in 1976. It occurred to me that Meridian must surely be sonically superior to Lecson. I phoned them at what I envisaged were their magnificent global headquarters in St Ives; I was invited up. I was nervous: I was meeting two of my heroes, entering a much more sophisticated world, and I was still working from home.

'I arrived early. I couldn't find the Meridian "campus". I drove round and around. Nothing. No corporate gargantuan office block, no car park packed with Ferraris. Nothing. Except a timber yard, and a series of nearby buildings that, no way, surely, could house these twin geniuses and their mega workforce?

'Late, frustrated and embarrassed, I phoned them in desperation. "Oh yes", they said, "was it you in the Cortina estate driving up and down, looking like a kerb crawler?". Yes, it was. "Ah well, we're easy to miss. We're in the pair of Portakabins inside the timber yard." As, indeed, they were.

'The Portakabins were cramped and warm and the people were friendly. I met my heroes, and the relationship began. And from these very modest headquarters, the foundation of a successful global business was being built. So much for preconceptions of giant stainless-steel-clad multi-storey corporate buildings. Preconceptions can be deceiving, I discovered.'

7. The BBC influence

By the 1970s, when the BBC's live FM radio music broadcasts were setting a breathtakingly high standard as a hi-fi source, its unique research and design facility influenced hi-fi product design too. Developed by the BBC for its own use, the LS3/5A speaker was an instant hit when Rogers (quickly followed by the other BBC-licensed builders) first offered it to the public in 1975. To own the LS3/5A was to buy into the whole BBC ethos.

Now, 30 years on, and long out of production, the original LS3/5A retains its hold, despite inumerable imitators and most recently an LS3/5A 'V2' with different drive units. But to read Trevor Butler's 1989 HFN/RR feature, telling the story up to the arrival (controversial among enthusiasts) of the 11 ohm version in 1988, is to understand just how this BBC creation came about – and why the magic could never be repeated.

A little legend: the story of the BBC LS3/5A *by Trevor Butler (HFN/RR, Jan '89)*

There can hardly be another single box which has provoked as much emotive comment, or given rise to so many myths and misunderstandings, as the BBC LS3/5A. The very name has caused confusion, but in fact it simply follows the BBC's coded equipment format. In this, cabinets have the prefix 'CT', filters 'FL', and loudspeakers 'LS', hence the first two letters

The figure '3' in the code indicates that the design is primarily for outside broadcast (OB) use. A figure '5' would mean studio broadcasting, as LS5/9. The number '5' after the stroke is the model number, the LS3/5 supplanting previous OB speakers like the LS3/1. So we arrive at LS3/5 which was the title of the initial model. Later the 'A' was added to indicate the first and only design alteration to the original specification. Any further specification change would result in a 'B'; but that hasn't happened, and isn't likely to, for reasons which will become apparent.

The concept of this speaker was to suit those BBC environments where monitoring on headphones was not satisfactory and yet there wasn't sufficient room for a 'Grade I' monitor. A Grade I monitor can be used for critical tonal balancing of programme material, setting of microphone positioning, etc. Current Grade I monitors are the LS5/8 and LS5/9. A Grade II monitor may be used for checking the quality of programme, but balance and mic positioning are normally Grade I-checked unless there is no alternative. It was recognized that what would be required was a small Grade II unit with some sacrifice of bass response and loudness reproduction, this being justified for the sake of achieving compactness. The likely users were, for instance, the production control areas of television OB control vans, where the producer needs to listen at a lower level than that used for the actual mixing.

There was no suitable available commercial unit, and so the Research Department of the BBC was asked to design one at its headquarters in Kingswood Warren. Less than a week elapsed between this request and the first prototype being offered for field trials and evaluation. This came about because the LS3/5 was based around an experimental loudspeaker which had been developed for some preliminary work on acoustic scaling tests at Kingswood.

By using one-eighth scale models, and one-eighth wavelengths (ie, 8-times frequencies), recordings can be made by which the merits of particular acoustic techniques can be assessed without the expense of a life-size environment. Naturally, though, this implies that the entire model reproduction chain, of tape player, loudspeaker, microphone and recorder, must be capable of operating at very high quality with a frequency range of 400Hz to 100kHz, in order to be able to model accurately a typical bandwidth of, say, 40Hz to 15kHz.

The model speaker, which the BBC used from 1972 until 1980, represented a major step in the modelling process. Although it had its limitations, primarily in terms of its tonal quality and maximum power handling, components of this small loudspeaker were found to be of a sufficiently high quality to help fulfil the demand for the unusually compact monitor needed in outside broadcast use. This was therefore packaged and called the LS3/5 and showed the model experimenters to have achieved good results.

A small number of these units were made in-house by the BBC and used in television mobile control-rooms, where they gave satisfactory service. The BBC got to the stage of inviting applications to make the LS3/5 under license by outside manufacturers. Indeed, Rogers issued a press release on 19th February 1974 which proudly announced that they would be exhibiting the new design at SONEX '74, an exhibition to be held that April. They offered a photograph and a provisional specification: 25W power handling with ±3dB, 80-20,000Hz and ±4dB 60-20,000kHz. Crossover frequency was quoted at 3kHz and the units were a 110mm bass driver with a Plastiflex doped Bextrene cone and a 27mm Mylar dome tweeter. The price was £52 each plus VAT!

Alas, though, there were to be early problems. Although the BBC had confidence in the KEF B110 bass unit at the time, when a subsequent batch of in-house LS3/5s was needed it was found that the low- and high-frequency units had undergone significant changes and a re-design of the speaker would be required before production could resume. Accordingly, the speaker was passed on to the BBC's Designs Department, then located in Great Portland Street, with a request to modify it so that it would once again be suitable.

The trouble was in three areas: the B110 had changed, exciting the cabinet in a different way, producing a coloration both from the LF unit and the cabinet; and the HF unit had developed a pronounced 'lispy' quality.

In an attempt to ensure that cabinet resonance would not cause problems, the side panels had each been damped with a bituminised pad, and the top and bottom panels likewise, except that two layers were required here. In addition, a PVC edging was applied to the chassis of the LF unit to de-couple it from the front panel and seal the join. In order to damp the air modes of resonance inside, all internal surfaces were lined with polyurethane foam. The cabinet was sealed to prevent air leaks, which might produce extraneous sounds from the high pressures produced – indeed, even the screw holes were made airtight. The cabinet problems were associated with the softwood parana pine fillets which connected the back panel to the front; these had an insufficient impedance and were therefore replaced with beech. The back panel was re-specified from the precious sandwich of spruce to multi-ply birch, thus obviating the voids often associated with spruce. This then became the CT4/11A.

The opportunity was also taken to sort out the treble lisp of the tweeter. It was felt that this unit, the KEF T27 SP1032, was vulnerable because it was exposed and could easily be damaged during rigging at a venue. It was decided to incorporate a protection grille and a suitable one was found, with some modification, from a Celestion HF2000. The tweeter is surrounded by a thick felt strip mounted on the baffle in order to prevent acoustic discontinuity presented by the edge of the cabinet setting up an interference pattern, since the T27 radiating surface is small and the radiator nearly omni-directional. The addition of the protection grille was wholly beneficial as it raised the output at higher frequencies and help cure the lisp. The effect of the Tygan cover on the front was taken into account in the design, and the loudspeaker should always be used with the grille on, to avoid discontinuities in the upper presence region.

Having carried out these changes, the crossover had to be adjusted to compensate and a new type, FL6/23, replaced the original FL6/16.

Sporting these alterations, the first variant of the LS3/5 was born – the LS3/5A. The 'A' suffix was necessitated because although the LS3/5A sounded similar to the LS3/5, the differences were significant enough for it not to be possible to use a mixed pair for stereo listening. Since only small quantities of the LS3/5 had been built, this did not present much of a problem and only 20 units had to be considered obsolete.

For those not fully acquainted with it, the design is still now very much as it was then, with just a few slight enhancements which came about over the years, as will be explained.

There were a few noted difficulties in 1977, and almost every summer saw the reject rate at the manufacturers rise slightly. The early 1980s saw a change when the surround-dip was seen to have moved slightly. This was resolved when the crossover resonator controlling it was tuned to a lower frequency and the damping resistor changed. Any alteration like this is issued by the BBC to the current manufacturers and is incorporated into their license. There have also been some adjustments to the value of the tweeter coupling capacitor; these are part of the relative balance adjustment. As the material of the tweeter alters, the 'Q' changes and there is a mild 'tippling' of the response. This coupling capacitor affects the shape of the network and decides whether it is under or over damped. To adjust the treble balance, an output from a tapped transformer on the FL6/23 is adjusted, and the coupling capacitor changed to maintain the crossover frequency.

Re-assessment

The major re-assessment of 1987 was widely reported in the specialist press; but this time the alterations had been requested primarily by the manufacturers. As one of the licensees (Richard Ross of Rogers) explained: over the years, whilst it had been possible to make an LS3/5A which sounded and measured within spec, and which was acceptable, the number of units, in particular the woofers which were within tolerance, varied. Because of the particular design of the LS3/5A, the B110s, although being to KEF's standards, happened to have the point where their tolerance was most variable occurring at the most critical point in the speaker's design. In hot summers the reject rate of the bass units could be anything from 10% to 85%, and, for the licensees, this was not satisfactory from an economic standpoint.

At the same time as the licensees were finding it difficult to make consistent units, the BBC was encountering its own problems. At the end of 1987 it was noticed that the units were tending to drift towards the limit of acceptability. Specifically, they were found to be about 2dB up at an octave around 1kHz, a particularly critical area for balance. There had always been a slight lift on the LS3/5A here, but now it started to become objectionable. It should be stressed that the units were still operating within limit for a Grade II monitor, but would have been unacceptable in a Grade I.

The crux of the matter was again the 'surround-dip', the precise frequency of which varies by a few hundred Hertz over time. This had become interactive with the box resonance to the extent that action was needed. A change had to be brought about so that speakers could be manufactured which the BBC would find acceptable, to provide them with the consistent loudspeaker they designed and wanted.

The BBC referred the matter to KEF, who set their Special Products Division to work. The problem was traced to variations in the consistency of the Neoprene used in the making of the SP1003 B110, and so a new B110 was specifically designed for the LS3/5A. This uses a PVC surround, more consistent and temperature-stable than the Neoprene but less compliant. A new spider voice-coil assembly was therefore required to give the new drive the same sensitivity as the older one, in order to achieve the bass performance. This is the B110 SP1228.

Crossover design is always a source of great debate and this has certainly been the case with the LS3/5A. Changes have been made, as reported, but the main specification and overall sound balance of the speaker have remained the same.

Crossover

A book could be written on this subject so far as the LS3/5A is concerned. The network is of unusual complexity. L1 and R1 are employed to equalize the rising axial response and frequency characteristic of the bass unit, while the group C5, L2, and R2 compensate for a hump in this characteristic. For the tweeter, L3 acts as a shunt inductor and as an autotransformer to allow for differing levels of sensitivity. C2 is adjusted to keep the crossover frequency constant and R3 is there to prevent ringing, with R4 and C6 to adjust the frequency response at the upper end.

The SP1228 has a considerably smoother response than the older-type B110, and hence needs gentler crossover equalization. It was decided therefore that the crossover could not only be re-designed to compensate for the change to the drive unit, but could also incorporate new technology. In essence, the equalisation is very much the same, with a similar-looking circuit. The earlier design used the already-mentioned tapped auto-transformer as part of the high-pass filter and to adjust the level of the tweeter in 1dB steps, but it was noticed that as the tweeter sensitivity was becoming increasingly consistent (to within 0.5dB), a simpler constant impedance resistive attenuator could be used to give the ±dB of adjustment in 0.5dB steps. One consequence of the simpler equalization is that the overall impedance has been reduced from the previous 15ohm nominal to 11ohm nominal.

KEF analysed the effect of component tolerances on the overall response and found that by tightening these in the most critical areas an improvement in consistency could be achieved. In previous units it had been possible to obtain a 2dB variation. For example, if the network was +1dB in the critical area and the accompanying drive unit was also +1dB the two compounded. KEF decided that by opting for computer-aided matching, it was possible to select components so that if the network was +1dB a drive unit with a −1dB figure would be chosen to give 0dB overall change. The new crossover is the FL6/38, SP2128.

Therefore KEF was able to offer matched components to the manufacturing licensees even though the company does not manufacture the speaker in its entirety itself. It so happens that all three current licensees use the KEF matched parts. At the end of the day, it has to be said that KEF did a superb job. They were issued with a BBC LS3/5A reference unit (No 6) of 1975 vintage and produced a set of 1988 parts which sounded so similar that they were within Grade I limits, and could be made much more consistently. Hence, LS3/5A remains.

Spendor used to make its own complete crossover units and says that it could start again if they situation called for it. It has now adopted the iron-dust inductors (not to be confused with ferrite) and has dispensed with its previous silicon-iron E & I transformer winding. The E & I laminations tend to be more costly, and the opportunity to buy the matched KEF sets was taken.

Rogers had for years used various ferrite and iron-dust cores, because its research showed that they were more economical and gave superior saturation qualities compared with the radiometal or grain-orientated strip steel, given that in the transformers there are quite small gaps with quite high fluxes, whereas in the ferrites there are big air gaps and a lot of magnetic material. Although there are probably a few more turns and the DC resistance rises slightly, the saturation properties are considerably enhanced. Rogers decided that with modern crossover techniques, it was simpler to make a 2 or 3% tolerance iron-dust core inductor than to make a gapped radiometal choke. This is partly because the design is complicated and any opportunity to make things less so should not be avoided.

It would perhaps have been simpler in the long term for the BBC to have completely re-designed the speaker, and to have produced an LS3/5B, but they did not want nor could they afford this option, since some three-and-a-half thousand of the existing design were in use up and down the country. And design change had to produce similar results, and the same response, because future models would end up alongside existing ones. Even today, when a batch is taken to a location, it does not matter whether some are from one generation and some from another – they should all be capable of matching as stereo pairs. That in essence is the whole purpose of the design, consistency through production and during use, anywhere. To sum up then, the recent changes have offered no enhancements in terms of specification, simply a means to provide better consistency in production to maintain the speaker's standard. This is now back on 'median' and so may sound a little different from those latter 'older models' of just pre-Christmas 1987, but will sound the same as earlier production runs.

The impedance has altered slightly, post-modifications. Whereas the original was a nominal 15ohms the newer model is nearer to a nominal 11ohms. Looking at the nomograph, we can see the original as 15ohms, using the old equalizer and with the old bass unit which had about a 7ohm resistance. The new bass unit has a lower DC resistance but, with the new equaliser, the curves are very similar in shape, although the average level is now more like 11ohms. This still means that the LS3/5A is voltage rather than current driven and needs an amplifier that will swing volts and produce reasonable power levels, but not into low impedances.

So an LS3/5A circa 1977/78 will not in any particular way be better or worse than one from 1983 or now. The consensus of opinion, from those who understand balance, is that the system is the same and offers the same qualities as it always has, in terms of its tonal characteristics.

In detail, the latest models are now marginally smoother because irregularities of the high treble have been sorted out, and the coloration has been reduced by a small degree with the new surround, but not so as to affect the tonal balance, because the perception of localised coloration is all part of the balance of the loudspeaker system and its equalisation. So if the tonal coloration were reduced to an extent in, say, the 1kHz region where it was noticeable, it could highlight colorations elsewhere.

The new design offers only, in real terms, a better consistency, executed by KEF to maintain the standard. No enhancement in terms of the specification was made, although commentators say the loudspeaker now sounds a little better because it is back on the median. Essentially it produces the same sound. This has been backed by tests carried out at the BBC and with manufacturers, with regard to the unit's stereo capability.

The total number of LS3/5As made since the first licence was granted is estimated to be around 60,000 pairs so it is not surprising that a huge interest has been generated around the world. In the BBC, the speaker has found many uses from the one-man OB to the control and balance of experimental quadraphonic transmissions from the Promenade Concerts several years ago; and in BBC Local Radio Stations, the design provides the main cubicle monitoring. Even so, the design has its fallbacks, like the passive and complicated equaliser in the crossover to restore the loss of low frequency caused by the cabinet size and limited cone area.

Licensees

The very history of the speaker has interesting connections with licensees who have been allowed to manufacture them. After early production runs at the BBC's own Equipment Department in Chiswick, the Corporation permitted a number of companies to apply to produce the speakers under licence, as it is obliged to do under its Charter.

The licence fee is a means of recouping the original development cost, not purely a way of cutting unit costs by mass-production, and the money is recovered by the Director of Engineering and not BBC Enterprises, the commercial arm of 'Auntie', which has taken over other money-making areas like publications and records. Recently, as many as four companies had licences although in essence only two actually had a production line at that time. This situation came about when Harbeth, formed by H D Harwood who was working on the LS3/5A at BBC Research Department, was granted a licence, while Rogers, Spendor and Goodmans were also permitted to manufacture. Goodmans, in fact, had ceased production and did not re-apply for its licence when the renewal time came, and Harbeth had yet to start making any.

Another licensee manufacturer, Spendor, founded by the late Spencer Hughes who had worked with Dudley Harwood at the BBC, did not apply for a licence at the first opportunity. The company was then already working to full capacity, but when a 'vacancy' next arose it did apply, encouraged by the fact that Mr Hughes knew the design and all that would be entailed, by association with it.

Rogers was involved almost from the start and now own the Chartwell brand, a company also previously licensed to make the LS3/5As. The parent company, Swisstone, acquired the defunct Chartwell, a previous competitor, in 1978, having merged with Rogers in 1975. Manufacturing to quantity demands, Rogers announced in 1979 that it had sold its ten-thousandth pair and proclaimed the LS3/5A the world's most successful small loudspeaker, with its total to date standing at 33,534 pairs.

The latest company to be permitted to manufacture is Harbeth, now under the control of Alan Shaw. Samples from its first batch were passed by the BBC and are now eligible for full production; all are of the computer-optimised type. This initial sampling process, a condition of all licensees, is to assure the BBC that their speakers are being made correctly. The licensee selects two units from the initial batch to send to the BBC. One of these is kept by the Corporation as that licensee's working reference, while the other is tweaked so that it matches the BBC's own reference, a unit from the very first in-house batch. This second speaker is then returned to the licensee and becomes the reference for all subsequent units to be compared with.

Earlier companies to have been licensed by the BBC have not fared as well. It is agreed that the LS3/5A is not an easy product to make properly and must be marketed correctly. Some names have fallen by the wayside because they found the market was not as large as they forecast, and some found it too difficult to make to the BBC's tight tolerances. These problems could be because people expect more than they see for a £250 loudspeaker, and that without the correct marketing, sales are just not realised.

Names like Audiomaster, who launched its models in April 1976, had a rather short-lived licence span, while RAM never got any units out on the street: they went bankrupt before the production line got underway. Falcon, who were making crossovers for Goodmans, made a batch for ailing RAM company and then found itself having to distribute the boards directly because RAM was not in any position to pay for them. A flurry of activity was seen from JPW, but no quantities to speak of ever materialised. Constant checking of the licensee's production is carried out, and there are some tales of 'nasties' being found. There's the case of a unit coming in for evaluation with a thicker-than-usual grille material causing a two-octave 1.5dB dip. Needless to say it was swiftly returned!

Of the three current manufacturers, Spendor says that although a percentage of its production line ends up in the UK, 80% of sales are to the export trade, the areas being mainly Europe, the USA and the Far East, including Japan and Taiwan. Rogers also exports to Japan, Europe, North America, Hong Kong and Singapore, with even more sales to Japan than to the United Kingdom, where, whilst a quantity goes to the BBC, the hi-fi retail outlets get through a fair volume too. Despite the advances of other designs, the LS3/5A remains a reference-standard loudspeaker in its class.

Acknowledgements
I am indebted to BBC Engineering for ensuring the accuracy of this article. Within the BBC, the work of two people, T Somerville and D E L Shorter, must be considered as having laid the foundation for current standards. The particular work on the LS3/5A was carried out by Messrs H D Harwood of Research Department and both M E Whatton and R W Mills of Designs Department.

Peter Thomas, founder and chief designer of PMC, on LS3/5A impedance:

'I do have some knowledge of many aspects of the design as I was part of the group concerned with the work at the BBC in the '70s and '80s, albeit that most of my involvement was with the cabinet design and manufacture rather than the electronics.

'There is some confusion regarding LS3/5A versions and impedances. The variance of figures in the industry could well have had something to do with the different methods magazines used to determine the "nominal" impedance. The load presented to an amplifier by the loudspeaker depends on both the crossover and the drive unit, and will vary with frequency. Different measurement and averaging techniques will also tend to give slightly different numbers. The nominal 15 ohms quoted for the first version LS3/5A is higher than the impedance of the drive units because of the crossover circuitry. (To provide a reasonable low frequency extension of the complete loudspeaker's frequency response, the crossover in the LS3/5A introduces significant loss above a few hundred Hertz. This is achieved by using series resistance, so the overall input impedance of the loudspeaker is somewhat higher than that of the drive unit alone).

'The first version of the LS3/5A uses a bass driver with a higher resistance and inductance than the later version, so it appeared to present a higher impedance load to an amplifier. The later version of the bass driver also needed slightly less correction to its frequency response, so the crossover has less effect on the input impedance. These effects combine to give the nominal "11 ohm" version.

'A recent eBay item would show this, as the speakers (Rogers) had a photographed label indicating 15 ohms, whereas astute investigation of the photograph of the speaker itself would suggest the units used might have led to a different impedance – this fact was questioned by a bidder and a further statement relating to a previous repair (hence a resulting impedance change) was added to the details of the item.

'The type of bass driver used in the two versions can be determined by looking closely at the loudspeaker with the front grille removed – both the outer surround material and the actual plastic cone appear visibly different. You can also tell by the different crossover and the SP1003/SP1228 label.

'The loudspeaker began as an LS3/5 (not externally available, although I have a pair myself) and the LS3/5A was an update (significantly changed). A further update was made still carrying the LS3/5A label.

'Parameters are, I believe, as follows:

'LS3/5: input impedance 9 ohm, B110/A6362 bass/mid at 4 ohm (rubber surround), T27/A6340 tweeter at 4 ohm

'LS3/5A, first version: input impedance 15 ohm, B110/SP1003 at 8 ohm (rubber surround), T27/SP1032 at 8 ohm

'LS3/5A, second version (1988): input impedance 11 ohm, B110/SP1228 at 6 ohm (neoprene surround), T27/SP1032 at 8 ohm.'

---

*US writer **Allen Edelstein** in praise of Rogers' bigger BBC-based monitors:*

'The Studio 1 is a development of the Rogers Studio Monitor speaker (I have the brochure in front of me now) which was a BBC LS3/6 with the approved addition of a Celestion HF2000 super tweeter to the Celestion HF1300 for extra extension and especially better dispersion at high frequencies (the Spendor BC1 added an STC super tweeter early in production for the same reason, though I think the HF2000 was smoother and more extended).

'The LS3/6 used a development of the 8 inch midrange from the LS5/6 (12 inch woofer, 8 inch mid, both slot loaded, HF1300), the first Bextrene-coned speaker, to produce a smaller monitor of similar quality. The driver was rated at a whopping 25 watts (it used a very light paper voice coil former I believe) and there was a recommendation of a maximum of 40 watts. I'm sure this is what led to the Studio 1, the need for more power handling, and there goes the BBC approval. I'll bet it also allowed Rogers to save money on the crossover and the insane quality control demanded by the BBC. Remember, a prime factor in BBC monitors was consistency speaker to speaker – you should be able to randomly choose two speakers of a model and still have a fine stereo pair.

'The Spendor BC1 was a development of the LS3/6 programme though not an official one. The work on the LS3/6 was stopped before it was finished (it was later completed and the Rogers was the result). Spencer Hughes left the BBC with the knowledge of the work and the BC1 was his application of the research to a real speaker.

'I heard the Rogers once. It was lovely, with a subtle warmth in the best sense. It was rich but, given the time, still felt as uncolored as any dynamic speaker. I think the bass was tighter than the BC1 (a problem throughout its lifespan) and the top octave was superior.

'Since I'm on the subject of BBC monitors, the most interesting one I ever heard was the LS5/8. It was certainly a very interesting design. It used a slot-loaded 12 inch polyprop woofer (the first time polyprop was used, I think) crossed over electronically about 1800Hz to a 1.25 inch Audax tweeter. I had a pair on loan from the American importer (he sold around three pairs a year at $6000, in around 1980, which was a lot then). It was typical BBC but with better bass, loudness, and dynamics and a little less "BBC sound" (there is a subtle BBC coloration).'

The late **Spencer Hughes** *, founder of Spendor, wrote this letter to HFN/RR in 1980:*

'Dear Sir,

'The Spendor BC1 was not, as it has so many times been described, a development of the BBC loudspeaker type LS3/6. Perhaps a short history of the lead into, and the development, of the two systems may be of interest.

'From the very early days, even before hi-fi, the BBC has designed its own monitor loudspeaker systems as commercial systems were not, and most are still not, accurate enough for broadcast work. These designs were based on available units matched by, what were in those days, very complex crossover networks and mounted in custom designed cabinets.

'During the mid-1960s, the development work carried out by the BBC had advanced to a stage which was beyond the capabilities of the available paper pulp cone bass units. The decision was taken to investigate the possibilities of using some form of plastic as a cone and surround material. It was assumed that plastic would be a consistent material unlike paper pulp, which to some degree seemed to depend on the mood of the pulp stirrer. Over the years it has been found that it was not quite that easy.

'The section of the BBC Research Department involved in this operation was headed by Mr D E L Shorter, now retired, with Mr H D Harwood now of Harbeth Acoustics, second in command and myself completing the investigating team. Some two years were spent making 12in unit cones in a variety of shapes and from a range of plastics; this could be a story on its own. The first successful unit was made from the now well-known Bextrene and used in the development of the BBC studio monitor type LS5/5. This loudspeaker was described in an article written by Mr H D Harwood in the March 1968 issue of *Wireless World*.

'My part, as a laboratory technician, in the operation, was to do most of the actual work both on the plastic investigation and the development of the LS5/5. With that experience I decided that it should be possible to make a loudspeaker from scratch in the home environment. With the aid of our electric fire, a compressor working in reverse and an iron bedstead the first vacuum former was built. Bins full of malformed cones were produced before any measure of success was achieved and the first 8in unit was produced. This unit turned out to be almost certainly the first commercial 8in Bextrene driver and still arguably the best.

'The first pair of BC1s was constructed using these units and Celestion HF1300 units. The cabinets were smaller than the current model and initial listening tests indicted that the performance could be improved by an increase in size, hence the present design. At this point it was all being done for fun.

'The second pair of BC1s was made for a friend who took them to Merrow Sound of Guildford. The third pair was sold to Merrow Sound and Spendor was on the way to a small niche in the audio world.

'Now some difficulties were beginning to arise as under the terms of my contract with the BBC, the design had to be offered to them. Fortunately the "Pop" era had just started and the main request was for more power, so the BC1 was turned down. Around about this time there was a special requirement within the BBC for one pair of speakers about the size of the BC1s. Being a kind soul, I suggested that my design could be used, so I was given the task of producing an official version of the BC1, later designated the LS3/6.

'This design used an 8in unit made by Research Department, the Celestion HF1300 and a redesigned crossover. The main change in the crossover was the addition of a large multi-tap autotransformer to allow adjustment of levels between the two units, normal BBC practice at that time.

'Some months later BC1s were fitted with an amplifier mounted in the back panel and the 4001G super tweeter added. This addition was for purchase tax reasons, but it did have two extra gains. Firstly, it improved the overall dispersion characteristics, secondly, from the broadcasting angle, it made any 625-line breakthrough to be more easily detected.

'Now the LS3/6 was offered to a number of commercial companies and eventually taken by Rogers, then under the control of Jim Rogers. With approval, and a little assistance from the BBC, Rogers added the Celestion HF2000.

'As Spendor was now a commercial company it was agreed that a royalty should be paid to the BBC for each BC1 produced. This was in recognition of the work I had done on the loudspeaker whilst still employed by the BBC.

'To perhaps prove the order of development of the two systems, it is of note that out of over two thousand BC1s supplied to the professional market there are over six hundred in operation with the BBC and as far as I know very few, if any, LS3/6 speakers.

'In addition to the above, the name Spendor is derived from the first names of myself and my wife Dorothy. Mrs Hughes provided practical assistance in the early days with her coil-winding expertise and now as Managing Director is responsible for all accounting, sales and general management. Derek Hughes, the son, another ex-BBC employee, deals with an amplifier design and assists me with research and development and general running of the factory.

'Yours, Spencer Hughes'

8. Music in *Hi-Fi News*

'A highly respected London music critic who wrote for Audio Record Review did not like the Quad electrostatic speakers in use for a demonstration set up by technical editor Donald Aldous, so that its music panel might better understand sound quality. "Don't you think they sound cold?" he asked the man next to him. He was sitting next to Peter Walker.' **Christopher Breunig**

Music reviews in *Hi-Fi News*. By Christopher Breunig

Record reviews did not become a part of *Hi-Fi News* until the end of 1962, when John Crabbe began a roundup feature. 'Recommended Recordings', highlighted new LPs which offered the best stereo sound – stereo recordings had become familar since their introduction in the autumn of 1958, although many collectors still had single-channel systems and had simply exchanged pickups for those unlikely to cause groove damage. By way of example, in September 1962 there were just 70 new Classical releases, some of these paralleling earlier monos: a small number relative to today's over-production but quite a strain on the budget nonetheless; with the additional purchase tax, a Decca or HMV 12in LP then cost 40s.

Conductors such as Ansermet, Beecham, Karajan, Monteux, Munch and Walter were re-recording their repertoire for stereo; operas were plotted for spatial separation; hi-fi enthusiasts looked to the latest *Scheherazade*, *Pastoral* or *Pathétique* with high expectations of sound quality.

The three principal magazines for record collectors at that time were *The Gramophone*, *Records & Recording*, which began in 1957, and *Audio Record Review* (in the mid-1950s *The Gramophone Record Review*). There was also an influential subscription publication, EMG's *The Monthly Letter*, which had unique performance/sound ratings. EMG was a London record retailer with its own exclusive 'Davey Loudspeakers and instruments [*sic*]'. Shops like EMG's and Henry Stave & Co would disappear with the abolition of resale price maintenance.

A hi-fi odyssey

In 1965 I moved to London, somehow fitting a pair of Quad Electrostatics and a substantial piece of furniture I had had made for turntable and Quad 22/II amplifiers into my Renault 1100 (and thence into a moderate-sized bed-sit). I had travelled considerably in terms of hi-fi since my original Pye Black Box: a Northern Radio Services system (based in Swiss Cottage, they were importers of the Stereophoner described by John Borwick) comprising Rogers HG88 amplifier; Lenco turntable, which had fine speed adjustment; and a bass cabinet with baffle-mounted treble unit, later replaced by small electrostatic tweeters.

Like many enthusiasts, in the late 1950s I had DIY ply rectangular column speakers with 8in Wharfedale units face-up – my neighbour's sat atop salt-glazed drainpipes! But Thomas Heinitz, *Records & Recording* critic and audio writer, put the notion of the Quad ESL, then £52 each, into my mind. In the early 1960s I could only afford one at a time. The Lenco was replaced by a Garrard 301 with Decca *ffss* arm, then – Heinitz's influence again – out went the Decca in favour of the Worden articulated arm. Worden was a concert pianist; he also designed a corner speaker.

Strange tonearms must have appealed: since 1986 I have kept Bill Firebaugh's Well-Tempered Arm and van den Hul moving-coil cartridges; before that the Zeta with Garrott-modified Deccas; and before that the bizarre Transcriptors with Shure V15/III. John Crabbe's reviews of the Ortofon SPU, the Empire 999VE and the Shure prompted ownership of all three in turn. My hi-fi odyssey would continue with Thorens TD150/SME 3009, the inevitable Linn LP12/Grace/Supex–Ittok/Asak; Cambridge Audio P40, Lecson and Naim amplification, Musical Fidelity's The Preamp with TVA1 yielding to DNM; dallying with Bowers & Wilkins DM3s, KEF 104s, Cambridge Audio R50s (Bert Webb's design), IMFs from John Wright, but always coming back to the Quad ESL.

Audio Record Review and *Hi-Fi News*
I wanted to be a record reviewer. I already had a short column in my hometown newspaper (*Gloucester Citizen*); cuttings from these were sent to John Crabbe in 1965 – *HFN* by then had a small team of uncredited reviewers but still only LPs of a very high technical standard were covered – and, some months later, to Peter Gammond, editor of *Audio Record Review*. Luckily, both took me on. *ARR* was in a small office off The Strand. The writer Burnett James, wheel-chair bound as a result of polio, was Music Editor, the cheery, ever helpful Donald Aldous its Technical Editor. Contributors included Peter Branscombe, Kenneth Dommett, John Freestone, Arthur Jacobs, William Mann and John Warrack – the first four familiar to longterm *HFN* subscribers, since the magazine team was absorbed into *HFN* in October 1970 as *Hi-Fi News & Record Review*; it had become part of Link House Publications at the beginning of that year and for its last few issues '*Audio*' had been dropped from the earlier

ARR title. The *HFN* record reviewers emerged from their anonymity in the January 1966 issue.

Burnett James's column 'From the Crow's Nest' contained some provocative ideas: he maintained that however good the performance, if the sound was bad he'd always prefer to listen to someone else's. And he liked to quip about reviewing: 'Ah! Toscanini. Write the review today, listen to it tomorrow!' Engineer Tony Faulkner believed that all writers worked on that basis; he urged that editors should mask the artists' names when sending out review discs.

One of Peter's innovations, in 1967, was the Audio Award, originally for 'services to music via the gramophone record'. Subsequently, one was given to a musician, another to someone involved with making recordings. In 1971 Sir Neville Marriner was the first recipient, at a private lunch, of a small commissioned sculpture in the form of interlinked treble clefs. From 1972, these were presented at an annual ceremony held in a suite in the Royal Festival Hall, a get-together for the magazine team and record company representatives, which continued for ten years. This was well in advance of the *Gramophone* Awards or the Classical Brits.

Whilst a writer for *ARR* I reported upon several recording sessions – mostly CBS thanks to the generosity of producer Paul Myers – and was privileged to hear Leonard Bernstein (the famous LSO quadraphonic *Le Sacre du printemps*), Pierre Boulez, Hans Werner Henze, André Previn, Rudolf Serkin, Sir Georg Solti; and much later watched Michael Tilson Thomas recording Mahler 3. An article I had written in 1967 about the regrettable deletion of many EMI recordings by Wilhelm Furtwängler was drawn to the attention of Daniel Barenboim who then kindly lent me his Furtwängler Melodiya LPs (made from German radio tapes confiscated by the Russians at the end of the war); I sat in at various EMI sessions with Pinchas Zukerman and Jacqueline du Pré when Barenboim was recording prolifically in the late 1960s.

The A:1 rating and Quality Monitor

In 1967 Peter, Burnett (in whose study sat a pair of the original Quad pre-electrostatic corner speakers – he loved good sound) and I had developed a numerical ratings scheme, up to '50:50', to summarize performance/recording. Later this changed to 0–50:A–D (H = historical). Perhaps because contributors tended to put fine gradations like '47' these were further rationalised to the *HFN* ratings current until November 2003, this time with letters A–D(H) for sound and numbers 1–4(H) for performance, with stars for exceptional merit. Confusing? Some readers skimmed the music reviews just looking for A*:1* ratings and promptly bought on those recommendations.

When Peter Gammond was *HFN* Music Editor (a post he held until the end of 1980) he and John Crabbe thought that readers might like illustration of how, or how not, to make good stereo tape recordings and the effect of using different types of microphone; in February 1972 the Conway Hall was hired and piano, chamber vocal and choral recordings were engineered by Bob Auger for an LP, *What is Good Recorded Sound?*, published on the Discourses label with an elaborate booklet; there was also an orchestral track licensed from Unicorn Records.

As the *HFN* music panel changed, some writers were not really bothered by sound: as John Crabbe observed, if they liked the performance, they subconsciously awarded high marks for sound too. One eminent contributor was found by Angus McKenzie to be happily listening to out-of-phase speakers fed with bell wire, his amplifier mains connected with earth/neutral reversed. Perhaps with this sort of thing in mind, a quarterly reassessment feature, 'Quality Monitor', appeared, at first written by Angus and then, from the end of 1970, by an augmented editorial team, when the critics' findings were further analysed – and some of us were 'put right' in no uncertain fashion! It was a feature I especially valued as a reader, and it was a pity that the advent of the compact disc meant that in 1984 it had to be dropped. This was because, although at first only a few contributors had CD players, it was essential to allocate page space to this new carrier. Before the main reviews we had CD assessments by John Atkinson, Ivor Humphreys, Angus McKenzie and others. Angus was especially critical, mostly giving 'D' ratings; Ivor, though, liked the stable pitch with pianoforte, etc. *HFN* writers were more wary of the digital sound that was fully embraced in other journals.

Other writers

Judged on thickness, *HFN/RR* was at its zenith in 1972: the December issue ran to 249pp, 35 of them music editorial pages, with pop (Fred Dellar, Arthur Jackson), speech (Mary Postgate), cassette tapes (Peter Gammond), 'Traditional' (the likes of The Chieftains, Ewan MacColl, etc) but a predominance of Classical. There were recording session reports – most notably the 1966 Bernstein/CBS Mahler 8, outlined in John Crabbe's chapter – general music news stories and 'Music on Record' features on artists and repertoire. Distinguished contributors included the composer Humphrey Searle, arts critic Charles Osborne and the fine music analyst Hugh Ottaway. Within the editorial office, Classical music reviews were overseen by Gareth Jefferson, Gary Bellamy and Geoff Jeanes (both to die tragically), and Ivor Humphreys, whom I succeeded in 1986 as Music Editor, staying until mid-2000. A younger generation of talented writers included Hugh Canning (now principal critic of the *Sunday Times*), Andrew Keener (an eminent freelance producer), David Nice and Edward Seckerson (both writers and broadcasters); English music specialist Andrew Achenbach and workaholic broadcaster/writer Rob Cowan left to edit the short-lived *Gramophone* off-shoot *Classics*, and they were as valued as Antony Hodgson and Robert Dearling, who had previously served on *Records & Recording*. The indefatigable Bill Newman, who had once worked with the Mercury recording team, undertook artist interviews and sent in innumerable uncommissioned reviews for which he never demanded a penny.

Jazz and pop writers, who determined their own review material, included Max Harrison, Ben Watson, Denis Argent, Pete Clark, Ken Hyder, Johnny Black and Ken Kessler. The music pages were cut back in 2000 – regrettably they never attracted the record company advertising support they deserved – whilst CD had spawned further competing music titles, *Classic FM* and *BBC Music Magazine* being the principal survivors.

Subsidiary publications and another record project
From 1966–71 *Audio Annuals* were published, between 1972–81 retitled *HFN/RR Annuals*. These carried Peter Gammond's 'Basic Classical Library' listings besides feature articles on various musical matters: Erik Smith's essay on record producing; Tristram Cary on electronic music; listening in the home, by John Crabbe. There was also an *Audio Diary* available for 1966–69 which included listings of musical terms, composers' dates and nationalities and an equal temperament frequency/pitch table for the piano keyboard.

Quadraphonic recording had prompted a favourable editorial response in November 1970, following articles published in *HFN* in August by Michael Gerzon and David Hafler – John Crabbe had been impressed by the 'extra dimension' given by one or a pair of rear speakers fed from the positive terminals of a stereo amplifier. But the record companies variously supported four different systems for quadraphonic LPs. *HFN* ambitiously set out to illustrate these options with a limited edition vinyl set, *Quadrafile*, with just under 25 minutes of music transferred to four LP sides respectively mastered in SQ, QS, CD-4 and UD-4 formats. This was a two-year project completed in 1976, with tracks licensed from CBS (Bartók *Concerto for Orchestra*), EMI (Menuhin and Grappelli; Pink

Floyd's *Money*) and Virgin Records (*Tubular Bells*) and a private recording made by Jerry Brook at the Unicorn sessions for Mahler 3 with Jascha Horenstein and the LSO. There were also three electronic sounds tracks produced by Tony Faulkner.

Quadraphonic LPs were soon dropped and the master tapes mixed down for stereo – the Bernstein/LSO *Rite of Spring* had been produced at Abbey Road with the orchestra encircling the conductor. However, some experimental Philips multi-channel recordings have now appeared as multi-channel SACDs on Pentatone.

Kostas Metaxas *on keeping up to date:*

'During a rehearsal for a concert at Hamer Hall in Melbourne Australia, I had the principal performer and virtuoso violinist Richard Tognetti, of the Australian Chamber Orchestra, come up to me once he spied that I was using an analogue tape Stellavox recorder. With his priceless Cremonese violin in hand, he asked, "Why are you still using these old things from the 1960s?". To which I replied, pointing to his 200-year-old violin, "For the same reason you're still using these old things from the 1760s..."'

Ron Goldberg *reflects on a scratchy speaker dem:*

'Here's one that I'm always happy to tell, about how audiophilia can be self-defeating even to the most dedicated. While working with the CEA some years ago, I was invited to hear a new brand of speakers at Jeff Rowland's headquarters in Colorado. The room was beautifully treated from an acoustic standpoint, and the electronics were what you'd expect from Jeff's own demo room. The speaker company was marketing high-end floorstanding models finished in onyx!

'I had brought my favourite demo CDs with me, but the rep for the speaker company refused to let me audition his speakers with digital source material – "a travesty!". Instead, he proudly insisted on playing an (admittedly interesting) LP he had picked up at a garage sale for $1.00, which was covered with scratches. I patiently took in his demo, which sounded like a scratched record that you'd find for $1.00 at a garage sale.

'Afterward, I insisted on hearing my discs; although they were CDs, at least they weren't scratched. I enjoyed the sound – good, but not great, I thought – but when the music stopped, the rep lamented that my demo wouldn't really be valid anyway. After all, I had not taken off my glasses; the resulting reflections would confuse my impression of his product.'

9. The era of hi-fi shows

'It was in the 1980s that I recall dubious practices and mysticism creeping into some exhibitors' rooms, headed by a couple of well-known names who would make great play of taping up the telephones, placing unused loudspeakers face down on the floor, and even deliberately walking bare-footed on LPs placed on the carpet, before picking them up and playing them.' **Colin Walker**

***Colin Walker** recalls UK audio shows, then and now:*

'The first Audio Fairs I took part in were in 1965 and held at the Russell Hotel in London, and The Majestic Hotel in Harrogate, these in the Spring and Autumn respectively, and both organised by Rex Hassan. They were for me, very exciting events, and a world apart from current shows.

'For a start, they were much smaller, the hotel rooms larger, and it was the general practice in those days to close the door and offer a 15 to 20 minute recital of varied music to a captive audience, after which they would file out of the room and the next batch would enter, having queued patiently in the corridor. This was a very civilised approach, compared with today's wide-open doors, with exhibitors seemingly engaged in competing to outperform their neighbours across and along the corridor.

'I think I am right in saying that there was no Japanese equipment in the country in the mid-1960s except possibly Pioneer. The main exhibitors included Quad, Leak, Rogers, Armstrong, KEF, Wharfedale, Celestion, Richard Allan, Fane, and I seem to recall a few American products – Fisher and McIntosh come to mind.

'I also recall at that time, the first live versus recorded comparisons, by Bob Fisher of AT&C to demonstrate their microphones using piano and strings played by students. In later years George Hooley did similar demonstrations using pre-recorded tapes interspersed with his live clarinet playing, these for B&W and later, Castle.

'In the late 1960s it was becoming increasingly difficult in Central London to unload and load the demonstration equipment at the hotels, and I think it was in 1969 that the show first moved to Skyways, one of the Heathrow hotels. It was Leslie Watts (JordanWatts) who first suggested this new venue at a meeting of the Federation of British Audio, whose meetings I used to attend as Richard Allan's representative. (I felt very much out of my depth in those days, in the midst of such luminaries as Raymond Cooke, Donald Chave and others. Ken Williman, who later exported the original Ariston was the rather pompous chairman.) 1970 saw the first show at Olympia, with fabricated rooms constructed for demonstration purposes. By this time, Japanese equipment was being imported, and I recall Pioneer having a football-pitch-sized exhibition space. The other feature of Olympia was the intransigence of the unions who built the exhibition. I well recall exhibitions opening more than a day late, and also the time B&W created a walkout by having the temerity to stick their own B&W sign on the wall of their room. Harrogate was always a civilised event which eventually expanded into several hotels under the auspices of Peter Hainsworth and Stan Smith. Stan was a professional musician, a trumpet player who had his own band and had played with mainly Latin-American bands. When the large, new exhibition centre opened in the late 1970s, most of the show was accommodated there, but many of the exhibitors preferred to remain at the Cairn Hotel.

'One after-hours feature of the Harrogate shows was the hospitality evenings organised for the exhibition by *Hi-Fi For Pleasure* magazine, which appeared at the time to have a bottomless pocket, as the tables groaned under the weight of the food, and they hired bands to entertain, including the Pasadena Roof Orchestra and the Syd Lawrence Band.

'It was in the 1980s that I recall dubious practices and mysticism creeping into some exhibitors' rooms, headed by a couple of well-known names who in their demonstration rooms would make great play of taping up the telephones, placing unused loudspeakers face down on the floor, and even, in one case, deliberately walking bare-footed on LPs placed on the carpet, before picking them up and playing them. It also became the fashion for many exhibitors to look deliberately scruffy and unkempt.

'Observations about visitors to the hi-fi shows include those who show intense curiosity with the rear panels of loudspeakers as though they held some secret ingredient, and endless questions about whose ancillary equipment you were using (and why!) instead of asking about the products you were representing. Others would come into the demonstration room clutching their favourite CD, asking for it to be put on, and sitting there in rapt concentration before moving on to the rest of the rooms to repeat the procedure, hoping no doubt, to hear subtle differences while trying to ignore the extraneous noises permeating from other rooms.'

Gordon Hill, consultant and former retailer, recalls a famous tale:

'There's the famous story of Harold Leak as told by Gilbert Briggs, "The Price Of A Full Stop". In early 1950s Britain, obtaining foreign currency was virtually impossible. After a lot of hassle, Harold Leak managed to wring some dollars from a reluctant Government so that H J Leak could participate in the New York Audio Fair, which was in those days held at the Waldorf. So he sent the Waldorf a telegram. "Will take room 18 dollars available".

'Being careful with cash, he omitted the period in between the 18 and the dollars with entirely predictable consequences. The Waldorf were not amused and it took a lot of effort on Leak's part to persuade the hotel that he did indeed have more than 18 bucks!'

Chris Short, Managing Director, Myryad, on a regular exhibitor:

'At almost any UK "hotel show" you attended in the 1980s, there would be John Gay tucked into an alcove in a corridor, behind a trestle table piled with unlikely accessories, additives and general "mid-fi" alchemy, busking the bemused with "Come on, you lot, we're not one of those here-today-and-gone-tomorrow operations: we're gone tonight!"'

Robert Becker of SOTA, on one of the benefits of shows:

'Once at a CES, a genuinely blind, future dealer of ours from Minnesota came to visit our booth and we tried to convey the remarkable isolation of the SOTA tables. While we were quite audibly banging on the cabinet, we handed the dealer the tonearm and asked him to start the record.

'He effortlessly placed the arm down and smiled broadly when he heard music undisturbed by our obnoxious attempts to dislodge the stylus, which played on and on. That was known later on in SOTA circles, including the dealers, we suspect, as our kind of true, double-blind test.

'We made the sale and we had a new dealer impressed in ways he never had been by a top table. I remember his smile today.'

Arthur Khoubessarian on Pink Triangle's first exhibition:

'During my time at Pink, we went through many, varied experiences. I am sure that a lot of them will have parallels from other people. So how about a humbling one?

'When Neal and I first started, we were in our early twenties. Naïve, we were in awe of the industry and the great and the good who peopled it. We had no illusions of the enormity of the battles which lay ahead. Indeed, we felt we were as small fry as you could get.

'We were doing our doing our first Audio T show in London. All our money gone. R&D, production and the cost of the show, which to us was a small fortune, had to come first. We dreaded anyone asking us to share a drink, for between us we had just £5 to last us the entire weekend! This is not an exaggeration. The burning question? How was the product and the infamous company going to be received?

'Well, the queue to get into our room went down the hall and round the corner for the entire show, and that was fantastic. But what really got us was just one comment. A gentleman, of some respectful number of years, had been sitting, listening intently for some considerable period of time (over an hour) to our offering. He then got up and came over to us and simply said: "It's a good thing Hitler didn't get rid of all of you!".'

***

Richard Black *on Tim de Paravicini putting up with punters:*

'Tim de Paravicini (EAR Yoshino) was at the Heathrow hi-fi show one year (about a decade ago, if not more) and was getting fed up with a succession of punters asking the usual, "So this hi-fi of yours – is it any good then?" sort of crap. He put up with a bit of this from one luckless sod before coming out with the immortal line, "If you can't hear what it sounds like, get the f**k out of my room!".

'Also at Heathrow, Tim was talking to that nice fellow who used to make Axhorn speakers, Mr Davies I think, and was explaining how good speakers should produce bass that really hits you in the stomach. As he said this, he hit Mr Davies in the stomach for effect, but unfortunately the latter hadn't seen the blow coming and hadn't had a chance to stiffen any muscles, and I rather got the impression that he was in some discomfort for a minute or two. Tim, predictably, didn't seem to notice.'

***

Tony Shuman, *Apogee Acoustics, on Jason Bloom's show technique:*

'After the birth of the full-range Apogee, we tried various means of attracting a larger audience to the product. The Caliper was an attempt to downsize the speaker while not giving up the overall effect. We introduced it at CES in Chicago. As with many of our products, work was done on the acoustical aspects right up to the end.

'Jason Bloom was the lead audiophile, Leo Spiegel was the chief technical guru, and I filled in where necessary. Frequency responses gave just so much information on our type of product; so much more was done by listening and tweaking based upon oral statements. Leo, requiring hearing aids, could only interpret our desires as we voiced them without being directly able to confirm for himself by listening for just what we wanted. I always thought that this was one of our interesting strengths.

'We arrived in Chicago the day before the show and began the setup. As visitors will remember, sound and presentation were always uppermost in Jason's mind. The speakers had been finished at the factory the day before we left and the front covers were glued on to the speakers such that they could not be removed. We completed the setup in the room and proceeded to listen to our latest product.

'It did not sound as we wished. We had made several changes to capacitors and resistors at the end of the final tweak and something had gone wrong. We could not remove the front covers to get to the network and could only barely reach the network. There was no opportunity to add or re-attach anything that was removed.

'After much discussion, Leo determined what he thought was the problem and I reached in and cut it out of the network, knowing that there was no going backwards. Blessedly, it was successful, and Jason was able to present to the world another Apogee triumph.

'Jason was known for his music programmes, which included unknown pieces of music that had great demonstration appeal. Often people would come in just to hear what he had found. It became important to him to come up with new pieces for each show. Oftentimes, a week or two before a show, Jason would go to a music store and rummage through the racks, buying large quantities of vinyl, in the early days, and then CDs. We would go into the sound room and listen to brief segments throughout the albums looking for the truly special. Lots of discards, but many memorable demos at show-time.'

Bascom H King, Consultant, on the Infinity IRS Loudspeaker introduction at Winter CES:

'It was at the Winter CES, I believe in 1978, that Infinity introduced the new IRS loudspeaker. Working with Arnie Nudell, I had designed the bass towers for this system. Each tower contained six 12in woofers and was driven by a 1.5kW power amplifer mounted on the rear of the woofer tower. This system had an accelerometer sensor on one of the woofers which was incorporated in a feedback servo system that sensed the acceleration of this control woofer. The resultant corrected signal drove all six of the woofers in parallel and resulted in distortion reduction and a flat response down to 20Hz.

'We had it all for this demo. Two large rooms in the basement floor of the McCormick Inn, The Soundstream digital recorder with some of their source material, Keith Johnson's famous analogue tape recorder with some of his source material, appropriately good phono equipment and records, and a great set of mono tube power amplifiers to drive the mid-tweeter panels of the IRS speaker.

'I had built these amplifiers for a mentor friend during my college days. They were a two-chassis push-pull 845 triode design based on a record cutting amplifier another friend and mentor used in his audio store in Santa Barbara, California. They were operated in class A with each tube idling at 100W with a plate voltage of 1000V and a current of 100 mA.

'At the time, there weren't very many 845 amplifiers out there and when people came in to hear the IRS, they would point to these glowing yellow thoriated tungsten filaments and say what are those amps?! I got great pleasure in saying "Oh, something I built for a friend a long while ago." Believe me, it was an honour to have my amps power the IRS for their maiden voyage.

'It was truly a great experience, one of the best moments of my audio career to see the line of people that, incidentally went outside and around the building, waiting to hear the IRS and to see the looks of astonishment when these speakers did their stuff.'

Ross Walker of Quad on an incident involving his father, Peter:

'We were at a show at the Russell Hotel, and a customer came up and he said to Peter, "What's the input sensitivity of your AM tuner?". And Peter said it's so many millivolts per metre, and the man said, "I don't think it is at all".

Peter picked him up by his lapels, lifted him up off the ground, shook him and said, "If you don't believe the bloody answer, then don't ask the bloody question!"'

Robert J Reina on ships passing in the night:

'When the CES was in Chicago, the Congress Hotel was the place to see what was new in high-end audio. Vegas is another story; I hate the place. Anyway, I was standing in the doorway of one of the display rooms at the Congress when from one direction Peter Moncrieff of *IAR* is walking towards the room and from the other direction comes Julian Hirsch.

'I cannot imagine two more polar opposites at their craft. Moncrieff was over the top on the techno/subjecto end of the spectrum while Julian was the audio equivalent of *American Bandstand* reviewing (it has a nice beat,

I like the lyrics, you can dance to it so I'll give it a 10). I was expecting something to happen, some sign of recognition perhaps or even some sort of eye contact. But it was like two ships passing in the night, neither was even aware of the other. I found the episode very ironic.'

Bill Peugh of Sumiko recalls the shafting of a noisy exhibitor:

'In 1995, Ken Kessler walked into the Metaphor suite at the CES. Preparing to play their new speaker for Ken, the room was suddenly rocked by the somewhat unrecognisable sound of a Saturn V rocket launch from the floor below. Seems someone with a large subwoofer had discovered the 1990s version of a freight train and was trying to play it as loud as the real thing. Kessler was incensed, not only by the awful sound shaking the floor, but also by the rudeness of a fellow exhibitor. He wanted the exhibitor banned. But then he got kind of an evil grin on his face, pointed at the new speakers he had come to hear and asked how loud they would play. "How loud would you like them to play?" was the response. Ken produced a just-released *Hi-Fi News* compilation disc, loaded it into the player, and spun up the volume control.

Suddenly the room was filled with the strains of Isaac Hayes' soulful voice demanding to know, "Who's the black private dick, That's a sex machine to all the chicks? Shaft! Ya damn right!"

'Ken was moving and grooving. "They say this cat Shaft is a bad mother. Shut your mouth! I'm just talkin' 'bout Shaft."

'The Saturn V was silenced and not heard from again for three days.'

Janet Belton on the trials of being a show organiser:

'Having organised the London Hi-Fi Show for over 20 years I have been faced with many strange situations, not the least being a complete power failure caused by a severed cable somewhere in the vicinity of the airport, just as we were about to open the show.

'However, I never cease to be amazed at the problems exhibitors can throw at you expecting an instant solution. The one that sticks in my mind most was from a charming Swedish gentleman who during the pull-out asked, "Would I please get the forklift truck up to his room on the First Floor of the hotel to remove his pallet of goods as soon as possible?" When asked how he thought this could be achieved the reply was a swift: "You're the Organiser, I'll leave the logistics to you. I have a plane to catch."

'My other lasting memory is of a member of the public stopping in the doorway of the Organisers Office, craning his neck to see what was in the room without actually crossing the threshold. When politely asked if we could help, he looked at the sign over the door, then replied, "Organisers? You couldn't organise a p***-up in a brewery!" and walked away!'

Robert J Reina on perplexing pricing:

'I always attend *Stereophile*'s Home Entertainment shows and frequently I'm assigned to write about new speakers. I always get dragged into a room by a company showing off a new design and looking for my approval. Once I visited such a room and the sound was mediocre at best.

'Judging by the construction of the speakers, the speakers looked fairly costly to manufacture. After listening to a lengthy discourse on the design parameters, I took copious notes. I then asked the manufacturer what the retail price was: "Seventeen".

'I honestly didn't know if the speaker was $1700 a pair, or $17,000. If I asked the manufacturer, or guessed and guessed wrong, I would have offended him. I was at a loss either way...'

Kostas Metaxas recalls a bathroom demonstration:

'I can remember one CES show at the old Sahara in 1991 where I was launching some new products and had booked two demonstration rooms. Everything was going well until I had a chap come into my room accompanied by a rather ugly woman who asked if he could use my bathroom. I didn't think much about the request, so I replied OK. The fact that both of them went in was a concern, but I figured that in a few minutes, they'd both be gone and I wouldn't make that mistake twice.

'There was quite a bit of traffic coming into the room, so I was distracted from the events in the bathroom for at least 30 minutes after which I became quite concerned and my thoughts turned to what could they be doing in there.

'This was Las Vegas. Drugs? Murder? At this exact moment, the British magazine reviewer Ken Kessler walks into my room to see and hear my exhibition when the bathroom door slams open, and the chap with the ugly girlfriend literally run out of my room in front of an excited Ken Kessler shouting, "Hey, that's Ron Jeremy!" who turns out to be the world's Number 1 porn star. This left an indelible impression on Ken who wrote up the incident in UK's *Hi-Fi News* as "Ron Jeremy having a businessman's lunch at the Metaxas Audio room".'

10. The John Atkinson Era

'It was a July 1966 review by John Crabbe of Ortofon's S15TE moving-coil cartridge that was the prototype for what I wanted to achieve with the magazine's equipment reviews. Yes, that review featured measurements, but they were not the point of the review.' **John Atkinson**

From October 1982 to May 1986. *By John Atkinson*

Monthly magazines, with their focus on the new, the exciting, the cool, are inherently ephemeral things. Some readers react to this reality by merely glancing at a few features as the magazine wends its way from mailbox to recycling bin. However, other readers pore over each issue's content, using it to stay abreast of what is happening, to feed their passion for the subject. Such readers are drawn to a publication that shares their passion, that doesn't talk down to them, that is unfailingly honest with them, that informs and educates as it entertains, that gives them more than they expect with respect to both breadth and depth of content. *Hi-Fi News* is quintessentially such a magazine, so it shouldn't come as a surprise to learn that it is celebrating 50 years of continuous publication in 2006.

Back in the late 1960s, my passion for music had led me to live performance which in turn had led me to recording which in turn had led me to what we called 'hi-fi.' The laboratory I worked at back then subscribed to scientific periodicals, but among the academic journals available was also *Hi-Fi News* (incorporating *Tape and Tape Recorders, Audio News, Stereo News, Record News*). I added my name to the lab's long distribution list and, several months in arrears, began a relationship that continues to this day.

I devoured those issues, starting with the trademark yellow covers. The 'process yellow' printer's ink was first featured as a band top and bottom, then as a picture frame around the featured photo, which may or may not have had a direct connection with audio. Those 1960s issues were packed with content: Rex Baldock on 'Audio A–Z,' Angus McKenzie on 'BBC Stereo' and reviews of LPs paying special attention to sound quality (the renowned 'Quality Monitor' column, which was later to be written in-house), George Tillett's 'American Letters,' Jean/John Walton on tonearm geometry and cartridge theory, Stanley Kelly on speaker design. There were thinkpieces, like Geoffrey Jeanes's 'Past Considerations: The

Gramophone as a Time Machine' in August 1968, constructional articles such as Trevor Attewell's Bassett subwoofer, Rex Baldock's Paraline, a small quarter-wave horn speaker, and Peter Atkinson's (no relation) ambitiously named 'A State-of-the-Art Loudspeaker.' There were the magazine's own recordings, such as 1972's *What is Good Recorded Sound?* and 1976's *Quadrafile.*

But most importantly, there were the equipment reports, from names I came to respect and trust, such as Ralph West, Gordon J King, B J Webb. I almost read the ink off the page of R W's February 1966 review of the Thorens TD150 when I came across it a couple of years later in a secondhand book store, while I lusted after the Quad 33 pre-amp and 303 power amp, reviewed by L H Hulley in April 1968, though the price of the latter (£55) was way out of my reach. There were the reviews of products destined to be classics. There were the loudspeaker impedance graphs which formally warned: 'Note: this curve does not indicate the frequency response of the loudspeaker'.

Joining the editorial team
In 1972, I left the lab to try my hand working as a professional musician. *Hi-Fi News*, which had absorbed its Link House stablemate *Record Review* in 1970 to become *Hi-Fi News & Record Review*, followed me, filling my time during the various day jobs I worked to supplement my musician's income. And by the autumn of 1975, when I was working at a ballroom residency in Brighton, my long daily commute by train made me thankful for a magazine whose content held me in its grip me from London's Victoria Station to Brighton and back again!

By the early summer of 1976, I was still working steadily as a musician, but was finding it harder and harder to get paid. My then-wife, Maree, called my attention to an advertisement in the *Guardian*: 'Wanted, News Editor for *Hi-Fi News & Record Review*.' I called the number and, to my astonishment, it was the editor, John Crabbe himself, who took the phone call. John was an Olympian figure, having given *HFN* an almost unparalleled consistency of approach since he took over from founder Miles Henslow in April 1965.

An interview was arranged, which ended up being conducted by then-deputy editor Paul Messenger, John being indisposed by emergency heart surgery; and on September 1976 I joined John, Paul, Record Reviews editor Geoff Jeanes (the same GJ who had contributed that 'Gramophone as Time Machine' article in 1968), art director Mark Stevens, and secretary Helen Eckersley, in their Dingwall Avenue, Croydon office. I remember that, as the office 'newbie,' I kept my head down for the next six years. However, glancing through back issues reveals that I wrote a lot of copy for the magazine. My first news article, on an East London record store, was published in November 1976, my first technical feature, on Dolby-B Broadcasting, and my first interview, with the then-director of the Brighton Festival Chorus, Laszlo Heltay, both appeared in December 1976. My first of two appearances on the magazine's cover was in January 1977, where I was pictured playing a viola da gamba, to promote an article I had written for that issue on the early instruments program at the London College of Furniture.

My system at the time I started reading the magazine comprised the then-ubiquitous Garrard SP25 turntable with an Audio-Technica cartridge, a Trio (Kenwood) KA-2000 solid-state amplifier, and a pair of Wharfedale Super Linton loudspeakers, all of which I bought, of course, as a package from a regular *HFN* advertiser, JJ Francis (Wood Green) Ltd ('specialists in Nagra equipment'). I still had the Wharfedales when I joined the magazine, but the Trio had given way to a Sony integrated (with matching Sony tuner) and the turntable had long since been upgraded to a Thorens TD150AB with its own arm and a Shure M75EJ MM cartridge. In fact, it was probably my awareness of the importance of the system's front-end at defining the overall sound quality level that led Paul Messenger to give me the job after my interview (although he now says that it was also the fact that the other applicant couldn't spell!).

As much as I loved the sound of this system, it was not at the level where it could be used for reviewing. My first reviews for *HFN/RR* – of the Audio/Pulse Model One ambience synthesizer and the Sansui QSD-2 surround-sound decoder, both published in October 1977 – had to wait for further system upgrades. Fortunately, Paul Messenger was working his way through a literal mountain of gear for his monthly 'Subjective Sounds' column, and I borrowed much of what he was writing about to educate myself on what we were later to call 'high-end sound'. Stand-outs were Gale GS401 and Rogers LS3/5A speakers and Lecson amplifications. Then, in the fall of 1977, Geoff Jeanes and I drove down to Salisbury where we both purchased Linn Sondek LP12 turntables from Naim Audio's Julian Vereker. I have since bought three more LP12s, and still use this classic belt-drive turntable today.

Doubts about the magazine
'Subjective Sounds' and the Linn were the initial triggers for my increasing dissatisfaction over the next five years with what the magazine had become

at the time I joined the staff. With his column Paul Messenger was pushing a concept that at the time seemed heretical to many but has since become the core of audio publishing: that the best way to judge audio components was to do what the eventual owners would do: listen to them. (J Gordon Holt in the US had founded *Stereophile* magazine in 1962 on exactly the same premise.)

The Linn became a factor because of a confrontation I had had with Linn's Ivor Tiefenbrun at the October 1976 Heathrow Show. I had gone into his dem room to introduce myself, but once I had done so – 'Hi, I'm John Atkinson, I have just joined *Hi-Fi News* as news editor' – had almost been driven out by Ivor, furious at any representative of a magazine that had just published a measurements-based review of the Sondek that, in his opinion, completely missed the point. The *HFN* reviewer, ex-magazine staffer Frank Jones, had apparently not listened to the turntable. At the show, once he had stopped shouting, Ivor sat me down and played the same LP, first on a Technics direct-drive turntable then on a Linn turntable. The tonearm and cartridge were the same, but there was a large difference in favor of the Linn.

The third trigger came in the summer of 1978. At that time, I believed – no, I *knew*, that amplifiers operated short of clipping did not sound different from one another. An editorial I wrote in the April 1979 *HFN* illustrates the man I was back then: 'The result of a subjective test can only be regarded as valid if all potentially misleading variables have been removed, but this is very often not the case,' I thundered.

Then, in 1978, I took part in a blind listening test organised by Martin Colloms, in which the panel tried to distinguish by ear between two solid-state power amplifiers – a Quad 405 and a Naim NAP250 – and a tube amp, a Michaelson & Austin TVA-1. The results of the test were inconclusive, the listeners apparently not being able to distinguish between the amplifiers (the test was reported on in exhaustive detail in the November 1978 issue of *HFN*). Having been involved in the tests, having seen how carefully Martin had organised them, and having experienced nothing that conflicted with my beliefs, I concluded that the null results proved that the amplifiers didn't sound different from one another. I bought a Quad 405.

As I mentioned in a debate that took place at the 2005 Home Entertainment Show in New York, over time I began to realize that even though the sound of my system with the Quad was the same as it ever had been, the magic was gone. Listening to records began to play a smaller role in my life – until I replaced the 405 with an M&A tube amplifier two years later. Amplifiers did *not* sound the same, even though the magazine I had been reading for a decade and had now been on the staff of for two years said they did.

Promotion – and some hard thinking

Paul Messenger had left the magazine in 1978 to edit *Hi-Fi Choice*, then an irregularly-published book devoted to reviews of a single product category. I was promoted to assistant editor upon his departure, then to deputy editor in January 1979. (Replacing me as News Editor was the multi-talented Ivor Humphreys – musician, musicologist, writer, audio engineer – whom, I am pleased to note, continues with the magazine as a freelance equipment reviewer to this day.)

By 1979, I was contributing a copious amount of copy to the magazine, including many show reports, where I tried to give readers a feel for what it would have been like to visit the show, a massive two-part article on 'The Stereo Image' in May and June 1981 and an article on how to construct a true-peak-reading Sound Level Meter, which I had designed using CMOS logic gates in October 1981, as well as writing many of the 'Quality Monitor' record reviews. 1981 also saw the first of what has become a regular series of appearances at audio shows where I lectured on various audio-related topics, conducted public listening tests, or chaired panel discussions. Also in 1980 and 1981, I was heavily involved in a spin-off from *HFN* called *Audio & Video Mart*, which was aimed at less committed readers: I wrote almost all the reviews as well as an in-depth technical feature for each issue, but *A&VM* only lasted three issues.

So, there I was in the early 1980s, keeping busy, but also starting to wonder if *Hi-Fi News & Record Review* had lost its way. A successful magazine should inform, educate, and entertain its readers. It publishes reviews so that its readers can short-list components that they might be interested in purchasing and therefore should audition for themselves. As well as being informed, readers need to be able to define what they want in terms of their personal tastes, before they can make buying decisions. The magazine must also educate its readers, therefore, in how to listen and how to identify what is important to them. And it needs to entertain them so that the mental heavy lifting involved in being informed and educated goes unnoticed by the readers.

HFN had been informing, educating, and entertaining its readers since the beginning. Founder Miles Henslow had written in the very first issue that 'we shall endeavor earnestly to represent the high standards that are essential for High Fidelity sound reproduction... We may mention many things but we shall recommend nothing that does not "measure up". We hope in this way to build and maintain a publication that our readers and advertisers will come to regard as sound and dependable'. In many ways, the magazine had lived up to that promise, becoming the prime source of audio information for 25 years for those passionate about recorded music. This was reflected in its published readers' letters pages, where arguments initiated by the magazine's features and reviews continued to rage. (It can be argued, and I have done so on many occasions, that the prime reason for publishing anything in a magazine is to generate letters that themselves can be published. A magazine that doesn't have a healthy letters section is a magazine that has died but hasn't yet noticed the fact.)

Yet, given the primacy of the word 'hi-fi' in its title and Miles Henslow's 1956 mission statement, it didn't seem right to me that the magazine's editorial identity was dominated by music and recordings, important as they are. When the commercially successful *HFN* had absorbed the failing *Audio & Record Review* in 1970, it was if the latter had actually absorbed the former. The content that was most popular with readers, the equipment reports, were pushed to the 'graveyard' at the back of the magazine, behind even 'Classical Cassette' reviews. Add to that the fact that the measurement-dominated equipment reviews, while always authoritative, were increasingly marginalised when examined in the light of readers' own experience, and you can understand my increasing frustration in the early 1980s with John Crabbe's vision for the magazine.

It is hard to write these words, since I have aways regarded John as both a mentor and one of the clearest thinkers in audio I have encountered. It was also John who defined for me the relationship between a magazine's editorial integrity and the advertisers who support it financially (readers, sadly, are never a significant source of income, given the high costs of distribution).

Back in 1964, John stated in an Editorial Leader that *HFN*'s reviewers 'have a mandate to write what they think, even if some feelings are hurt', expanding on this sentiment in a subsequent conversation to define the matter thus: 'If you tell the truth about components you review, there will always be a small percentage of companies at any one time who are not advertising in your pages. But if you publish the truth, you will have a good magazine. And if you have a good magazine, you will have readers. And as long as you have readers, disgruntled advertisers will eventually return. But if you don't tell the truth, you won't have a good magazine. And if you don't have a good magazine, you won't have readers, at least not for long. And if you don't have readers, you won't have advertisers. In publishing, as in all things, honesty is the best policy.'

(I was later to learn that that prototypical newspaper columnist Walter Lippman had written on this subject in 1922, before John was born: 'A newspaper can flout an advertiser... but if it alienates the buying public, it loses the one indispensable asset of its existence.')

But being honest is not in itself any guarantor of publishing success. You also have to publish editorial content that readers wish to read. And back in 1982, it appeared that this was no longer true with our magazine. Other titles had also successfully ridden the high fidelity wave and *HFN/RR*'s advertising revenue and circulation – the two metrics by which publishers calculate the success of their ventures – were in steep decline. Our July 1982 issue, which heavily featured in-car audio, was the smallest issue ever. Something had to be done.

A new publisher and a new editor

To cut a rather long and complicated story to its essentials, in October 1982 *HFN/RR* acquired a new publisher, Paul Messenger, and a new editor, myself. Paul guaranteed me a clean slate, editorially: as long as the financial numbers improved I could do what I felt necessary to makeover the grand old lady of audio publishing into a modern miss. I had already eliminated the yellow border in January 1982, but the first step was to commission freelance graphic artist Paul Carpenter to transform the look of the magazine with a new logo and a fresh interior design. Then, it was time to redesign the content, to reject old dogma in favor of material that mattered.

In my first Leader as editor, in the December 1982 issue, I nailed my colours to the mast. Even as I reassured readers that John Crabbe may have taken up a new career as a freelance writer, his new position as Consulting Editor would mean that his considerable experience and expertise would still contribute greatly to the authority of *HFN/RR*, I wrote that 'The state of hi-fi development is such that it seems impossible to obtain anything approaching perfection, and several aspects, at present, even seem to be mutually exclusive. There are systems capable of low coloration, low distortion, accurate presentation of stereo imagery, impressive resolving power, and dynamics indistinguishable from real life. However, I have yet to hear a system without at least one major deficiency from that list, so it would seem naive at this stage of the game to strike any definitive posture concerning the hardware. *HFN/RR*, in its third age, will continue with its policy of nonalignment, to recognise that "different folks need different strokes", and that with its new editorial team representing as wide a range of opinion – rather than dogma – that can be found, its pages will contain argument, not confrontation, and considered criticism, not repetitive cant.'

In place of the rather haphazard arrangement of content that had been the norm since the beginning, I fitted each issue's content into an iron frame: contents always on page 3; editorial leader; readers' letters; news; audio columnists; audio features; equipment reviews; music features; record reviews. I started running a feature on the final page facing the inside back-cover advertisement. All magazines now take advantage of this prime editorial real estate, but not many did so back then.

Not surprisingly, I moved the equipment reports to the centre of the magazine. If reviews were what readers most wanted, I would place them in the centre of the arch of content. Ironically, it was a July 1966 *HFN* review by John Crabbe of Ortofon's S15TE moving-coil cartridge that was the prototype for what I wanted to achieve with the magazine's equipment reviews. Yes, that review featured measurements, but they were not the point of the review. Instead, they reinforced and explained the subjective findings in a manner that really only Martin Colloms in the early 1980s was equalling. This new-old approach to reviewing, tying together both the subjective and objective approaches to equipment reviewing, reached its apogee during my tenure as editor with, appropriately, the Apogee Scintilla loudspeaker in September 1985: almost 10 pages of technical analysis, listening comments and measurements from three writers. On a more personal note, I tried a different style of subjective reviewing in August 1983, with a report on the Krell KSA-50 power amplifier, in which I tried to illustrate the descriptive points I was making using specific musical examples. This is something that is ubiquitous these days, but seemed very daring back then.

I made more of existing writers like Martin Colloms, Trevor Attewell, Barry Fox, and Angus McKenzie. I introduced new writers to the magazine's readers: the technically incomparable Malcolm Omar Hawksford; the inimitable Ken Kessler, who made his triple-pronged debut in July 1983 with a column called 'Classical Glass,' devoted to valve components, followed by the first 'Golden Turkey Awards' in September of that year, and the first 'Anachrophile' column, devoted to the BBC LS3/5a in November '83; the soft-spoken Ben Duncan, who contributed an awesomely complex DIY pre-amplifier design, which I had to split into many 1984 instalments, followed by exhaustive research into the sounds of passive components like resistors, capacitors, and wires. We started a Hi-Fi Show at Heathrow Airport in 1983, which continues to this day.

Behind the scenes, I instituted a major change in the way the magazine was produced. Through 1982, typesetters had keyed in the edited text for an article or review, first on Linotype machines, which spit out hot metal type, then on optical typesetters, which produced a photographic 'galley,' a continuous strip of column-wide print, then on computerised typesetting machines, which also output photographically printed text. But in 1982, with the magazine's staff starting to use word processors, it seemed a good idea to see if, rather than a printout of the edited article text, a file on a floppy diskette could be sent to the prepress facility and read directly into the photo typesetting machine. That way, the text would not have to be keyed in again. The first article I tried this with was an interview with Telarc's Jack Renner in the January 1983 issue. With the help of the pre-press company this worked, so from then on an increasing proportion of the magazine's content was sent out for typesetting on diskette. This had to be a stealth operation because neither the magazine's management nor the print unions approved of this process, but it set the path for the future.

With Ken Kessler and Ivor Humphreys providing inspiration and Moth's Mike Harris the fulfilment and, when necessary, the manufacturing, I started the 'Accessories Club', which would offer readers inexpensive products that dealers didn't stock. The first of these was the Mission Isoplat, which we offered in the April 1984 issue.

The riskiest of the products we offered was the *Hi-Fi News & Record Review* Test CD, which was co-produced by Martin Colloms, Tony Faulkner and myself, and released in July 1985 and pressed by Denon in Japan. Even with the deal Denon cut me, the FOB price of the discs with jewelcase and booklet was £8 each – the magazine's management was understandably nervous when I told them I had already ordered 1000 CDs! Fortunately, the test CD sold like hot cakes – it seemed like everyone wanted to hear Mike Skeet's garage door recording – and I got to keep my job!

It was compact disc, launched in the UK in the spring of 1983 that stimulated the resurgence of interest in what we were beginning to call high-end audio. Despite its teething problems, the sonic promise of the medium was that it would lead to new approaches to amplifier and loudspeaker design. Which it did. I resolved that *HFN* would ride that wave for all it was worth. One casualty of that decision, which I regret to this day, was to replace the long-running 'Quality Monitor' feature with a CD equivalent. If I'd had the space, I would have continued doing both. But I didn't.

There was a lot of change in a short time, but the readers responded positively. By the spring of 1986, the magazine's finances and circulation had both risen considerably. I had a lot more I wanted to do with *HFN*, but fate stepped in the form of Larry Archibald, publisher and owner of the small American magazine *Stereophile*. Larry offered me not only a clean editorial slate but also the opportunity to buy into the company that published *Stereophile*. It would have been folly to turn Larry down, so on May 16 1986, I left the magazine that had come to occupy my life.

In the ten years to then, I contributed to 116 issues, offering nearly three-quarters of a million words on hi-fi and music. I reviewed 200 CDs and more than 450 LPs; I reviewed loudspeakers, amplifiers, CD players, cartridges, headphones, accessories, and one turntable; I wrote numerous features, including reports from 27 hi-fi shows; and I interviewed over 60 musicians, composers and engineers. The most memorable of these included cellist Julian Lloyd Webber, guitarist John Williams and recorder player Michala Petri, all of whom picked up their instruments and played for me (surely the ultimate in hi-fi?); mouth organist Larry Adler, whose wit sparkled for what seemed like hours; Julian Bream, the archetypal performing genius; the late Boyd Neel, who had a fund of anecdotes about British musical life in the 1930s and '40s; and James Galway who, tired after a hectic tour, dismissed all my carefully-prepared questions in ten minutes with monosyllabic replies.

My final review to appear in *HFN* was of the KEF R107 loudspeaker, in the July 1986 issue. The late Raymond Cooke, KEF's founder, subsequently told me he had read the review aloud to KEF employees. I assume he meant it as a compliment! Looking back, it was one heck of a ride, and 50 years after it made its debut, *Hi-Fi News* is still one heck of a magazine.

John Atkinson is Editor of Stereophile, a US audio magazine based in New York. He also produces classical and jazz recordings made using minimalist microphone techniques.

11. On the front line: retail reminiscences

'He unpacked the amp, only to discover there was no volume control knob. A volume spindle, yes – but no knob. I can only imagine how often, and with increasing desperation he shook the box, the packaging, wrapping and so on. No knob.' **Howard Popeck**

***Bill Peugh**, Sumiko, on legendary retailer Mike Kay:*

'Hyatt Water Tower Hotel in Chicago, CES 1979. Mark Levinson, the man, was holding his CES Dealer Meeting in an Exhibit Suite. This was an exclusive group. Most of the groundbreaking dealers of high end in the US were there, including a young Peter McGrath of Sound Components, who would soon become legendary for his stunning recordings and a huge Levinson dealer, and Mike Kay of Lyric Hi-Fi in Manhattan. Mike stood above the rest as the man most responsible for the growth of high end at the retail level and the biggest dealer of all.

'The subject of the meeting was the recent price increase of the Mark Levinson ML-1 pre-amplifier. The ML-1 was considered to be the first solid-state pre-amp on the market that challenged the sonic superiority of the day's best tube designs. Its build quality was second to none. But a 50% price increase had caused some dealers to question whether or not they could still sell it.

'In the front of the room, a successful young New England dealer stood up. Beaming with pride, he offered that he had sold two pre-amps in the preceding month. In the back row, Mike Kay leaned toward Steven Zipser from Sound Components and said quietly: "What? He had a bad week?".'

***Howard Popeck** of Subjective Audio recalling the early days of Musical Fidelity:*

'As Musical Fidelity's first-ever dealer, I was there at the birth, so to speak. Building a growing business is not without its problems, as I discovered during the demise of Subjective Audio. In MF's situation, quality control in the early days, although exemplary now, occasionally left something to be desired 20 years back.

'The Musical Fidelity Synthesis integrated amp was a winner, from the off. It was heavy, comparatively well-built, sounded superb and was great value for money. And we had the lion's share in the London area. Demand was high.

'One particular buyer was a young teenager. As it turned out, he had saved hard and his parents and family had contributed. It was either a Bar-Mitzvah gift, or something similar, I really can't recall.

'Dunstan, our ever-patient and resourceful engineer, did the installation. What seemed like the buyer's entire family were there in the room to witness the great event. Dunstan had, by his estimation, an audience of about 15 souls. They'd all contributed to the purchase, so they wanted a performance. And they got one! He unpacked the amp, only to discover there was no volume control knob. A volume spindle, yes – but no knob. I can only imagine how often, and with increasing desperation he shook the box, the packaging, wrapping and so on. No knob.

'Rising to the occasion, Dunstan played the amplifier, turning the volume spindle with increasingly sweaty fingers. With great presence of mind he took a straw poll amongst the assembled throng as to what the best listening volume was.

'When a consensus was arrived at, he set the knob-less spindle and then clamped his mole-wrench to it, so the wrench was balanced perfectly but precariously, vertical, thereby defining the optimum sound level, and offering, with reason, a degree of volume control.

'He explained he'd be back the next day with a volume control knob, but cautioned any of them from being to heavy on their feet in that room for fear that the mole-wrench would quickly rotate clockwise, thereby deafening the entire room and no doubt destroying the speakers too. Clearly, dancing to celebrate the new purchase had been eagerly anticipated and equally clearly, it was now temporarily but most certainly out of the question.

'The customer, no doubt impressed by Dunstan's ingenuity, went on the purchase more items from us.'

Richard Colburn *on meeting the Audio Gods:*

'I started my audio career in September 1971, when I walked into Minuteman Radio in Cambridge, Massachusetts, and was hired on the spot. I can't explain this, the manager simply liked me. (I had sketched out a dream system for him during my counter-top interview. It was KLH 9 electrostatics, Marantz 9s, a Marantz 7C and a Thorens TD-125/SME/ Shure V-15 Type II combo.) He must have been impressed, so I started the very next day. At the time, we sold JBL, KLH, Rectilinear, Marantz,

Crown, Revox, Sony, Sansui, Kenwood, etc. Shortly after I began, I started pushing for more exotic gear. We eventually took on Dahlquist, Nakamichi and Mark Levinson.

'On a Thursday afternoon sometime in 1973, we got a call from a man named Jon Dahlquist. He had this new speaker that he wanted us to hear. Being an open-minded lot, we told him to bring them in. They were located on Long Island, about a four-hour drive from us. He informed us that his partner Saul Marantz was going to bring the speakers up in his car on Saturday morning.

'*Saul Marantz!* We were abuzz from the time of the phone call over this impending visit. Saturday morning rolls around and lo and behold, in walks the man himself. It was as if Apollo of the Audio Gods had arrived, the sun shone in through our door and we became very happy. After falling all over ourselves over the very kind Mr Marantz, we listened to the DQ-10. Needless to say, we were astounded and wrote an order that very day. We were quite successful with the line. Later on, when I heard of Saul's death, I was crushed. The first truly high end gear that I owned was a Model 7 pre-amp (tube) and a Model 250 2x125W power amp.

'Not long after that, I received a phone call. On the other end was a man with a heavy Japanese accent asking if we were a Revox dealer. I informed him that we were and asked if he would like to have a demonstration of an A-77. He replied that he had a cassette deck that would perform as well as a Revox open-reel machine. I told him to bring it in. Turns out that the man was Ted Nakamichi.

'When he arrived he was accompanied by his father Etsuro – or "Ed" as he insisted that we call him. So Ed and Ted did the demo of a Nakamichi 1000 versus the A-77. It was really close, but we were so impressed that we took on the line. We were really successful with those machines, especially with the 700 model. In later years, Ted told me that we were the second dealer in the country to buy the line, the first being Harmony House in New York. Their marketing plan was simple: sell to all the Revox dealers.

'We took on Levinson in 1975. Now you have to remember, we were in the midst of hi-fi Armageddon by this time. There were five hi-fi stores in Harvard Square and the competition was fierce. Mark Levinson showed up at the store and demo'd his JC-2 for us and we were stunned. How could something so simple (and expensive) sound so damn good? We didn't ask too many questions, we took on the line and sold quite a few pieces. We were visited frustratingly often by members of the Boston Audio Society. They were a nice enough bunch, but they expected to purchase audio nirvana for about $0.48. Well, that wasn't going to happen at Minuteman

Radio. We had the Levinson hooked up to a Stax pure Class-A amplifier driving a pair of Koss Model One electrostatic speakers (a phenomenal product). One weekend, we invited the BAS over to the store for an evening with Mark Levinson. After his presentation, the guys attacked him for the price of the JC-2. Too much! Too much! Well for that bunch, no wonder. Anyway, Mark replied over and over again, "If you don't like it, don't buy it". After that disaster, Mark took three of us out to dinner in downtown Boston. We rode in his 1966 Maserati Quattroporte.

'I left Minuteman to work for Suffolk Audio in late 1973 but returned to Minuteman in 1975 as manager. While I worked for Suffolk, they sold lots of British hi-fi. We had brands like IMF, Quad, Celestion, B&W, Radford, Linn and Decca. We also sold that nut-ball tonearm from Keith Monks – mercury, fer crissakes! We took on SAE for big power. The Mark IIIC was getting a lot of play and we really liked the way it sounded.

'Now, Jim Bongiorno of SAE was quite a character. We had him in one night for a seminar which had a lot of MIT students in attendance. Well, the technical questions were flying fast and furiously and Jim was getting a little bit agitated. Finally, he answered a question as to why he had done the output circuit a certain way. He replied calmly, "Because you're an asshole." It was incredible, a truly hilarious moment.'

Jim Dovey on plain sailing – or a day in the life of a hi-fi dealer:

'The phone rang one morning – it was a call from Ricardo of Absolute Sounds – Mr Big in high-end audio distribution. The question – could I arrange a home demonstration of a pair of Apogee Scintilla loudspeakers for a very important client in the City?

'The request sounding innocent enough, and being a big fan of these ground-breaking products, I happily agreed. I was given the name and telephone number of the client in question and, within the hour, an appointment was made. It was only when the day of the "dem" approached the significance of the address began to sink in: the Penthouse Suite at the Barbican Tower, right in the heart of the City of London. Past experience had taught me about the potential pitfalls of deliveries and demonstrations at "high rise" flats but nothing, absolutely nothing, had prepared me for the events to come.

'For those readers who are not familiar with Apogee Scintillas, they are full-range ribbon loudspeakers of considerable size and bulk, as tall as an average person, very wide and unspeakably heavy.

'On the day, my very large and strong colleague arrived with suitable transport. The speakers, cables and toolkits were loaded and off we set.

'The problems soon started! On arrival at the Barbican Tower, the caretaker announced that the public lifts were too small to carry the loudspeakers and that we would have to use the service lift. That was fine, we thought, until the caretaker explained that the service lift terminated at the floor below the Penthouse Suite and we would have to carry the loudspeakers up to the last floor.

'When we eventually got both loudspeakers to the floor in question, we discovered that the staircase was in fact a fire escape which led to the roof of the tower. The staircase was very long, steep and badly lit and was too narrow to allow a person and a speaker to ascend side by side at the same time. How were we going to get the boxes up there? We discussed the possibility of aborting the project there and then, but as we'd spent over an hour getting that far, we were reluctant to throw in the towel.

'My colleague had a brainwave – he had a tow-rope in his vehicle, so why couldn't we try pulling the boxes up the staircase? Off he went, back to the vehicle to collect the rope, which fortunately was long enough to lash round the boxes one at a time and allow us to raise each speaker on a push-pull basis. After another half-hour of serious exertion we eventually got both boxes to the top of the stairs and at last arrived on the roof.

'We then, prematurely, started congratulating ourselves on our ingenuity and endurance and took a short rest.

'On opening the door at the top of the fire exit stairs, we were greeted with daylight, the real world and an awe-inspiring view looking down on the dome of St Paul's Cathedral.

'After the initial excitement of seeing this wonderful panoramic view of the city, it did not take long to realise more major snags. The walkway from the door we had just visited was about two feet wide and it ran alongside the edge of the roof with a retaining railing about three feet high. This was a pretty scary walk on your own, particularly if you were afraid of heights, but carrying two large heavy boxes it was positively daunting!

'Just to add insult to injury, there was a strong wind, with occasional gale force gusts, that threatened to fly us and the large boxes off the roof into obscurity. After two nerve-wracking journeys along this walkway, we arrived at the client's beautifully landscaped roof garden and, guess what? The only access to his patio doors was across a muddy, densely planted shrub border. Having navigated the boxes around the shrubs we at last entered the suite some two-and-a-half hours after arrival at the building.

'We were ushered into an area which resembled a room at the Tate Gallery, full of paintings of men eating live babies and an assortment of erotic statues. A lengthy game of hide and seek then ensued to find a location for the speakers amongst the statuary. We eventually found a satisfactory solution and had at last reached the stage where all we had to do was to connect them up to the client's system.

'Where is your amplifier we asked? We just knew the answer would not be simple. "My wife doesn't like looking at hi-fi, so the amplifiers are hidden," the client said. Our hearts sank. The two Krell monoblock amplifiers were in fact located in a service duct, behind a false wall panel under the floor! We now had a desperate need for a midget with hi-fi experience to make the necessary connections!

'The service duct was only inches bigger than the amplifiers and it took another hour and many painful contortions to make the connections, but at last we had music!

'The client was amazed at the quality of sound and was soon totally sold on the idea of owning the Apogees. Success, we thought, until the client's wife suddenly arrived home and announced that "she would rather leave home than gaze upon these ugly loudspeakers.".

'Our client then said he was sorry he could not go ahead with the purchase without his wife's consent and thanked us for our trouble! If only he knew how much trouble!

'The realisation then hit us. We had to pack our bags, re-box the speakers, reconnect the client's system and reverse that dreadful journey across the roof, back down the staircase to ground level.

'The day had proved to be such a physically demanding experience that my colleague and I drove back out of the City to Watford without speaking a word to each other. My memories of that day, although many years ago, are still vivid and I often wonder what would have happened if the Apogees had been blown off the top of that tower and decimated half the population of the city. Oh, to be a hi-fi dealer.'

Richard Colburn on The J Geils Band and their hi-fi systems:

'It's 1973 and the J Geils Band are huge in the Boston area. I'm standing in the middle of Minuteman Radio one day and in walked Magic Dick. Being a fan, I was thrilled to be able to wait on him. I wanted to start my demo with a J Geils record figuring that he would be impressed. Dick told me not to, he was sick of those songs. I ended up selling him JBL-L100s (what else would a rock'n'roller buy?), a Marantz 1200 integrated amp and a Thorens/SME/Shure setup. Gradually, all of the members of the band sought me out and bought the identical system from me. The best guy to deal with was Peter Wolf. He was really funny and had me in stitches most of the time. When he picked up his system he brought along his girlfriend at the time who was none other than Faye Dunaway. She was sweet and really into music.

'About a week after he took delivery, Peter showed up at the store with a broken stylus. He was sheepish about it (something about a party) and I ended up giving him a new stylus at no charge. Well, a week after that, he shows up again with a broken stylus. I looked at him and said, "Gotta charge ya". He smiled and replied, "I know". I ended up selling him about 12 styli over the next year!'

Tom Barron *of PMC on a hard question:*

'I was in the Sound Organisation store one day when a man came in and approached one of their salesmen.

'"Do you stock Karman Hardon equipment?" asked the man.

'"No, sir, we don't," came the reply.

'"Why's that?" said the man.

'"Because the products we stock give it stiff competition," said the salesman with a wry smile.

'The man left as the rest of us in the store collapsed with laughter.

Howard Popeck *of Subjective Audio recalls an unexpected customer reaction:*

'One afternoon, I demonstrated a system to a distinguished, immaculately-suited American high-flyer. His employers had phoned to tell me that on his behalf they would pay for his chosen system – and there was no budget limitation. His chauffeur waited outside while I went through the preliminary briefing.

'It's hard not to be influenced by the personal appearance of the customer. You try not to be judgemental, but you can't help it. Anyway, part of my first stab at a system composed the ultra-rare, mighty and visually imposing Wharfedale Option-One active speakers. The visitor, reluctant to impose his desires, invited me to choose the music. Naively, as it turned out, I selected opera, jazz, full orchestral, piano and so on. The demo passed pleasantly enough, but the visitor, although impressed, didn't seem highly motivated.

'During a pause between tracks I heard this man mutter, seemingly to himself, and with an air of regret, "I used to be young – dammit". I said something vacuous like, "Yup, I know how you feel", and started to select the next classical track. But he caused me to pause by asking if I had any 1960s West Coast/Bay Area acid rock? What, like Jefferson Airplane, Moby Grape, Quicksilver Messenger, Skip Spence – that kind of thing?' He smiled – broadly. By chance, I was and remain a deep enthusiast of that music, and I had some to hand for my own after-hours entertainment.

'I slipped on Jefferson Airplane's *Bless Its Pointed Little Head*. I sat next to him, turned to look at him, and this captain of industry had tears in his eyes. He told me he'd been at that very gig, at the Fillmore, as a kid. He took off his jacket, shortly after giving me his Amex Card.

'We didn't exchange a word, side after side, and side by side. He was transported. Hours passed. He told me I'd influenced his life in a way he'd never thought likely, or possible.'

Richard Colburn on rectification:

'Since Minuteman was a Rectilinear dealer we had a lot of walk-in customers simply asking for them. Their Model III had gotten some good press. I was behind the counter and a young man walked up to me and asked in a heavy southern drawl if we carried "them Rectum Recliners". He asked this with a straight face, but I couldn't keep mine that way. I burst into a laughing fit that lasted about five minutes. He was nonplussed, not having realised he had said anything funny. He thought I was a nut though. I managed to stumble and laugh my way through a demo, after which he bought a pair of Rectilinear IIIs. I often wondered if his rectum was well rested.'

John Reddington on the importance of retail staff training:

'At a product training session at Laskys in the 1970s, I asked the question "What is a transient?". One bright spark shouted out, "A type of van". The same question a few months later met with the response: "A man who dresses up in women's clothing".'

Richard Colburn recalls a tough amplifier test:

'Bored in the store... while at Suffolk Audio we often went hours without seeing customers. You have to understand that British hi-fi was kind of a novel thing to be selling in 1974. We had taken on BGW amplifiers for a while. They were a professional company that made a run at the consumer business in those days. The amps sounded pretty good and were really reliable. For some reason we ordered a 1300W mono amplifier for an instrumentation company.

'We opened it up just to take a look. Unable to resist hooking it up, we decided to test out its reliability. We hooked it to a 1000ft spool of speaker wire and then to a Quad electrostatic – talk about an inductive load! We expected fireworks and smoke, but the thing worked. We could actually hear a signal through the Quad. It was muffled, but it played. Amazing.'

Howard Popeck *of Subjective Audio recalls a small piece of opera education:*

'It's with considerable embarrassment that I recall both my musical ignorance and my inverse snobbery about musical styles. Styles that I neither understood nor wanted to understand, for no good reason at all in the early days of Subjective Audio. I could tell a good sound, of course, but that was due in the early days at least, to an intimacy with the equipment and its capabilities rather than an inherent understanding of the musical processes struggling to escape undamaged from the various components.

'Anyway, one Saturday morning, I had a small, but for me, deeply significant life-changing experience, courtesy of one of my customers. Saturday after Saturday this wise old gentleman, now deceased, turned up to listen to things of interest and to satisfy his curiosity, to share tea and biscuits, discuss various philosophies, and occasionally buy something. Working from home, it was pretty much a relaxed environment, one which we never entirely replicated in our shop.

'My customer observed that whenever I put on one of his opera records, I then went out to make the tea. Another opera record, and I seized the opportunity to replenish the biscuit supply. You get the idea.

'Finally, one day he asked me why I didn't stay in to listen. I replied in some immature, crass way something to the effect of "It's just big women wearing horned helmets belting out something indecipherable in a language I don't understand". He gently suggested I take the record off, sit down, have a biscuit and then shut up for a moment.

'He asked me how I reacted to the blackbirds singing in my garden. I replied truthfully that I responded deeply, happily, joyfully and gratefully. He then, back-footing me, asked if I knew what the f**k they were singing about? It was the only time I heard him swear. Amazed by the perceptive wisdom that supported the question, I replied that I hadn't the first clue. I just loved the sound for what it was, not what it did or didn't mean.

'From that day on, I've never viewed opera in that ignorant way again. It doesn't mean I like it, but I acknowledged then as I do now the depth of musical ignorance I share with so many others and how I have to continually remain on the lookout for my own preconceptions.'

Richard Colburn remembers a B&W customer::

'One strange loudspeaker: people these days have no idea about early B&W speakers. When we sold them at Suffolk Audio, they had a transmission line speaker called the DM-2A and an electrostatic/dynamic hybrid speaker called the DM-70 (shades of MartinLogans to come).

'The 2A was a box, but the DM-70 was truly unusual. It looked like a space-aged washing machine. It was short and squat with gently curved front baffle. The lower section held a 12in bextrene woofer while an electrostatic element that matched the curve of the box perched on top. It was unusual, but it sounded fantastic. I sold a pair to a gentleman who played in the BSO. He wanted his in white!

'So, we dutifully ordered him a pair. Thing was, he lived on the third floor in a Back Bay apartment. The speaker wouldn't fit up the stairs. We ended up hiring a piano mover to get the speaker in through his front window. Can you imagine white DM-70s being hoisted up into the air in plain view? People on the street simply stopped an stared in fascination. It was surreal. The man truly had a great system though.'

Arturo Manzano of Axiss, on selling speakers to US servicemen in Europe:

'During the heyday of audio in the early 1980s, I was the working for Teledyne Acoustic Research as their European Sales Manager in Wiesbaden, Germany. It was my responsibility to take care of all of AR's military business, selling to all those GIs, about 500,000 of them dispersed thoughout Europe.

'What was amazing at this time was their insatiable desire to own audio equipment. The PXes and Audio Clubs would throw these massive Tent Sales where we would sell a 40 foot container of speakers in three days! This was not unique to AR but was also the case with all the major name audio companies that sold to the military.

'At times I wondered where all that product was going and one day I found out. After shipping a container to an audio club, which shall go unnamed, I took a short tour of this ancient Italian city with my rep and as we were walking we heard music. As we turned the corner... lo and behold, there in all their glory, stacked upon each other, box upon box was the entire shipment of speakers!'

12. KK's high end odyssey

'My body was still holding out after three incredibly intense days during which I'd had no more than five hours' sleep. Who could go to bed when some new audio thrill lurked around every corner?' **Ken Kessler**

Living in the USA. *By Ken Kessler (HFN Dec '84 & Jan '85)*

The journey is over, and I think I've got a pretty good handle on what goes on in the USA. John Atkinson said: 'Ken, go over there and find the pulse of the nation. Tell our readers how the other half lives. Win yourself a Pulitzer'.

I've had the honour and the privilege of spending 24 days touring the United States, meeting as wide a cross-section of its audio community as was physically possible. I stopped counting after I'd met 30 people, stopped trying to remember the names of the hotels, and gave up on fighting my body; I want to sleep for a week.

I want you to learn about a whole world of hi-fi that, in a lot of ways, has been denied to us in the UK for a number of reasons with origins lost in the past. But we're now part of a global village, whether we like it or not, and any isolationism on our part has no place in the remaining decade-and-a-half of this century.

If my capabilities with the written word are up to par, you should get a taste of what is happening in the only country besides the UK which has a hi-fi industry striving for improvement. The desire has been to capture the personalities of the people who make the hardware with which you're already familiar. I hope you enjoy meeting them as much as I did.

PART 1: THE WEST COAST

The batteries began to wear out just south of Barstow, flying into Los Angeles. Sony were right, and the Walkman Professional did eat batteries, but they cost less than the fee for those horrible rubber contraptions that pass for headphones in-flight. The Walkman went into my flight bag and I knew my eleven-and-a-half-hour ordeal was almost over. I was feeling just like a tourist and loving every minute of it.

Lyrics don't come true all that often; I can count on one or two hands the number of times I've experienced the sentiments of my favourite songs. (In other words, I've yet to turn off my mind, relax and float downstream, shuffle off to Buffalo, or shimmy like my Sister Kate.) But I do understand what Chuck Berry meant when he sang about 'touching down on an international run-way, jet-propelled back home…'.

Regular readers know that I'm a Yank, but they're probably wondering why I get all touristy at the thought of heading Stateside for a tour of the American hi-fi scene. What they don't know is that I've lived in the UK for over a third of my life (and it's 20 years since my Bar Mitzvah), so I'm at the same disadvantage as any of you when I head west. The place sure has changed since '72.

As I'd never seen the West Coast – I'm New England born and bred – the start of this trip, California from a suitcase, was as new to me as it would be to many of you. I didn't know what was more alien: seeing California for the first time or visiting my hi-fi Never-Never Land.

That's what the trip was all about, a *Whicker's World* visit to the Land of the True High End, a country where not one but two companies manufacture loudspeakers that cost more than a three-bedroom terraced house. It's a place full of Peter Pans and the occasional Captain Hook, and I didn't mind playing Wendy so long as I could keep my beard, and dress in other than nightgowns.

Randall Research and Infinity

This jaunt just might be the first of its kind. It's one thing for a single manufacturer to take a dozen journalists abroad for factory tours; it's something else entirely for a dozen manufacturers to take one journalist abroad. With the organisational abilities of Ricardo Franassovici to hand, aided by the immensely capable Debbie, the impossible became reality, and a dozen competitors pooled resources, altered schedules, and provided *HFN* with the opportunity to visit and write about the cream of America's audio crop.

Randy McCarter, the 'Randall' in Randall Research, collected me at the LA airport, taking me straight on to the freeway in the direction of Irvine, California. I looked for Ponch and John but didn't see them anywhere, so I must assume that their omnipresence on *CHIPS* is exaggerated. Randy didn't disappoint, though, for he looked as healthy and Californian as television would have us believe all West Coast denizens are. He was a bit let down because I didn't have a handlebar moustache, monocle and tweeds, but he didn't hold it against me.

I didn't know it at the time, but Randy set the pace for the whole of my stay in the land of oranges and Porsches. He's a music lover and hi-fi nut first and foremost, and his upbeat attitude was not uncommon.

His reasons for starting Randall Research were echoed time and again by other manufacturers, and it proved a common thread with just about every person I met. Randy made his first set of leading-edge signal cables for himself, to improve the sound of his own system. Making them commercially available was a happy accident.

Those of you who have read Martin Colloms's cable reports in *HFN* know that the Randall Research products are highly regarded and very exclusive. You've probably wondered, too, how a metre of phono-to-phono can cost as much as a decent basic integrated amplifier. I found out within minutes of reaching the Randall headquarters.

Randall Research is, like many of our specialist manufacturers, a cottage industry type of company. But cottage industry in California means a bit more than working out of a cluttered garage. Though the company has fewer than 10 employees, the works look as modern and tidy as the most mechanised of the mass-market favourites. The difference is that Randall Research isn't mechanised at all. The modernity only extends as far as cleanliness, functionality, and a bank of test equipment that would do justice to most electronics specialists, let alone a cable maker.

Where Randall departs from the in-house robot approach is in the methods of manufacture: Randall cables are hand-constructed and each and every pair must pass a listening test administered by none other than Randy McCarter himself. The raw cable comes in on big drums from a source closely monitored by Randall for consistency and quality, the terminations being fitted by a soldering wizard named Neil. All the connections are made with silver solder, and hygiene is the by-word. When I saw Neil doing the work while wearing white gloves, and heard Randy talking about the acidity in finger tips, I knew that here were cables for use in high-risk hospital wards.

The attention to detail was staggering. Randall tests for more than directionality, and the selection process ensures that no consumer need ever go through the time-consuming process of figuring out which way the leads sound best. The combination of time and materials makes Randall leads costly, but no-one can argue their value in a high-resolution system.

Randy's background, besides severe audiophilia, includes engineering design in the aerospace industry, and he knows the merit of attention to detail. His research into cable design is an ongoing proposition, and the first thing he quizzed me about was the appearance of linear crystal copper and the response to it in Europe. As I was once a Boy Scout, I had enough sense to take with me the October '84 issue of *HFN*, which contained MC's feature on the stuff, so Randy didn't have to rely on my garbled, non-technical comprehension of the topic. He spent the next day or so muttering, 'How do I get ahold of some?'.

We took a break from hi-fi to partake in a peculiar Californian pastime called 'partying'. In between glasses of whatever we were drinking, I learned that Randall Research might soon come to mean more than just cables, which explained all of the heavily-modified tube amplifiers and loudspeakers dotted around the factory, referring directly to Randy's predilection for installing outrageously advanced capacitors everywhere he can. He has a sideline in constructing his own caps, which must be about as far as you can go with DIY tweaking, and these could be sprinkled liberally throughout his upcoming products. He was deliberately vague about the future, not wanting to be questioned by the public about products that could be six months or a year away, but I will blow the whistle a bit and say that I saw a pair of Dynaco Mk IIIs that bore about as much resemblance to the originals as Colin Chapman's first Lotus did to the Austin 7 upon which it was based.

It's too easy to have a good time in Southern California (though occupational guilt plagued me much of the time) and I didn't really want to leave. Would the next stop be as entertaining? (Wrong question, Kessler – you're here to do a job... remember?)

I worry too much. The next morning Randy reunited me with Arnie Nudell of Infinity, and I rather guessed that the second stop on my tour would involve more painless education. What I didn't know was that a bumper harvest of audio produce awaited me in Bel Canyon, including a marathon session with the legendary Infinity IRS loudspeakers, a full-frontal assault on the state-of-the-art.

It must be said at the outset that Arnie Nudell inspired this entire trip. I met him last March when I went to the Paris show to see the new Infinity loudspeakers, and we hit it off immediately. In typical American fashion, he said, 'You really must visit us in LA'. Naturally, I took this as basic American hospitality and filed it in the back of my mind; Arnie was obviously unaware of the unlikelihood of my ever having enough spare cash to fly into the setting sun. Little did I know...

What Arnie had planned for me had nothing to do with factory tours or indoctrination into any given way of thinking. He's got this not-so-secret weapon that does all the talking for him, and he figured that it was high time a British journalist got a taste of what Americans call the 'true high end'.

Before describing Arnie's show of strength, it's best to describe the rest of his system. Bearing in mind that he regards the vinyl LP with the same contempt most of us hold for pre-recorded cassettes, it's no surprise to learn that the head honcho of Infinity only listens to first-generation copies of master tapes in 15ips open-reel form. How he got hold of the many thousands of tapes is another saga, but rest assured that this magical software collection does exist, and it takes up two walls in his hi-fi room. He plays these back on an Otari machine, fed into an Audio Research D250; he keeps an SP10 for those rare moments when he needs to listen to other sources.

It's hard to imagine a higher resolution basis for a no-holds-barred system; this naturally presupposes the existence of loudspeakers up to the task of translating such a pure signal into sound waves. This is where the real fun begins, for the termination to this chain is the design that has but one challenger to the throne. The speaker is the legendary Infinity IRS, and it is simply the most physically imposing item of hi-fi equipment that I've ever seen.

The IRS consists of four structures which tower to a shade over seven feet. Two columns each contain six 12in bass units (driven by 1500 watt amplifiers), while the others are massive panels housing EMIT and EMIM drivers to cover the high and mid frequencies. These are as close to a genuine line source as you can probably get and the desired effect should be a sound as perfect as today's technology can provide. They scared the hell out of me! The weirdness set in without any warning.

Less than 48 hours earlier I'd been standing on the platform at Canterbury East, rain coming down just to remind me of what I'd be leaving behind. And here I was sitting in Arnie Nudell's hill-top eyrie facing the most overwhelming loudspeakers ever seen in a domestic environment. And we weren't alone. Joining us for the marathon listening session were Bascom King of *Audio* and Paul McGowan of PS Audio. This hands-across the-water business was starting to get serious.

All-nighters, as the Americans are wont to call the absence of sleep, are best left to the young and fit. I knew that my first visit to California was going to be a minute-by-minute experience, but I didn't anticipate this throw-him-in-at-the-deep-end approach while still jet-lagged. John Miller, one of Infinity's designers, must have known what to expect, because he left after dinner...

It went something like this: Arnie rubs his hands with glee, knowing that he's about to turn his victim's perceptions inside-out. It must be like the sharp city cousin taking the country bumpkin out for his first night on the town. Believe me: prior to the IRS, I was an audio virgin.

I don't know if it was the master-tape copy of *Dafos* that did it or if I lost my grip entirely when I heard – or, rather, felt – a 16Hz signal doing a breakdance on my chest. The rest of them just smiled, having lived with the IRS long enough to know that it does things that most audiophiles can't even imagine hearing from a sound system. In ten hours with the IRS, interrupted only by a dinner involving positively carnal Veal Prince Orloff and wines wearing blankets of dust, I learned more about soundstage and bass extension and imaging and openness than I'd ever thought possible. Infinity wanted a tool for analysis; they've got one.

To show just how revealing the system can be, we spent some time listening to a prototype pre-amp that Paul had brought along to the session in breadboard form. It's destined to become PS Audio's first foray into high-priced, high-end hardware, and there could not be a better test for it than to see how it fared 'against' the SP10. After hearing only a couple of tracks, all of us had managed to identify with great consistency and unanimity a number of areas needing more work. The system Arnie has assembled has that kind of authority.

What all this has to do with Infinity *vis-à-vis* the real world is simple. They try to take what they learn from the IRS and incorporate it into the rest of the range. Things like 1500 watt servo amplifiers aren't likely to turn up in their $100 speakers, but polypropylene drive units do, so the claim isn't so outrageous (or Madison Avenue) as it might seem. But that wasn't what I'd hoped to learn during my stay.

As with Randy McCarter, I learned that Arnie – and Bascom and Paul and John – is a 'supertweak', a die-hard music lover who will drop ants down his jockey shorts if he thinks it will give him better sound. Who else but a total music-hi-fi looney would stay up until 6am discussing upper midrange colorations and phase anomalies? This was repeated throughout my visit, and I learned right off that our American cousins are as finicky, dedicated and terminally psychotic as any of us. They just do it differently.

James Boyk and Doug Sax

Three days into the trip and it was time to call on occasional *HFN* contributor James Boyk. A man of many talents, James is a tube fanatic, an LS3/5A user, a professional musician, a lecturer in sound-related topics at Caltech, a gourmet, and the man behind Performance Recordings (all analogue and all tube). He's got strong ideas about recorded sound and he's as hung up on microphone technology and usage as de Sade was on discipline. James's house is a hi-fi Aladdin's Cave, and I found tube goodies in every corner. There's an air of the mad scientist about him, and when he unfolds his six-and-a-half foot frame from within the confines of an MGB-GT, you get the impression that he likes to defy convention. Oh, does he defy convention...

How many people do you know who give live-versus-recorded demonstrations in their homes? None of this 'Here's what she'll do' nonsense, or 'This is what I do to annoy my neighbours' – uh-uh. James bangs out some fantastic stuff on the piano, and then proceeds to suspend your disbelief by playing back a tape of that piano in the exact spot you're seeing. OK, so maybe the presence of the actual instrument in the precise location in which it was recorded provides an unfair visual clue, but so what? He made me feel so-o-o good when his demonstration proved my ravings about the LS3/5As to be savagely understated.

James Boyk worships Alan Blumlein with the same passion Italians show for Enzo Ferrari. His work with microphones is an act of homage to the great man, and his recordings are continuing proof that Blumlein was a genius. It wasn't enough for James to let me hear his recordings; he wanted me to visit another master, and this turned out to be one of the many unexpected pleasures that filled my time. With no announcement, James took me to the Mastering Lab to meet Doug Sax.

James and Doug are old friends with like attitudes about recording; they use each other's skills and talents in their never-ending quests for analogue refinement. When CD entered the conversation with James, I'd get wonderful lines like 'CD finishes the jobs transistors started', and leave it at that. Tubes and analogue and 12in slabs of black vinyl are what these guys care about, and eccentricity has nothing to do with it.

We didn't stay long at the Mastering Lab, but I did get to hear their monitoring system, a melange of different drivers filling a whole wall. The sound, like that in 'normal' studios, is painfully revealing, but the valve electronics counter most of the screech you get in typical installations. Most of the pieces in use have been heavily reworked, and you sense this undefinable air of concern and respect for the music that lets you know that somebody really cares. I guess those gold records on the wall are proof that the tender loving care pays off...

Back at James's house, I had another surprise in store: Roger Modjeski, of RAM Tubes and Music Reference, turned up bearing a set of computer-matched EL34s for me to try back in the UK. Roger was another tube legend I was dying to meet and the three of us traded thoughts for most of the afternoon.

The whole valve-versus-transistor issue doesn't exist on the West Coast.

By my reckoning, tube electronics accounted for 95% of the sounds I heard, and no apologies or windy explanations were needed to deal with this overwhelming preference. It illustrates how a man like Roger can set up an operation that sells computer-graded sets of tubes without him being written off as a sufferer of severe psychoses. One of the most interesting tidbits I gleaned from Roger (besides his promise of a Music Reference Preamp for review) was that Absolute Sounds will be supplying RAM tubes by special order to UK customers.

My body was still holding out after three incredibly intense days during which I'd had no more than five hours' sleep. Who could go to bed when some new audio thrill lurked around every corner? I'd seen an Infinity Black Widow with a titanium arm tube; a one-off pair of Infinity RS1s (with twelve bass units per side) in Cary Christie's home – just what you'd expect to find in a system belonging to one of the company's executives; I'd ridden in an obscenely rapid Porsche Turbo Cabriolet at speeds wa-ay above the 55mph limit which chokes the USA; seen a Marantz 10B tuner in like-new condition; picked up some Decca cartridges that were lying about unwanted; ate flannel cakes (they look and feel like their name) in Hollywood's oldest restaurant; saw more Dynaco equipment than I could possibly covet in a lifetime; and had country-style bagels and lox of all things in a 'rustic delicatessen'. As Jay and the Americans once sang, 'Only in America...'

Jan Mancuso is a public-relations-*cum*-researcher who spent many years with the folk at Monster Cable. She took me under her wing in San Francisco, assuming, quite rightly, that this poor boy would be in rough enough shape after the excesses of Southern California and in need of a little help. Her husband Rick had the barbecue going and I supped on beef from a slab of meat that would have fed most of Kent. The local wines are better than the French would have you believe, and there was enough garlic on the bread to render me unapproachable for 48 hours. Little did I know that this sustenance would be needed to prepare me for the shock of staying in an hotel unjustifiably bearing a name similar to the title of an Eagles' LP.

In Amsterdam it's called 'the red light district' and in London it's probably what you'd find in Soho. San Franciscans call it 'The Tenderloin', but the meat for sale isn't the kind you serve with salad and a roll. Jan put it very simply: 'Ken, if you must go out at night, just make sure that you don't turn right out of the hotel. Stay to the left and you'll stay alive.' Terrific. (If any of you want to know how many tiles there were on the floor of the bathroom just send an SAE to me at the usual address.)

At home with Dave Wilson

I did live through it, welcoming the morning sun with glee that I haven't known since childhood. The next morning meant a visit to the Wilsons, home of the $40,000-plus WAMM loudspeaker, and the sole opposition to the giants I'd heard in Los Angeles. Jan collected me and gave me my first ride over the Golden Gate Bridge, which is actually red, on up to (or was it down into?) Novato. She showed me Marin County, where the most oft-expressed line is 'It's only a cold sore', and on through *Grapes of Wrath* territory which seemed a million miles away from the quasi-Monte Carlo look of California's southern half.

The Wilsons are a gracious couple who seem far too normal to want to house a multi-array loudspeaker system straight out of Flash Gordon in the middle of their living room. You go in expecting, say, a pair of small ARs and you walk straight into these massive constructs wearing electrostatic panels, KEF mid-bass drivers, teensy Braun boxes, and – just a bit behind them – towers housing woofers the size of Pirelli P7s.

Dave Wilson tells me that he's actually sold seven or eight pairs of WAMMs, and he seemed just as surprised as I did, because (like the IRS) they weren't designed with commercial sales in mind. The Wilsons' main concern is the record label which bears their name, and they felt the need for a high-resolution system which would reveal all. The rest of the system consists of a modified Revox open-reel machine, Goldmund arm and turntable, a variety of cartridges, and more Krell-power than John Atkinson and Jimmy Hughes can muster between them. The effect is as devastating as that of the Nudell leviathan, but the sound is rather different.

As with the IRS set-up, the music machine in the Wilson home lets everything through. Time was short, and Dave wanted me to 'understand' the WAMMs as quickly as possible, so he had some tapes and discs ready for the demonstration. The most telling performances of all were the first he played, two recordings of his wife, singer Sheryl Lee, made with different microphones. Like James Boyk, Dave is a stickler when it comes to microphones, and this little experiment – in addition to bringing home the point that music reproduction starts in front of the performer – demonstrated exactly what a top-flight system can provide in the way of extreme subtleties.

What was just as fascinating were the marked differences between Dave's speakers and the IRS system. Both did things with soundstage (like telling you where the walls were in the place where the recording was made) that you can barely approach with lesser systems. Both offered dynamic range and sheer power worthy of the amplifiers doing the driving. Both systems – though taller than a telephone kiosk – reproduced full-scale images rather than floor-to-ceiling exaggerations. Both managed to 'disappear' in spite of their horizon-filling dimensions. But while the IRS offered you the truth, the WAMM grabbed you by the throat and made you listen to it. It would appear that these two approaches might be conflicting, but I would imagine that they would appeal to different kinds of listener rather than different kinds of music. The IRS lets you talk or go to the kitchen for a snack; the WAMM says, 'Don't move, sucker, I'm playing'. I want both of 'em.

The temperature in Novato was 95° or so, much cooler than the 100–105° I experienced in Los Angeles. Thank goodness for the muggy summer we've had; it prepared me for the sauna-like atmosphere of California and I only came close to dying but once or twice. (Los Angeles is air-conditioned; San Francisco isn't. Dave made sure we came early so the Krells wouldn't bake us.) The Wilson home was quite a refuge from the *Blade Runner* depravity of LA, and about six stages cleaner than the hell-hole of a hotel where I left my luggage, so I didn't really want to head back over the Bridge. Fortunately there was another respite in store in the form of Noel Lee and the Monsters.

Noel Lee and Monster Cables

Noel is one of the few US hi-fi celebrities I had met prior to my visit, having attended a UK Monster Cable press luncheon earlier in the year. Noel, on that occasion, appeared to be an archetypal US marketing wizard rather than a 'hi-fi person', and I was wondering how I would be able to deal with a specific example of an American genotype, having grown a bit rusty in my behaviour with my fellow countrymen. (Note: do you know how hard it is saying 'I'm from England' when you've got an accent like Dick van Dyke?) Noel sure had us fooled.

The Monster launch had some of the press rotters muttering about the super-slickness of the whole presentation, and I think Monster's head man had been written off as pure PR. Well, Noel has the last laugh: he's so tweaky that even our own Russ Andrews would find him a challenge. Noel's main claim to fame is turning the mass-market (as opposed to those already converted) on to quality cables. It's safe to say that the Monster brand is the world-wide leader, and it has the rare distinction of being commercial, successful and acceptable to the world's audiophiles. Should I have been surprised to learn that Noel is as whacked-out about fine-tuning and fiddling about as Christopher Breunig, *HFN*'s resident detail fanatic? Thankfully, Noel's interest in hi-fi doesn't get in the way of his biological needs, and I learned that he lived up to his reputation as audio's *Guide Michelin*. This, too, was merging into a pattern, for Arnie Nudell places audio somewhere below premium wines; I'd love to see the two of them together running up gourmet-type tabs in a Michelin three-star restaurant.

Noel showed me around the Monster operation, a quart-sized business in a pint-sized office, and there I discovered point-of-sale and promotional material that rivals even the efforts of Ortofon UK's John Reddington. The Monster Mentality is so comprehensive that parts of the warehouse made it seem like Noel has strong interests in the rag trade; if he ever publishes a catalogue of Monster clothing, it will probably bump cable sales down to second place.

Most of the products were familiar, but new to me were the many cables Monster have created for the professional market. Initial response from West Coast recording studios has been wholly favourable, and Noel was pleased to learn that studio types aren't quite the anti-sound-quality dim-bulbs we've been led to believe they might be.

Other fronts under attack by the Monster include in-car – much more important in the USA than over here – and moving-coil cartridges, the latter leading to a scoop that could irritate some US magazines. (I've been told that the UK press is known for getting the news and reviews out quickly, instead of sitting on them for months as do the US journals.) Monster has been enjoying much success with its first moving-coil design, the Alpha 1. Along with the various Talisman cartridges, I saw more of these $400-ish m-cs in use than any others, and the whole audio community was looking forward to the final version of the Alpha 2, a $650 device joining the Alpha 1. The new model was seen and heard in one of the over 40 prototype forms at the CES Show, and it took until the end of September before shipments of the production model reached the shops. The Alpha 2 sports a gemstone cantilever and a Namiki MicroRidge stylus, and hearing it in Noel's SOTA/Dynavector/Spectral/Threshold/Acoustat/Entec (how's that for a run of exotic names?) system indicated that here was something special.

Sadly, no samples were available at the time, but the gods smiled: a few days later, just before my departure from San Francisco, the first case of Alpha 2s arrived, and Noel gave me the first one to leave his possession. It goes into the Zeta as soon as I can dig it out of my valise.

I figured that this was a hot enough item to make the whole trip worthwhile, but Noel had more in store. One of Monster's other new lines is a range of sound-absorbing panels marketed under the name Sound-Ex. These panels are domestically acceptable screens which one dots around one's soundroom, either free-standing or hanging from the walls, to fine-tune a room with a live or resonant character. Noel was fooling around with the panels when it dawned on him that their absorptive properties could be used to cancel out crosstalk between speakers, without the negative effect accompanying active electronics used for this task. He stood one in between the speakers, the narrow edge facing the listener, and he was overjoyed to hear everything snap into place. The only reason he's letting me spill the beans on this new item (to be called 'Hocus-Focus Acoustic Imagers') is because he got the patent approval just before my departure.

The guy's a tweak, no doubt about it. He also knows where you can get the best Italian and Chinese food in the Bay area, loves jazz, and has one of the best-looking secretaries in the industry. Pure class.

Noel collected me from the 'hotel' the next morning, and he didn't even ask me to sit in the back of his estate though he knew where I'd slept the night before. (It really was that unsavoury.) We spent the morning discussing the professional products and the implications of Hocus-Focus, when the time arrived to drop me off in Oakland for a visit with Rodney Herman and Robert Becker of SOTA. The most upsetting thing about this part of my trip was the overwhelming joy I felt upon hearing Rodney's English accent. Had I lived in Canterbury that long?

The SOTA turntable

Up to this point, I'd met speaker and cable manufacturers, record producers, and a couple of people involved with electronics; SOTA was my first exposure to Americans with heavy involvement in turntables. Yup, the conversation couldn't help but turn to a certain Scottish design, its impact on the world of audio, and its hold on the UK scene. I suppose the biggest kicker of all was that Robert could be mistaken for Ivor Tiefenbrun at a distance; his turntable, however, could not be mistaken for a Linn.

Messrs Herman and Becker made it clear that the SOTA is a response to American consumers and retailers who begged for a turntable that not only offered world-class performance, but could be set up easily and hold its state of tune for a long, long time.

Had I met the SOTA people a few days earlier, my UK-formed instincts would have rebelled against this notion, but I'd learned enough in my short stay to know that American consumers and retailers do not particularly share the British love for the hair-shirt approach to hi-fi. The SOTA's reception in the UK has been a bit chilly, and I think a lot of it has to do with the absolutist approach we adopt here, often forgetting that many people are not prepared to invest in expensive components that offer neither the styling nor the ease of use that are taken for granted in much cheaper, less serious designs. For starters, Americans are houseproud, and the SOTA is styled for American tastes. Additionally, though I found tweakers everywhere I went, I learned that they do not account for all of the high-end sales activity as they do in Great Britain; non-audiophiles – or people who want super sound but don't want to get locked into the hobby aspects – buy equipment that our equivalents wouldn't even consider. In essence, comfortable, non-hi-fi-oriented Americans have higher audio standards than the well-to-do English.

The chaps at SOTA have aimed their products at a much broader base than any of the other manufacturers of high-end turntables, carefully balancing form with function, audiophile acceptability with commercial viability. If there has been some resistance to the SOTA in the UK (partly due to cost, I would imagine), no such resistance exists in the USA, and I saw and heard more SOTAs (and Oracles and Goldmunds) than any other turntables, regardless of origins.

Rodney and Robert are a perfect team, Rodney being the engineer/audio person and Robert the hard-nut businessman. They employed Dave Fletcher of Sumiko as a consultant when designing the SOTA, and the input from all three has resulted in a turntable that's now apparently back-ordered throughout the USA. At present they're doing a lot of work with their vacuum design, the Star Sapphire, and have paid special attention to the negative effects of sucking on the old LP. (Did you know that too much suction affects the composition and stability of the vinyl? Neither did I.) At the time of my visit, they were wrapped up in playing with new mats, as visitors to their room at the Penta Show can attest.

Because I'd spent all of my time so far meeting members of the manufacturing fraternity, Robert and Rodney figured it would be a good idea if I saw how the retailers in the USA practised their trade. They chose db Audio in Berkeley (pronounced 'Burr', not 'Barr'), which is one of those shops that carries items from budget level on up to silly money. They were super-tweaky in a lot of ways, but were just this side of 'audio salon'; that would have to wait for a couple of days. (UK dealers take note: American retailers have to suffer the same sort of indignities that you face. They get timewasters who come in on Saturdays when the shop is really busy and hang around until closing time or whenever their wives finish shopping, which ever comes first. They get pennypinchers, which you might have thought did not exist in such a prosperous land. db Audio's James Alexander and I swapped stories but I've got to admit that his topped mine. Imagine the shop giving away a four-figure system in a competition and having the winner saying 'Can I change it? It's not what I really wanted!'. I spent an enjoyable evening with the SOTA folk and members of the db crew at a restaurant where I had to go outside to suck smoke. We ended up at one of the db salesperson's homes to play around with some new toys, like the Lead Balloon turntable stand and the Streets power amplifier. It was here that I listened to the Eminent Technology linear tracking tonearm, an airbearing design that turned up more often than any other arm, usually fitted with a Talisman cartridge. The room was about 12 x 12ft, but that didn't stop its owner from stuffing it with a pair of Acoustat electrostatics.

I got to bed around 5am, because James figured that I had to see The Tenderloin, if only through the window of an all-night café – better to do it with a San Franciscan, I figured.

Joe Abrams and Dave Fletcher

Mere hours later, I was in the company of Joe Abrams and Dave Fletcher of Sumiko, the Talisman, Tweek, and The Arm people. They, too, have a penchant for fine food, and by this time I was up a kilo or two on my pre-flight weight. Over lunch, I figured it was time I gave the Walkman Pro a workout that included more than mere playback, so I recorded the conversation; I'd been warned that Dave Fletcher knows all the sordid, scurrilous bits that make the hi-fi industry so enjoyable, and he didn't disappoint. Unfortunately, playback of the tape a day or so later revealed that it contained little I could relate through these pages, but I did glean such gems as:

1) Dave Fletcher is the man who told Ivor T about single speaker demonstrations. This, of course, comes from DF, not IT; I mention it because Dave said it with such a straight face.

2) Dave Fletcher reintroduced m-c cartridges to the West by being the first to sell Supex outside Japan.

3) Dave Fletcher does the best impersonations of audio celebrities in the world; his only serious rival is Ian Anderson of Billy Vee.

If this sounds like self-promotion on his part, what the heck. The guy has more stories than Aesop, and he had me in hysterics. When the conversation turned to hi-fi, though, I found out that Dave – who worked on the SOTA, designed The Arm and the various Talisman cartridges, and a few other mighty items – is as serious as the next man. He's got this clown prince air about him, and I think Joe helps keep him from, say, savaging recalcitrant journalists, but he's also got a pair of the finest ears in the industry, more about which anon.

Joe and Dave gave me sneak peeks at the new straight-tube, fixed-headshell Premier MMT tonearm (a reply to serious criticism from the UK, perhaps) and the upper-market Talisman cartridges coming in above the Alchemist, both in prototype form. One real knock-out was the new VTA adjuster which will be fitted as an optional extra on the Premier; it's foolproof, accurate, and so utterly simple that it defies belief. He also told me about future plans for Tweek, and showed me where he personally tests each and every Talisman he sells. (Those individual frequency response charts are not drawn with a ruler.)

Joe and Dave had the same idea as their friends at SOTA, and the next day they took me to an American lunatic-fringe dealer, the kind of shop that keeps Audio Research D250s, SP10s, and Oracle Premieres in stock. The shop was Music By Design in a rather chic area called Sausalito, and it looked more like a ski chalet than a hi-fi shop. Peter Litwack is the kind of dealer that the UK press has been campaigning for all these years, so someone must be reading us. (Yes, there were copies of *HFN* in both of the shops I visited.)

I made two promises to myself before going on this trip. One was to eat local food whenever possible; the other was to hear as much hi-fi as I could that I'd never find in the UK. db Audio let me hear the Spica loudspeakers, a $400 American challenge to our SL6/ProAc Tablette calibre minispeakers; Peter set up the big and expensive Vandersteens, a current hot fave among US audiophiles. The rest of the system contained familiar pieces, like the Oracle Delphi, Audio Research electronics, and – again the Eminent Technology arm with Talisman cartridge. It was here that Dave Fletcher demonstrated those golden ears of his.

We were listening quite merrily, when Dave shook his head and said, 'The absolute polarity is wrong.' Joe and Peter said that he did this all the time, and invariably would point it out every time a different LP was put on the turntable. Both leads were reversed, and lo and behold, the image tightened up and the overall perspective improved. The implications were horrendous, and Dave proceeded to prove that half of everything we hear is wrong.

This topic emerged again when I visited Counterpoint a few days later, and I dug up J Peter Moncrieff's work on the subject. The topic has been discussed in the UK as well – I remember John Atkinson and Ivor Humphreys trotting around hi-fi shows demonstrating the effect after their features on the subject appeared in *HFN* some four years ago – but nothing impressed me as much as Dave's little demonstrations. The only time I ever bothered with it at home was when I got a Sheffield LP that suggested it in the liner notes; what keeps me from doing it all the time is the aggravation of swapping leads, going back to the chair, comparing, swapping again, etc. But I'm going to label a few LPs for absolute polarity so I'll know what I'm hearing each time I review equipment.

The Vandersteens were impressive, with the kind of deep, deep bass so beloved by Americans, but the overall balance was surprisingly polite and 'British'. The speakers were not much smaller than a large fridge, so they could cause domestic problems in rooms smaller than a typical Odeon.

One other goodie at Music By Design was one of the two black and gold Oracles in existence, awarded to Peter's shop for exemplary performance as an Oracle outlet. Peter wouldn't tell me the price.

The best thing that happened to me at Peter's shop was finding my favourite LP of all time amidst the demonstration discs, *Get It While You Can* by Howard Tate. I did some serious listening to the system via three of my favourite tracks, and it added a nice note of familiarity to my trip.

A note of sadness also entered here, for Peter broke the news to us that Peter Snell had died a few days before. Peter Snell had a reputation as one of the truly 'nice guys' in hi-fi, and the loudspeakers that bear his name had a strong following; indeed, they had started to appear at shows in the UK and were strongly supported by companies like our own Musical Fidelity.

I said goodbye to Dave and Joe and rejoined Noel Lee for a change of pace: real music. San Francisco is one of those places like London, where there's too much music happening for anyone to hope to attend all the concerts one would like to hear. The artist we heard was San Francisco native Rodney Franklin, a jazz musician who does wonderful things with the piano. Noel knew the man in charge of the sound and promised that the concert would delight the fussiest of hi-fi types. He was right, and we were treated to a couple of hours of sheer pleasure. Franklin cooked up a magic mix consisting of the theme from *Hill Street Blues* and some genuine blues, the two sounds segued into such a natural match that it was easy to forgive the titular pun.

It's worth mentioning that over 75% of all the music I heard on the radio during my stay came from British musicians. The UK is hot stuff in the USA, and I saw more of Boy George, Wham and Depeche Mode than I thought possible. What brought it all home was a walk with Noel through the North Beach area, a sleazoid West Coast equivalent of New

York's Bowery, where even the do-gooders think twice before entering unarmed. Everywhere you looked were English-style, circa 1976 punks, with only the accents wrecking the image. There's something warped about skinheads who don't drop their 'h's or suffer glottal stops, but at least they weren't violent...

I actually had an almost-free weekend in San Francisco, until I realised that I was supposed to be writing this epic as it happened, so Saturday was spent in my hotel room pecking away on this fantastic little Canon electronic portable, which I seduced away from the company by offering to field-test it. I think I've sold about a dozen of them now, and it took great effort to wrest it away from Audio's Bascom King. But Jan Mancuso and Gary from Threshold rescued me from my labours, and I spent the evening eating too well, yet again. I also learned that the Threshold/Nakamichi collaboration has been given the go-ahead, and we should soon be seeing Nelson Pass-designed electronics bearing the Nakamichi logo.

My last morning in San Francisco was spent with Joe Abrams of Sumiko – eating again. It seems that the Sunday Brunch – a cross between a big breakfast and a gigantic lunch – is an American tradition, and Joe and his charming wife (and wee daughter) took me to the best brunch in the city. They rolled me – tummy full of bagels and chopped liver and fresher-than-fresh coffee – to Noel Lee's to collect the Alpha 2, some leads for Martin Colloms, and some final words on HocusFocus.

Noel showed me yet another new toy, a wild creation called a light sculpture, introduced me to Peter Lee (another die-hard audio fanatic), and drove me to the airport, promising to meet up with me in London on his next visit. It dawned on me that I'd met over a dozen of the nicest people I'd ever spent time with, in a span of under ten days. All I could think of were those daft anti-American cracks I used to hear about how Americans say 'Have a nice day' with parrot-like precision. It occurred to me that I prefer a 'Have a nice day' to the surly grunts I get from British Rail employees, shop assistants, and other malcontents. Maybe it has something to do with the water.

But don't start clapping – you're not rid of me yet. In spite of the readily-apparent prosperity and the optimism, I kept on thinking about funky old England, where naked ladies grace the newspapers, FM radio doesn't suffer from compression, and our actors stay on screen or stage. Incipient schizophrenia reared its head, but I patted my return ticket and reminded myself of how lucky I am to live in the UK and still have reasonable access to this other kind of life.

My next stop was San Diego, and I was learning that Disneyland extends from Canada to Mexico, and from the Pacific to the Rockies. San Diego (depending on the commentator) has a reputation for a wonderful climate and breathtaking women, and it's close enough to the Mexican border to guarantee that the cuisine of that variety will be authentic. Rich Riccio of Counterpoint saw to it that I got my dose of mandatory heartburn when he tricked me into eating a particularly potent Jalapeno pepper.

Counterpoint

Counterpoint had to put up with me for a couple of days, because my planned meeting with International Audio Review's J Peter Moncrieff did not materialise. I was looking forward to visiting Counterpoint, because I've got a soft spot for their SA7 preamp, and I knew that they had six or seven other tube products which I'd never seen or heard.

The Counterpoint offices and factory are up-to-date, computerised, slick and thoroughly professional, which didn't quite blend in with the image I've always fostered about valve amp manufacturers. I was expecting a couple of rabid tubeophiles soldering away in a basement. Instead I walked into a light, airy office with not one but two delightful secretaries, a bunch of computer terminals, a wonderful listening room (Linn LP12, Magnepan-equipped) and wall-to-wall carpeting. So much for whacko eccentrics being the only valve lovers. (Sorry, Beard, Grant, and TVA – I was only kidding!)

Mind you, there's this rather odd fellow named Bobby out back testing circuits who reminded me a whole lot of Jim in *Taxi*. I suppose he's needed to keep things in perspective. Sonovagun when it comes to electronics, but sports a haircut that would make most skinheads think twice.

The big noise around Counterpoint was the SA8, a hybrid valve/MOSFET design with enough power to satisfy the most highly motivated South American dictator. It's too pretty to resemble a tube amplifier, but then the output stages are solid-state, which accounts for its compact dimensions. I listened to it twice, once at the factory through the Maggies and again at Rich's home via Acoustats. I think Rich agreed with me when I described it as the perfect choice for solid-state users who want to go valve, but who haven't yet reached a state of total belief in tube principles.

Other toys new to me included the SA3 and SA5 pre-amps (the SA3 is now available here), the SAπ phase inverter and the mouthwatering output-transformerless, direct-coupled SA4 monoblock power amplifiers. I didn't have enough time to audition all of the pieces, though I managed to hear the SA7's bigger brothers, but it was the SAπ that captivated me. I probably wouldn't have noticed it if it hadn't been for the experience days earlier with Dave Fletcher and the absolute phase experiment. The SAπ (which I will soon be reviewing if Rich Riccio remembers to post it) might seem like an expensive way to acquire the convenience of not having to get up from your chair each time you need to reverse the speaker leads, but it seems almost mandatory when you realise that you could – theoretically – have to do this for every LP you play; the only way around it would be to label every disc in your collection for absolute polarity. The SAπ, which is available on special order from Counterpoint outlets, could cost around £300 or £350 over here due to the dollar's strength, but I don't think anyone who's reached the final stages of tuning his or her system could do without it any more than they would settle for bell wire instead of killer cables. An added bonus for those who think its role is too minor to justify the cost is its suitability as a bridging adaptor for most amps, and its suitability as a line level, unity gain buffer stage.

The mere fact that Counterpoint is willing to manufacture such a limited-appeal item speaks volumes for their attitude toward sound reproduction. Though the company is sharp and professional, it is still run by audio fanatics who strive for advancing the state of the art. They spend many hours listening to tubes (throwing away about 30% as unsuitable); they do the same with capacitors, and they spend so much time on QC that it probably occupies 25% of the man-hours spent in production. Perhaps it has something to do with the screams heard from the UK about the build quality and inconsistency of the early SA7s – either way, they've done some in-depth work on the unit and the SA7 in its latest form might be one of the decade's great bargains.

There was plenty of time to get silly in San Diego, and Rich took me to all those places that were previously nothing more to me than names in Beach Boys' recordings. I stayed in a squeaky-clean motel that was as far removed from that toilet in San Francisco as one could possibly imagine. We dined on time-delay, two-alarm Mexican food – goes down a treat, but rips your guts open the next day. 'All over la Jolla', as the Wilson Brothers sang.

Rich wanted me to enjoy and exploit every minute of my stay, even managing to squeeze in a hi-fi experience on the way to the airport. He detoured by way of Leucadia, where I got to meet the good folk known as The Mod Squad, manufacturers of the megabucks TriPlanar tonearm, Tiptoes turntable and speaker supports, and a bunch of modification programmes that show no fear of the subjects' designers. LS3/5As, Ittoks, Quad 405-2s – this crew will modify anything. I'm really glad Rich treated me to that all-too-brief half-hour, because I got to see products I'd be unlikely ever to find in the UK, and I learned that there can be no tweakier a soul than Steve McCormack.

Steve, along with Joyce Fleming, house the Mod Squad in the same building as their retail shop, Music By The Sea. It's full of oddities, and Steve told me that I was one of the first people ever to see the new Superphon pre-amp, the initial product from Stan (formerly the 'S' in PS Audio) Warren's new company. I couldn't tell Ozark to delay the flight to St Louis, so I didn't get to hear what looks like a very serious minimalist design, but so what – Steve had Stax ELS-F81 electrostatics on display and that more than made up for any lost opportunities.

Each time I left a city, I found it difficult; I was enamoured with every soul I met. But the flight out of San Diego had an extra trace of sadness because it meant leaving not just some more new friends but California as well. I'd grown to love the Left Coast, even though I don't consider terminal sunshine to be a necessary part of my life, and I could only hope that I'd get to return one day to see everybody once more and call on the dozens of companies and people I had to miss this time around.

Audio Research and Magnepan

It was time to head east toward the middle of the country, Minneapolis, the home of Audio Research and Magnepan. That nightmare of a travel agent was having more fun with me, booking me on six-hour flights when there were direct flights available that would have taken a lot less time. And when I heard that I was going to fly Ozark Airlines, I had visions of in-flight drinks consisting of moonshine, and in-flight meals consisting of black-eyed peas and grits.

I don't know why, but Ozark served the best food I've eaten in a dozen years of flying, and the hostesses looked nothing at all like Ellie Mae Clampett. (Darn...)

Mel Brooks's movies have always had an effect on me, and I could have sworn there was a fanfare in the background as I went to meet one of my biggest heroes, William Zane Johnson of Audio Research. I felt a bit embarrassed, because the stopover in St Louis was a lot longer than intended, and he had to hang around the Minneapolis airport waiting for me. But it didn't seem to bother him or his wife Nancy, and we dived straight into some wonderful conversation about Things Hi-Fi. (This journalism kick does have its rewards, in spite of the wear and tear on my digestive system. Not two weeks earlier I'd met two other audio giants, Arthur Radford and David Hafler.)

Bill Johnson is a larger-than-life character, just the type of person you'd expect to manufacture an amplifier the size and stature of the D250. There's a solid, Midwest, Henry Fonda air to the man, a wonderful contrast to the dreamier nature of the West Coast audio community.

With over 30 years in the business, an abiding love for music, and a genuine respect for traditional values, Bill immediately gives the impression that he's a man worth meeting. His memories of the industry would give any hi-fi historian a couple of books' worth of material, and his ideas about what the industry should be doing remind you that he's one of the chairpersons on the board of the US equivalent of the Federation of British Audio. He *is* hi-fi, much in the way that Peter Walker is in the UK, and I could have done with a few more days just to pick his brain on general topics, let alone specifics.

Bill has this wonderful way of making a point, sort of like the school teacher you wish you'd had instead of the pedantic old buzzard who made you read Trollope without telling you why. And you want to hug the fellow when he tells you something like: Last year, worldwide sales of bi-polar transistors were around $75,000,000. For the same period, tube sales were $1,500,000,000. So. much for valve obsolescence, huh?

Bill Johnson is probably the best spokesman in the world for presenting the valve argument, and for one very good reason: even if you thought he was talking through his hat, you'd soon dismiss it because he's too sane to be written off as a mere audio nutcase. I don't want to suggest for a moment that Bill is deadly serious and austere to a fault. He cracks into a big grin with disarming regularity – and you almost forget that this man designs some of the most complex valve-based audio in the history of the art...

There were few shocks in store, because the Audio Research range of products is a stable one and its calm, conservative approach precludes the introduction of new models with Japanese regularity. I knew the complete line-up; all of the products having been on sale in the UK for some time. There was one prototype to be seen, a valve head-amp being developed by long-time ARC employee Jack Hjelm, but the real buzzes were found in a small room with the word 'Archives' on the door.

Nobody would deny that Audio Research has a track record second to none. The company's products consistently earn top ratings, and the name has never been absent from the upper reaches of hi-fidom. But the prototypes that never saw the light of day reveal a spooky insight into the mind of William Z, and it's, anybody's guess what might have happened if his 300- or 400-watt monoblocks had ever reached the market. He was grinning from ear to ear as he unveiled dreadnought after dreadnought, pointing out with pride that even these never-to-be-released one-offs bore proper badges and fascias.

The archives housed a quantity of past ARC products, including some of the earliest of his modified Dynacos (I saw Dynaco amplifiers everywhere I went) and all-tube mixing desks, some of which are still in use out there. He showed me the ARC tuner based on the old Dyna FM unit (heavily modified, of course) and not one but two of the ultra-rare D150 amplifiers. (Note: Bill doesn't quite agree with the mythology surrounding the D150, an amplifier which fetches thousands on the second-hand market; he reckons that even the D70 will embarrass it.) I used a lot of film in the archive room, and it took all I could muster to keep from offering myself as an indentured servant just to have the privilege of dusting the room's contents.

I'm sure some of you would like to know what Bill uses both in the factory and at home for analytical and pleasurable listening. Revealed to all, we have:

At the factory:

Oracle and VPI turntables. Infinity IRS (yup, the big 'uns), Infinity RS1; Magneplanar Tympanis; Apogees; whatever ARC electronics strike his fancy (My session in the factory included listening to bi-amped Apogees powered by two D250s.)

At home:

VPI and Goldmund turntables, Eminent Technology and Goldmund arms, Talisman and Dynavector cartridges (the latter being same rare model that looks like a Koetsu on steroids); ARC SP10 and SP8 pre-amps; two ARC D115 amplifiers; Infinity RS1 speakers.

Needless to say, I heard remarkable sounds an both occasions, with the home system offering all one could ever need in a domestic environment, and the in-factory system offering analytical qualities on a par with the WAMM and IRS set-ups.

I was having too good a time, but as the expression goes, it flies when you're having fun, and I was ready to meet yet another hi-fi great, Jim Winey of Magnepan.

Jim collected me from the ARC offices, and we joined his wife for another one of those high-calorie feasts. We had to eat quickly, though, because Jim had a treat in store for me – tickets to hear the Minnesota Orchestra, conducted by Neville Marriner, with Malcolm Frager on piano.

My track record for classical concerts hasn't exactly been admirable, mainly because the mere mention of the Barbican gives me a rash. Well, I learned that the hick image attributed to the denizens of the Midwest must be dispelled, because the concert hall was one of the best I've ever visited. Whoever designed it didn't forget function in favour of form (y'hear that, Barbican?) and I was overjoyed to hear some music that outperformed my hi-fi.

The concert was marvellous, at least to my layman ears, and the blend of Mozart and Tchaikovsky contained enough familiar pieces for me to hum along, Linn-style. Inserted between the two was a piece by a Minnesota native, Stephen Paulus, and it was nothing short of magnificent – sort of like Gershwin on acid. We had tenth row seats, and it proved yet again that those who ignore soundstage and image specificity have never heard live music with both ears.

I spent the next day with Jim at the Magnepan factory, and here too was a collection of hardware destined to render any anachrophile speechless. Jim has a room full of old amplifiers acquired ever the years, and I saw such rare beasts as the Quatre, a Quicksilver, some obscure Audio Research pieces, more Dynacos, some Threshold and Conrad-Johnson units, *ad infinitum*. But as with Audio Research, there was a dearth of scoop material, because Magnepan doesn't introduce new models just for the sake of it. I did get to hear, though, what will eventually become the next generation of Tympani, and it sounded outrageously sweet via Spectral, Threshold, Monster Alpha 1, and severely modified Linn LP12, with Magnepan's own Unitrac arm doing its share.

Jim is an awful lot like Bill, the uniquely Midwestern traits showing him to be a no-nonsense type who won't suffer fools gladly (which begs the question about him spending time with yours truly). He approaches everything with a clear head, an eye for detail, and a hang-up about quality that borders on the maniacal. He took me step-by-step through the manufacturing procedure of the speakers that bear the Magneplanar name, and I can attest to the fact that these products – though they sell in large quantities – are entirely hand-made, including the mounting of the voice-coils an the membrane and anything else that might at first look like it could have been done by a machine.

Jim Winey must have a wild time teasing Europeans. He comes across a bit like a 'good ol' boy' just this side of *The Dukes of Hazzard*, but he's as sharp as they come. Like Arnie Nudell, he knows his wines (and I don't think he developed a taste for good vintages just because of his last name) and he has an abiding love for music that explains why he has a season ticket for the Minnesota Orchestra's performances. He has a wicked grin and a terrific belly laugh, and I enjoyed watching him spar with his wife over what she'd let him eat. Again, it was a turnaround to find that such a high-grade specialised product was the brainchild of a realist rather than an eccentric scientist-type, and Jim joins the select group of manufacturers like Noel Lee of Monster who have blended commercial credibility with audiophile acceptance.

It dawned on me as I killed time waiting for my next flight that my trip was half over. In 12 days, I'd visited as many cities, met over 20 of America's hi-fi elite, slept in six different beds (about two hours each night, due to excitement rather than, uh, grounds for divorce), heard more products new to me than at any hi-fi show, and written the first half of this feature. The Canon Typestar was holding out in spite of my efforts to destroy it, but my brain and body were beginning to show signs of strain.

And I thought audio journalism was supposed to be a piece of cake.

(We leave our intrepid hero in seat 180 on an Ozark Airlines stop-everywhere flight, somewhere between Sioux Falls and Sioux City. Feeling about for his Bic-sized cannister of anti-mugger Mace and tightening his much-depleted money belt, KK prepares for the landing at La Guardia...)

PART 2: THE EAST COAST (AND HARRY PEARSON)

Part of the arrangements required that I check in with the folk back in the UK, which I did much to the delight of British Telecom, and I neglected not one duty, though I tried. By this stage I was really missing my wife and our cat (and my hi-fi) and I'd grown to hate the travel agent with a passion bordering on the pathological.

Why-oh-why did I have to fly from Minneapolis to New York City via Sioux Falls, South Dakota, Sioux City, Iowa and St Louis, when there were direct flights available? But I wasn't going to let this ruin the time remaining, because I still had some bona fide greats ahead of me, next stop being Futterman...

Harvey Rosenberg is as mad as his amplifiers, those whacking-great OTL units available from New York Audio Laboratories. But then you wouldn't expect some three-piece-suited, accountant type to be responsible for carrying on the tradition founded by Julius Futterman, his $10,000 OTL-1 system being as far beyond the lunatic fringe as any component I'd seen. But there was more to this wise-cracking New Yorker than would first appear, and I was about to experience some of the biggest surprises of my entire visit. Unfortunately, it started with the hotel.

Remember that dump I stayed at in San Francisco? Compared to the hovel in New York it was Versailles. Most insulting about my Manhattan *pied-à-terre* was the name, because by this time I was starting to get homesick and overly aware of my acquired 'Britishness'. The hotel was named after a now-departed member of the Royal Family, and I can only assume that his grave site shows signs of turmoil. I don't know if it was the graffiti in the lift, the bell-captain who looked like Mr T's big brother, or the Ortofon-SPU-sized cockroaches. (John Atkinson assures me that the cockroaches uptown are better dressed; mine wore stained macs.)

Harvey dutifully transported me from La Guardia to said hotel, showing me various landmarks along the way, like the hookers who populate the area where I was to stay. Unlike the girls in The Tenderloin, the NYC variety of streetwalker is a truly beautiful creature, and I fell in love about ten times. They do, however, have a survival quality about them that makes their San Francisco counterparts look like Roedean scholars in comparison.

I survived the night, noting how wonderful New York is by daylight. And one image alone – espied on my way to my first appointment – says everything there is to say about New York City and its attitudes about hi-fi and sound reproduction: 'DOLBY STEREO Porno Movies'.

If you're getting the impression that New York is little more than a cesspit-cum-bordello, well, that's only my vision courtesy of the travel agent. Harvey intended to show me as much of the New York audio scene as he could in the day-and-a-half we had together, and he put his own products aside temporarily to introduce me to a tweaker unlike any other I'd ever met.

Edison Price is a music lover with the kind of lifestyle that enables him to indulge in *haute audio*. His company designs advanced industrial lighting systems and he has access to facilities that would be welcomed by any audio manufacturer. In a room at the back of his offices, I found yet another hi-fi toy store, littered with goodies, like a pair of Marantz Model 2 power amps (mucho rare); a pair of the big Stax Electrostatics; Futterman OTL 1 amps (so what else is new?); SOTA, AR, Denon, and other turntables; more cartridges than most shops stock; and other sundry audio jewels worthy of the finest systems. It would appear that Edison takes his hi-fi very seriously, and is currently engaged in co-designing a tonearm that will set the world alight. Unfortunately, the product is so hot that my scoop will have to wait until an issue later in the year but I got to examine this product and bemoan the fact that everything I learned is temporarily 'off the record'. Watch this space...

Harvey, Edison and I went to lunch in a swish bistro, where we discussed audio topics ranging from tonearm design to journalists' iniquities. Armed with photographs of the prototype, we left Edison with promises of maintaining contact. As he has a complete set of *HFN* listed among his most treasured possessions, this shouldn't be too difficult for either of us.

I was expecting our next stop to be New York Audio Laboratories, but Harvey detoured by way of Lyric Hi-Fi, a legend among audio emporiums. The shop – with three demo rooms – actually stocks the Infinity IRS, the $11,000-plus Goldmund turntable, and a host of other pricey goodies aimed at Manhattan's professional sector. Mike Kay, the owner, has been hawking high-end equipment for a generation, and probably has more stories than Mother Goose, but it was Saturday afternoon and we only had time to make a quick tour.

By this time I was frothing at the mouth, just dying to hear the many OTL amplifiers in Harvey's stable. I suppose that the various diversions had one good benefit in that I got to know Harvey well before seeing his products. Harvey is a sharp, compact fellow, a sort of kosher Sumo wrestler, and he seems incapable of making any statements devoid of wry wit. Upon espying two or three hundred salamis hanging on a wall in Katz's delicatessen, I asked Harvey how long they'd last. 'About 15 minutes' was the reply. (This, I was to learn, is as much a New York trait as a Rosenberg trait. While standing in line to pay at Katz's, I told the girl that it was the best food I'd tasted in two years. The guy behind me said, 'You must be from Noo Joisey.')

For all of his New York street smarts, Harvey has had his fill of city blight, and has located New York Audio Labs in a sleepy village about 45 minutes away from the hustle and bustle. This, of course, has not slowed him down one bit, and he gave me a rapid-fire course in the history of tube amplification, output-transformerless design, what's wrong with audio, and why the name Harvey Rosenberg could enter the roster of hi-fi fame. I should mention that, prior to meeting Harvey, I knew two things about him. The first was the result of months of correspondence, in which it was demonstrated that Harvey – like Edison Price and Steve McCormack – is a supertweak, not even leaving his Triplanar tonearm in standard form. The other information was acquired along the way, hearing from others that Harvey was spiritually linked to the lunatic fringe, pursuing an audio goal with little bearing on reality. In other words, the general attitude was that Harvey had succumbed to the madness and should best be treated as a harmless tinkerer.

To those people who grouped Harvey with the dreamers, I'd like to say 'watch out'. Harvey is fully aware of his status as an audio madman, and delights in it because he's got a secret weapon. While the world at large has written him off as the purveyor of nothing more than $10,000 audio juggernauts, Harvey and his crew have been perfecting a hybrid tube/MOSFET design to be known as the Moscode. Their first product, a 150-watts-per-channel unit, has just reached the shops, and is a killer. Beautifully made and a joy to hear, the Moscode's sole virtue isn't its sound. The damned thing sells for a mere $899, putting it way below the price category where it competes sonically.

All this is wonderful, you might be thinking, but what's it got to do with us? Every other company I visited at least distributes its wares in the UK: when's the last time anyone ran into a Futterman stockist?

Remember, you read it here first when JA reported on the 1984 SCES show: New York Audio Labs will be having its products built under licence in Great Britain. This means that the products will (1) be readily available; (2) will sell for a price close to that in the USA; and (3) employ British manpower. Naturally, Harvey is excited, because he loves England and this gives him an excuse to visit our shores regularly. He sees himself as filling the gap between the super-middle-price products of the Hafler/Audiolab variety and the lower reaches of the high-end.

Like Counterpoint, who also market a hybrid, Harvey is aware of the reticence some people show towards 'going tube'; a hybrid like theMoscode makes it much easier for them. I heard it driving LS3/5As and Quad ESL-63s, and the sound was magnificent – open, clear, and with the kind of bottom-end that solid-state fanciers are loathe to sacrifice. (By the way, Harvey is the main force behind the Quad Owners Club. He publishes a semi-regular journal about the products and how to modify them, and he hopes that Peter Walker will forgive him for his heresies.)

I didn't want to leave Harvey, because the man is so *meshuggeneh* ('crazy' in his lexicon) that I was having a ball. But the next day held a meeting that I had been dreading for months, and I had to get through it no matter what diversions I could create.

Meeting Harry Pearson

What drug should I have purchased from the chemist to prepare me for a session of the gravest importance? How does a writer prepare for an encounter that could make or break a career? I'd recently been asked to write for the American publication, *The Absolute Sound*, and I was bound to spending a day with the terror of the industry, *TAS* editor, Harry Pearson.

I'd had enough of this torment in the past few years. My driving test, my trial period for *HFN*, my four days at the Penta Show. Never known for my bravery or intestinal fortitude, I looked forward to meeting Mr Pearson much with the same set of nerves I'd employ if visiting Harlem when wearing a Ku Klux Klan robe. There are more tales about Harry than any other man in the industry – he ties with Ivor Tiefenbrun, to be more accurate – and he's been described as an audio equivalent of Napoleon, Attila the Hun, and Rasputin. Physical illness overtook me on the way to Sea Cliff, Long Island, though how much of it was due to the inferior calibre of the American rail service I'm not quite certain. (Apologies to any BR employees whom I've offended in the past. Compared with the Long Island Railroad, you lot are Rolls-Royce chauffeurs.)

Harry works out of a typically Northeastern wooden building, much in the vein of the houses seen in the film *Moby Dick*. I'd grown up with that sort of architecture, so it shocked me to learn that this man didn't operate out of a turreted castle with moat and Nubian slaves. At the very least I expected armed guards of the banana republic variety, sporting Kalishnikovs, peaked hats, and Zapata moustachios. Instead, I find a (somewhat portly) Martin Sheen lookalike wearing a T-shirt and white boating-type trousers, about as menacing as Bob Monkhouse. So this is where the mighty *TAS* is created...

Do I sound disappointed? No way. Psychologists would call it 'relieved', and that's what I was. Remember, I was under scrutiny for the first time since I'd left the UK; up to this point I'd been pronouncing all of the judgements. I was taken aback when, before doing anything, Harry suggested we take a walk into town to collect some victuals, and he proceeded to stuff my face with culinary excesses like Häagen-Dazs chocolate ice-cream (I now know what he means by 'chocolate midrange') and the richest brownies I've ever tasted. We did not talk about hi-fi. Harry saved the audio portion of our time until later in the day, preferring instead to figure out just what type of person he'd invited.

The trip was turning full circle, for I was to hear a system not a million miles (3000 was more like it) removed from that at Arnie Nudell's back in Southern California. Infinity IRS speakers are the most obvious similarity, only Harry's room is what the British would deem just large enough for a pair of SL6s. Power came, via a pair of Conrad-Johnson tube amps of the megalith variety, with signal from the Koetsu/Goldmund front-end via Audio Research SP10 completing the path.

Both JA and Absolute Sounds' Ricardo Franassovici had heard the system earlier last year, and had warned me.

'Expect to be carrying jellied kidneys behind your belt,' cautioned my editor...

Do you know the expression 'Oy gevalt'? It's Yiddish for 'By Jove', and it barely conveys the physical experience of 16Hz bass at full whack. Harry and I didn't have much time, so he picked key recordings for my initiation, and I've never heard the Human League 12-inch 'Don't You Want Me' with such impact (see *HFN* October '84 issue). Harry chose this to illustrate one particular aspect of his *modus operandi*, which is separating layers of sound from each other – part and parcel of his focus on soundstage as a prime criterion for top performance.

You can almost tell what type of tape the studio used when the recording was made.

Harry's system – because you're almost sitting 'in it' – provides resolution like no other system I've ever heard. My anglicised tastes deemed the bass a bit more than that to which I'm accustomed, but it showed me just how far behind most reviewers are when it comes to selecting the tools of the trade. Unfortunately, this high-resolution system is as cost-prohibitive as the marvellous Hewlett-Packard equipment employed by Martin Colloms!

Just for the record, I found Harry to be the Southern Gentleman some commentators told me he would be. (Even Harry Pearson has friends among the enemies.) After the ice had broken, we got along famously, but then Harry doesn't have to suffer too much exposure to me because of the interference of the Atlantic Ocean, so I didn't have time to get on his famous nerves. Like the rest of the US audiophile community, HP, as his readers know him, has an absolute fetish about fine food and good wine, and I've got to admit that caviar makes a better pasta sauce than Bolognese.

So, my ego restored from its stand-by mode, I had to face an after-dark ride on the LIRR. I made it back to the hotel with only one altercation with an NYC native, who backed down when he realised that I was too far gone to worry about mere physical pain. I cast aspersions on his sexual preferences *vis-à-vis* his mother, and he backed off not expecting this from an obvious tourist.

The next day was spent in the appetising atmosphere of the aforementioned sewer, putting the Typestar to good use. I hadn't been using the Sony Walkman Pro as much as I thought I might, because the conversations were so casual, but it served nicely as a note-taking device, enabling me to recall many of the tiny details I'd otherwise have forgotten. I wandered around New York for a few hours, revelling in the only rain I'd seen since I left Canterbury, and readied myself for a visit to the Village under the guidance of a rather special New York native peripherally linked to the audio world. It was deemed mandatory that I escape the confines of that flop-house, and my last memories of the East Coast's largest brothel/flea market/wino-ery/pothole nursery were beyond favourable, but I had enough strength left to resist falling in love with New York in spite of the temptations.

I left with but one grave disappointment: everywhere I went I heard that nauseating ditty by Frank Sinatra about his adoration for the Big Apple, instead of the more appropriate, artistically superior 'Manhattan', by Rodgers and Hart, sung, of course, by Ella Fitzgerald. I ended up humming it to myself for the entire four days.

So, on to Boston

The home stretch was in sight, and I was just about to reach my turf. Though I'm not a Boston native, I know the place pretty well, having grown up in its shadow and having a sister who's lived there for 15 years. Flying in to Logan (the Amstrad of airports) brought a semi-lump to my throat, just shy of the boulder beneath my chin when I descend into Heathrow or Gatwick. Here, for certain, I could buy half-sour pickles unlike those to be found anywhere on this great planet, and I had them for breakfast, much to my father's dismay. (They're soaked with garlic and provide heartburn within 10 minutes of consumption.)

Fred Pinkerton of Boston Acoustics took me from Logan to the Boston Acoustics factory for a lesson in how KEF and Wharfedale's US equivalents deal with speaker manufacture. Because Boston is a real-world company rather than a dream factory, it presented a 180° turnaround from what I'd been seeing since I arrived in the USA. The attitude is one of concern for the layman rather than the hard-core audiophile, and my entire visit was peppered with pointers about keeping the customer satisfied and the product serviced.

Boston Acoustics is part of a great American audio tradition akin to our BBC speaker tradition. It's one of the branches on the family tree that was planted when Henry Kloss and Edgar Villchur created Acoustic Research, Boston Acoustics stemming from the Advent limb of the tree, which grew out of the KLH branch.

Fred introduced me to Frank Read and Andy Petite, business and design brains respectively, and – over lunch, of course – they filled me in on the history (straightening out a few historical errors along the way) and market philosophy of their company. It was refreshing to find – within minutes of joining Fred – that Boston has a crystal-clear game plan, which means selecting a specific part of the market and not diluting their efforts by trying to be something they're not.

In Boston's case, it means filling the hole left by the virtual disappearance of Advent from the market sector, which I like to think of as 'audiophile on a budget', but which translates in the US into a sector that has no UK equivalent. It seems that Boston products sell to discriminating consumers who are not audio hobbyists nor intending to become such. They seem to do well with a new creature called the Yuppie, young urban (or upwardly-mobile) professionals who show great concern for those values known as style and taste, with strong emphasis on quality, much like the archetypal Habitat shopper in the UK. The only slight wanderings the company has made include a line of in-car speakers (a far more serious business in the US than over here), and a new product that's so simple and obvious it made me wonder why nobody, to my knowledge, has done it before.

America has experienced the growth of a new market which has yet to materialise here, and that is the videophile presence, which I mentioned in reference to Monster's Noel Lee and Sumiko's Dave Fletcher. Boston realises that – just as in the UK – most laymen are unaware of the unpleasant results one achieves if loudspeakers are placed right next to a television set. The magnets wreak havoc with the colour, sometimes leading to permanent damage. But even education will not prevent consumers from placing speakers right next to the telly if aesthetics or practicality dictate, so Boston has come up with a solution. The well-received and very popular Boston A40, a natural selection for videophiles wanting speakers dedicated to their television sets, is now available as the A40V, a special version with heavily-shielded magnets. It's simple, but effective, and it shows exactly how Boston uses its marketing talents for both the consumers and themselves. [It's only fair to mention that England's B&W were neck-and-neck with Boston in introducing such a model in the US – *Ed.*]

The factory itself was large and bustling, and I learned that very little – the cabinets, for example – comes from outside. Because Boston's chosen area of warfare is the 'affordable' sector, they're hung up on efficiency, and the factory is designed to operate so that costs are kept down – as are the designs themselves. It explains how the A40 sells for so little, in spite of the high quality of the internal components, and Andy told me about how few products are returned because the design brief includes indestructibility as a major virtue.

Andy is a pure electronics/audio man, Frank a businessman, and Fred a combination of the two. I was a bit taken aback by their scepticism regarding things tweak, but it's consistent with their attitude about not pandering to fashion or trends, and anyone who speaks with Andy knows that practicality, traditional values, and simplicity are not neglected when he designs a product.

The company has its own attitudes about sound reproduction, and flat frequency response coupled with smooth tonal character are the main characteristics that Boston treasures. But even this seemingly conservative crew had the odd surprise in store, and I was informed that Boston has its own moving-coil cartridge on sale in the USA. Apparently it's been available for some time, but it was new to me and my poverty-stricken look resulted in a gift of the dearer of the two models, complete with van den Hul tip.

Boston Acoustics had put up with me for a good six or seven hours, when it came time for Fred to drop me off at the next hotel: I wish he hadn't. I suppose that slumming is a fun sport for those who are so used to luxury that they need the odd foray into the lower reaches just to keep from getting bored. I, on the other hand, have no such need to experience the low-life side of things. The latest example of non-palatial splendour selected by the travel agent I now reckoned to be irredeemably perverse, was an establishment whose walls were festooned with apologies for the look and condition of the rooms. I was later informed by a Boston native that these signs have been part of the hotel for many, many years. OK, so I had to suffer black-and-white, non-cable television for a couple of nights, and the cockroaches were smaller and better behaved than the street-fightin' bugs of New York, but the peeled-porcelain-and-mould look of the bathroom did little to make my showers a pleasure.

As I said before, though, Boston is getting near to home turf, so after doing my daily portion of this article, I phoned out for relief in the form of fellow vinyl junkies, Paul Bazylinski and Fred Jeffery. Little did my friends realise that I was exploiting them for this article, for their record retail experience completed the pack of individuals chosen to exemplify the American audio scene. A glance back shows that I've visited amplifier, turntable, cable, cartridge, tonearm, speaker, and record manufacturers, as well as record producers, hi-fi retailers, and a couple of audio journalists. What better way to add to the set than with a record retailer and a part-time retailer/hardcore collector?

I got a crash course in all that had happened on the vinyl scene since my last visit, and I learned that CD hadn't exactly set the world alight in their neck of the woods. They loaded me up with collectables, threatening to burst my luggage with even more goodies the next night, after my visit to Apogee…

Apogee and Krell

There's a soft spot in my heart for Apogee, because I like to think that I'm the man who discovered them for the UK. I first heard them in March 1983, and raved about them upon my return. My claims for these full-range ribbon designs – all $7000 worth – were written off as terminal lunacy, but those to whom I addressed my feelings have now changed their tunes and the line is soon to be launched here… especially since Apogee introduced the half-priced Scintilla.

What a gas – I covered 11,000 miles to ride in a British car. Jason Bloom of Apogee is one of those rare Americans of impeccable taste with a masochistic streak that enables him to survive the indignities of owning a notoriously fragile vehicle miles away from its homeland. A dead ringer for a much younger, more stylish Jack Lemmon, Jason listens primarily to jazz – with a vengeance – has a wonderful wife named Sara, makes the world's finest coffee, and intends, quite seriously, to share the responsibility for creating the world's finest loudspeakers.

After a brief spell at Jason's home, where we just chatted about things in general and dined on the best Jewish delicatessen I've had since George's closed down in the mid '70s, we went to the Apogee factory. It was there that I met Leo Speigel, one of the main designers, and heard the new Scintilla, having had a wonderful demonstration of the big 'uns back in Minneapolis at the Audio Research factory. The Scintillas proved frighteningly good, easily on a par with my traditional favourites, the Stax ELS-F81 and the LS3/5A. The company used a system consisting of Koetsu/Goldmund/Levinson products, with JA's beloved Krell supplying the juice. Considering that the room was hardly gigantic and hadn't been tweaked for maximum acoustical supremacy, the sound was such that no listener could fail to note that the Scintillas are world class.

Leo Spiegel is a fascinating man with a background in high-tech military design, but he's now committed to refining ribbon loudspeakers; his in-depth knowledge of metals and magnetic fields and other areas all make their presence known in the Apogee products. Jason is the company's fuss-pot and listener, and he approaches a music session with the same serious frame of mind that you'd like to see in a surgeon before he slices open your skull. We spent a few hours with the Scintillas, which proved themselves time and again to be capable of yielding an utterly convincing sound and image. The Scintillas are 'manageable' dipoles, physically presenting no great shocks to Quad '63 owners. A bit of a pig to drive, the Scintilla can be wired for either 4 ohm or 1 ohm operation, the latter mode necessarily limited to amplifiers of Krell persuasion.

Which leads nicely into my last call of the trip. Krell just so happens to use a pair of Scintillas at its factory, and Dan D'Agostino uses the full-range jobs at home. Jason and Sara drove me down to Connecticut to meet Dan, a journey which tied in well with their plans to collect a Krell pre/power combination. The time spent with the D'Agostinos (wife Rondi is a doll) turned out to be as much an Apogee experience as it was a Krell, so forgive me if the two companies – which are entirely separate – blend together slightly in this part of my travelogue.

The Krell factory is so neat and tidy that I was sure I'd find a permanently stationed government inspector. Modern, open and airy, it's as solid and 'right' as the amps themselves. Dan pointed out various techniques designed to make Krell products unburstable, brimming with the kind of overkill feel you expect from Germans rather than those of Italian extraction.

Dan is obviously a proud papa, and he speaks about his products with the kind of familial protection in his voice that calls to mind Don Corleone and his handling of the wayward Sonny. I was actually scared witless about meeting Dan – not the weediest of men – because I was told that he expected a snotty tube lover with no time whatsoever for solid-state gear. Hell, even I can hear the virtues of pure Class-A amps devoid of output capacitors. Besides, would you tell your boss you think he's retarded?

I was told that Dan was a practical joker, and I sat there helpless when my UK babysitter phoned up to find out how we were doing. Dan said: 'Kessler hates the stuff and Jason is driving him to the train station at this very moment.' The sharp intake of breath heard from the London end sucked smoke into the phone.

Dan had the Apogee Scintillas playing at the factory, using the pre-amp and amps Jason was about to collect. Jason was stunned, saying that he'd never heard them sound so good, and let nothing distract him as he worked his way through Dan's LPs. We went out for lunch, where I was introduced to 'steak fries' (chips with the skins still on them) and onion rings of the truly celestial variety. This sustenance was needed to prepare me for the visit to Dan's home, where the big Apogees lurked.

The Apogees, as mentioned before, can be used in normal 4 ohm mode, or 1 ohm for the hardcore, the sound (with the right amps) being a bit more open. Jason mentioned that Audio Research's Bill Johnson was thinking about modifying his D115s to work in this mode, so it must be serious stuff. Whatever, Dan has his Apogees tri-amped with more Krells than I've ever seen in one room, including a separate amplifier for the *0.1 ohm* midrange ribbon. Hints had been dropped prior to my departure eluding to the magnificence of this system, so I readied myself for some heavy-duty audio madness.

I don't want to imply for a moment that I was getting the slightest bit jaded. Within a three-week period, I'd heard at least six systems that, to my ears, represented the end of the road, though all were different. WAMMs, IRSs, the outrageous OTL 1 Futtermans driving LS3/5As, James Boyk's anachrophilic magic via Dynaco and LS3/5As, the prototype Magnepan Tympanis, the famous TAS reference system, speakers bi-amped with two Audio Research D250s – I knew that I'd been privileged like few others.

Listening to Dan's system was as much a revelation as hearing any of the others, and the same observations held true: it's possible for there to be more than one wonderful system, in spite of consumers and readers and sales reps wanting life to be made simple for them by the existence of only One Choice. I can't say, for the life of me, which system was the best I heard, for each and every one of them had unique virtues and weaknesses that would make their presence obtrusive depending solely upon the listener. No system I heard was flawless, and no points system yet devised will enable me to offer you a pecking order of those I heard. But I can assure you that the Krell/Apogee system (and this is coming from someone who still worships valve electronics despite thinking Dan D'Agostino is an amazing guy) ranks with the very best.

It shines in a couple of areas, brightly enough to make it truly great. I have never heard sound as effortless in my life, with no sign of break-up from any part of the chain. Part of this is no doubt due to the Krell attitude about killing flies with Uzis; there were enough amplifiers in Dan's set-up to satisfy three salivating audiophiles. Another aspect is most assuredly the Apogees, which offer transparency in a league with the Stax ELS speakers and some other fine dipoles. The cartridge, a Koetsu Silver, and the front-end, a Goldmund turntable and arm, were set up to perfection, and Dan said that the positioning of the speakers had been an ongoing situation since they arrived.

Jason was grinning from ear to ear, suggesting that even he didn't know how good his own products were, and we went through LP after LP looking for the sonic buzz. (How was I to know that Gil Scott-Heron was so damned funky?)

That says a lot, Dan's love for the black funk poet. It gets down to the passion of Italians, and he approaches music the way he builds amplifiers and creates tomato sauce. The man has a fetish, a fastidiousness that makes certain British efforts seem embarrassing, and if ever an analogy is needed, then Dan is to amplifier construction what Rolex is to watches.

It was amusing to hear from other people their puzzlement at Krell's astounding success in the UK, and I asked Dan to give me some idea of its place in the US market. I was surprised to learn, for instance, that there are at present no outlets for Krell on the West Coast, which explains why the only Krells I saw before reaching the East were in Dave Wilson's system. But Dan has a small core of dedicated dealers which he weighs against competition much heavier than that in the UK. There are at least a dozen solid-state units on sale in the USA which vie for the same audio dollars. The strength of Krell, besides its innate virtues, is Dan's attitude, a very American statement which shows two upraised fingers to those who think he can be dissuaded from assaulting the high-end.

I took an instant liking to Dan and Jason, and not just because we were on a similar wavelength due to my affinity for New England; after all, Dan is still the ultimate solid-state proponent. But these guys love music so much, having chosen to manifest this love via sound reproduction apparatus instead of performing, that I couldn't help but relish their company. They seemed more concerned with hi-fi in the purist sense rather than the hard-nut business sense, and it works for them in spite of what efficiency experts and economists might think. Like many of the other companies I visited – indeed, most of them – they succeed, despite being ultra-specialist, because their products are so very fine. Here were more people I didn't want to leave, people who made me feel like a friend and fellow audio casualty; not just another journalist.

Summing it all up

The turmoil and trauma had subsided a bit, and I'd stifled the conflict of returning to the UK or staying in the USA (or is it the other way around?). My own hometown included, I found the country to be an amazing place, the day-to-day people and activities far removed from the unfortunate, Reaganite society which we as Europeans are led to perceive. It was always exciting, the general atmosphere being one of optimism, and I've got to admit that I was sorely tempted by what is most assuredly a much easier life. But we've got something no-one else has, and I learned it time and again. No matter where I went or who I met, no matter how wonderful the audio equipment I got to sample, one thing emerged that even my American friends would not dispute: Americans know how to make the hardware but the Brits know how to set it up.

13. Reviewers and the audio press

'Audio reviewers are notorious for doing anything for free food and drink. One such renowned audio "glom", who was criticising a competing reviewer for similar behaviour, once told me: "XYZ Reviewer would attend the opening of an envelope if there was free food!"' **Robert J Reina**

Robert J Reina *on a demonstration of reliability:*

'There have been a handful of audiophile products over the past 20 years that have had spotty reliability reputations. One such group of products was a line of expensive tube gear. The US distributor spent a good deal of time trying to remedy this brand's cloudy reliability image in the US. One day, he announced the distribution of a new high-powered flagship amplifier from this company. He brought it over to a reviewer's house to demo it and invited other members of the audiophile press to listen.

'He wanted to show off this puppy and end this lack of reliability rumour once and for all. Except, when he reached over to turn the amplifier on, he unwittingly pointed his face away from the amplifier, grimaced, and shut his eyes before he flipped the switch. In front of most of the New York Metropolitan Area audiophile press.'

Bill Peugh, *Sumiko, on an editor's bass instincts:*

'In 1994, Metaphor Acoustic Designs debuted at the Las Vegas CES. I had made appointments with all of the most important reviewers in an attempt to garner coverage for the new company. One of the most powerful editors, one who could break a company with a few keystrokes, came by to hear the new speakers.

'Rather than play the usual audiophile fare, I decided to take a chance. I knew the editor was a bass player and that he was also a huge fan of Little Feat. Out came the *Waiting for Columbus* album and "Fat Man in the Bathtub" was cued up.

'Initially the editor was very tense, but within about 30 seconds he had drifted off and was playing air bass. This lasted for about 30 seconds. The editor then seemed to remember he was in public and sat bolt upright in his seat. He returned to his self-conscious reviewer type listening position. This time it took less than 30 seconds and once again, the editor was matching Kenny Gradney note for note.

'After the editor left, my two partners, Gerry Boyd and Karl Schuster, eagerly inquired what the editor thought. I replied: "I don't know what he'll write, but I know what he thinks."'

Robert J Reina on reviewers' free food (and Music Hall's Scotch):

'Audio reviewers are notorious for doing anything for free food and drink. One such renowned audio "glom", who was criticising a competing reviewer for similar behaviour, once told me: "XYZ Reviewer would attend the opening of an envelope if there was free food!" In fact, I've grown tired of certain reviewers bragging about how many times they've been out to dinner with a manufacturer and never paid for a meal. That's outrageous. I recall recently reviewing a speaker personally delivered by the designer. I then went to dinner with the designer and he was shocked that I picked up the tab – and paid out of my own pocket, not my magazine's. What's more, after writing a favourable review, I purchased the speaker, and noted in my review that I felt the speaker was such a bargain that it cost me less than the dinner with the designer!

'Roy Hall (of Music Hall, US importer of Creek, Epos, and Shanling) figured out early on how to lever this typical audio writer behaviour to get more coverage at Home Entertainment and CES shows. Roy is an expert on single malt Scotch whisky and has turned many writers (including yours truly) on to the drink. For some time now, Roy had developed a reputation for bringing good whisky to audio shows and opening his special bottles when audio writers enter the room.

'Over the years, Roy has upgraded his whiskies and tended to bring more expensive and more obscure bottles. At one point, he sent out press releases announcing the bottles he was bringing to an upcoming show to the audio press. His strategy worked but eventually backfired. Now, Roy always gets good audio writer attendance in his room at shows.

'The problem is, the magazine show reports tend to spend more space covering the whisky and don't mention the equipment that much.'

Karen Sumner of Transparent Audio remembers a review for adults only:

'Ken Kessler and I knew each other even before we met years later in the audio industry. We were fellow coffee house inhabitants in Portland, Maine, long before Ken moved to Canterbury and married a British girl. We were two shadowy figures passing each other, but not actually meeting in Portland. I can't help but think that our "Portland" connection somehow empowered Ken to take some liberties with my "image" when it came to talking about me and Transparent products in print. He wrote a review of our cables in *HFN* in which he made a "dominatrix" reference and created a vision of me dressed in black leather and boots, wielding a whip, and sitting astride someone who would dare not to like my cables.

'It was a great Transparent Cable review so we couldn't resist including it on our website. It wasn't long after including the review that we noticed we were having difficulty getting on the website. We discovered that the Net Nanny had blocked our site because of the dominatrix references. As far as the web police were concerned, we were X-rated.

'Next time I saw Ken I said: "Ken, because of you, kids can't get on our website. The Net Nanny has blocked it!"'

Allen Edelstein *recalls Percy Wilson's parable for audio critics:*

'Here is the Zanzibar Fallacy, as told to me by Percy Wilson, with about 30 years' time to alter the story but not the concept. To set it up, I phoned Bud Fried from work one day in the early 1970s just to bull a little. He says, "Guess who's coming to dinner? Gordon Holt and his wife, David Hafler and his wife, Percy Wilson (who he explains is one of the grand old men of British audio) and his wife and Jane, Bud's wife." I had met none of these people. Do I want to come for drinks and maybe dinner if there's room at the restaurant?

'I cursed my way to his home in Philadelphia rush hour traffic but I made it and got to go to dinner too. Gordon even gave me his home phone number and I got to know him and help a little with *Stereophile*. Percy was staying in the city centre and needed a ride. Bud recruited me, making Percy promise to tell me the Zanzibar Fallacy during the ride, a favourite of Bud's, and now mine, too.

'So I drove Percy and his wife in the back seat of my 1973 Chevy Vega and he told me this tale:

'There was a sea captain, well-beloved by his crew. Outside the wheel room was a small cannon and every day at 12 noon the captain had the cannon fired. One day, he gathered his crew and told them he was going to retire outside the main city on the island of Zanzibar where he was going to build a retirement home and, if anyone was near anytime, they should come and visit.

'One morning, one of his crew was nearby and came to visit. They greeted with great gusto. And the captain showed him around his new home. On the second floor, the captain had built a copy of the wheel room complete with cannon on the porch outside. It was just about noon. The captain checked his watch, went out on the porch, and at 12 noon set off the cannon.

'The crewman said how great it was to be here but he was really curious. How did the captain know when it really was 12 noon to shoot the cannon? "That's easy," said the captain. In the main city of Zanzibar there was an horologist who studied time. And he had an amazing clock collection. The captain just made sure his watch was co-ordinated with the horologist's and then he was sure what time it was. And he advised the crewman to check out the clock collection if he had the time.

'The next morning the crewman visited the horologist. The collection of clocks was amazing. It was just before noon and at 12 o'clock all the clock alarms went off in an Ivesian (my term) cacophony. He went over to the horologist to tell him how much he admired the clock collection. But then he asked him how did he know the time on the clocks was correct? How did he know for sure when it really was 12 noon?

"That's easy," said the horologist. "Outside the city lives a crazy, retired sea captain and every day at 12 noon he shoots off a cannon. I just make sure that my all clocks are set for 12 o'clock when the captain's cannon goes off."

'Percy told this story because he was afraid of too much circular reasoning in our evaluation of audio gear. There is often too much circular reasoning in all human evaluations, especially when it gives the answer we hope for.'

Karen Sumner, *Transparent Cable, on 'Women in Audio' tokenism in the audio press:*

'It is still unusual to see women in our industry holding executive, engineering, and sales positions, but there have been some incredibly strong women who have been major contributors in sustaining and building companies in our industry with their drive, talents and experience. Kathy Gornik of Thiel Speakers, Sheryl Lee Wilson of Wilson Audio, Rondi D'Agostino of Krell, and EveAnna Manley of Manley Laboratories come to mind.

'I was always included in this group when *Stereophile* had their annual token "Women in Audio" panel at their hi-fi show. The agenda was usually: "Women love music. Why aren't there more women in high-end audio?"

'At the last event of this type, I decided to filibuster this concept on two levels. During my first opportunity to speak I said: "Many high-end audio systems, particularly those put together by men who believe what they read in hi-fi journals, have absolutely nothing to do with music. These systems are an end unto themselves where the object is to make sound and to change it, not to listen to music. Most people, including women, just don't have time or the interest to make sound and to spend endless hours changing it. Our industry and the press that 'promotes' it need to become more centred on the universal value of music to engage more people in general, not just women, if we are to survive and prosper."

'On my second opportunity to speak I delivered the final blow: "How can any woman find it appealing to join a boy's club where even the journals such as *Stereophile* still segregate women into a women's group?" I challenged *Stereophile* to integrate us into appropriate panels along with key visionary men of the industry at their next hi-fi show, rather than put us in a sideshow. There was silence, then confusion, and the "magic" was lost forever.

'There have been no more "Women in Audio" panels. I'd like to think my performance helped bring an end to the "Women in Audio" panel at the *Stereophile* show; however, I have yet to note that there has been much integration of women and men in their subsequent hi-fi show panel discussions. Perhaps that's progress.'

Robert Becker on the unheard of ejection of an editor:

'Once an opinionated editor-in-chief who had rashly impugned the construction of our earliest product, a roundish pre-pre-amp rightly called "the Piglet", didn't take no for an answer at a CES one winter.

'He couldn't understand that we used parts approved by the celebrated designer, John Curl, and that his claims about "cheap parts" were totally unfounded, especially since he had never checked with us.

'On and on he went until I said, "I have better things to do and would like you to leave."

'He stopped, puffed up in his elephantine flummery, and refused, to which I puffed up (though smaller in those days) and said, "I paid for the room. You will leave. Should I call security?" No one in the history of audio had ever thrown a reviewer out a CES room, let alone threatened to bring in security.

'In shock (though this guy always looked in shock), the reviewer meekly looked to David, representing Sumiko across the room, and said, "Do I have to leave?" Fletcher, whose contempt for pretentious, know-it-all audio reviewers (that covered 95% of them) knew no bounds, smiled and put on his best peacemaker tone. "That would be best," he said quietly.

'The reviewer, first overcome by my fierceness, didn't know how to respond to David's softness and left muttering to himself. He happily rarely ever reviewed our products, as I recall, so fierceness worked fine.

'Over the years, David and I developed quite a repertoire in playing good cop and bad cop, though we eventually reversed roles from this early episode. Unfazed and resolute in his scientific convictions, David made a much better bad cop than I.'

Robert J Reina on annoyingly persistent manufacturers:

'Audio writers are constantly besieged by manufacturers trying to get their products reviewed by magazines. A friend of mine, who, at the time, was responsible for audio review equipment acquisition at an audiophile magazine, was constantly harassed by a manufacturer who wanted to send the magazine a new record-cleaning machine he had designed. My friend kept ditching him.

'Somehow this manufacturer found out my friend's home address, and drove from Florida to New York and rang the doorbell of my friend's apartment at 8am on a Saturday morning, record cleaning machine in hand. My friend called me the next day outraged. "The nerve of that guy! What if I was in bed with a woman or something?"

'Knowing the details of my friend's social life at the time, I dropped the phone laughing.'

Laura Dearborn recalls her most rewarding interview:

'After my book *Good Sound* was published, Steve Harris asked me to do some interviews of hi-fi luminaries for *Hi-Fi News*. The first one he asked for was of John Bicht, then of Versa Dynamics record player fame (go to www.versalab.com for more information about him).

'It was at the January CES show in Vegas that we finally met up and John agreed to the interview but I had to return to his showroom 13 times to finally get to talk to him. Sounds like a bad luck number but I really needed the money! And then we ended up totally besotted with each other, and have remained so ever since. (We married in 1991.)

'The best reward I've ever received for having a dedicated work ethic!'

14. Steve Harris: the modern era

'My experience on other magazines – I'd been Editor of Hi-Fi Choice for four years, and before that, Editor of What Hi-Fi? for three – hadn't quite prepared me for the organic complexity of HFN/RR.' **Steve Harris**

From May 1986 to June 2005. *By Steve Harris*

When I took over from John Atkinson in May 1986, he'd just finished putting together *HFN/RR*'s '30th anniversary' issue. It's hard to believe that nearly two decades have passed since then, two decades packed with incident for both the industry and the magazine. Mind-boggling advances in technology have often led us nowhere, except perhaps into periods of cliff-hanging uncertainty about the future.

The first decade certainly whizzed by. For the '40th anniversary' issue, June '96, I found myself reminiscing like this: 'My experience on other magazines – I'd been Editor of the handbook-format *Hi-Fi Choice* for four years, and before that, Editor of *What Hi-Fi?* for three – hadn't quite prepared me for the organic complexity of *HFN/RR*. Copy arrived unexpectedly, but allegedly by longstanding arrangement, from contributors I hadn't yet had a chance to meet. Manufacturers launched into me with grievances I knew nothing about. Legal threats were uttered over readers' letters published months before... Today, I count it as a privilege to have known at least some of the great figures who made the magazine what it was in the early days, but all deserve recognition.'

Sadly, since I wrote those words in 1996, even fewer of those pioneers are still with us, and it's simply impossible to pay adequate tributes here. But I have to say a word about Angus McKenzie, who passed away only in January 2005. I'd known Angus before I joined *HFN/RR*. As Editor of *Hi-Fi Choice: Cassette Deck*s, I would try to persuade him to review more budget two-head cassette decks. Angus always wanted to fill the book with the more expensive three-head decks – the off-tape monitoring made the three-head models ten times easier to test! He was a rather daunting character, but despite having being blind since his mid-20s, Angus was a world expert on tape and tape recorder performance; I found out later that he was held in awe by many of the Japanese companies and that he and his wife Fiona had even been invited to Akio Morita's home. Angus' main contribution to *Hi-Fi News* was his passionate FM Radio column, and I still remember seeing browsers in bookstalls pick up *Hi-Fi News* and turn straight to his page. He would lambast the BBC for such crimes as allowing hum on one channel in a live concert broadcast. He had to give up the column when his marriage to Fiona ended, but after this he set to, learned Braille, became adept with a computer and acquired a guide dog. With his dog, Angus could happily cross London alone by underground to visit the Hi-Fi Show. He even produced a cassette tape to help other blind people identify sounds and find their way around the tube network. He also worked to raise funds for Guide Dogs for the Blind.

I also have to mention the late Donald Aldous, who by the time I joined *HFN/RR* was only an occasional contributor. But he was extremely kind and helpful to me, the 'new boy'. 'Fight on!' he would say, in the face of any difficulty, 'Fight on!'

Hi-fi in schism

Among the correspondence that poured on to my desk in my first weeks as Editor were many letters responding to one particular article – Martin Colloms' May '86 report on an amplifier listening test he'd conducted as part of a lecture/demonstration to a London AES meeting. More than 90 people had taken part in the experiment: when played a piece of music repeatedly, they'd been asked to indicate whether there was a difference or not. The results of this 'blind' test had been submitted to an independent statistician, whose report allowed MC to proclaim, yes, 'Amplifiers do sound different.' However, not everyone agreed with him!

The debate which Martin was exploring had already been going on for years: the 'subjectivist/objectivist' confrontation. In 1978, James Moir and Quad had carried out a blind test on amplifiers in response to the purely-subjective reviews which had started appearing in many magazines. They'd concluded that listeners could not actually hear differences between two correctly-working amplifiers under 'blind' conditions. (As JA has noted, an earlier *HFN/RR* amplifier listening test had also been inconclusive.) But by 1986 the subjectivist/objectivist conflict had extended to loudspeaker cables and of course to CD players.

Hi-fi enthusiasts were sharply divided between pro- and anti-CD camps, and in high-end circles no-one yet regarded CD as an acceptable source. One of my first duties at *HFN/RR* in spring 1986 was to get hold of the new Philips true 16-bit CD players for MC to review. Later that year I started working on a book called *Jazz on Compact Disc* [Salamander, London & New York, 1987], which meant listening critically to hundreds of CDs, and I remember the relief I felt when I switched to a Philips 16-bit player (a CD360) for this. The task would have become an overwhelming chore with the grey, opaque and fatiguing sound of the old 14-bit player. But in 1988, just as the record industry was beginning to cash in on CD, a group of Japanese companies spoiled it all by trying to launch Digital Audio Tape (DAT). The record companies rose up in anger against a medium that would immediately allow the public to make 'perfect' 16-bit digital copies of copyright material (recordable CD was still many years away in the future) and refused to produce pre-recorded DAT cassettes.

We'd felt obliged to review all the DAT machines we could get hold of, even though the format was making no headway in the market. DAT was an immediate success with professional users who wanted a convenient, low-cost digital recording system, but as a consumer product, it was dead. For the first time, but not the last, we had got mired in the uncertainty of 'new formats', promising always jam tomorrow but never jam today.

In the end, I don't think that DAT harmed CD music sales much at all. But as early as 1991, when DAT was still in contention, Philips initiated another new format, the Digital Compact Cassette or DCC. When Sony weighed in with MiniDisc, we had a wearisome 'format war', which, unfortunately, set the pattern for the 1990s. With DCC and MiniDisc came a concept which was (and is) alien to the mindset of the audiophile. Both formats used 'lossy compression' or 'data reduction' schemes in order to record a given amount of music with a smaller amount of digital data; instead of trying to reproduce the original sound, they try to fool the ear. Today, we've got used to it. We live in a world of data reduction, from DVD movies to JPEG still images to MP3 music.

Meanwhile, we soldiered on with our CD players. They were getting better, slowly, but would they ever be completely well? Then one day in the spring of 1989, I got a call from Paul Miller: 'Something you've got to hear!' When I got there, Paul showed me a Sony TA-F630ESD amplifier he'd got in for review. As an added feature, Sony had given this rather ordinary amplifier a digital input, taking advantage of a new, low-cost chip from Philips. This 'digital amplifier' was actually the first product to use a 1-bit PDM or Bitstream DAC. Paul played some CDs through this DAC and it was a revelation. The sound was fluid, listenable, three-dimensional – yes, everything my CD player at home was not.

Sadly, the promise of that early Bitstream experience was never fulfilled in production players, and subsequent generations of Philips models got mediocre reviews at best. Philips' component division went on to incorporate the PDM DAC into ever-cheaper one-chip solutions, and in the process threw the baby out with the bathwater. Locked in a technology race against the Japanese majors, the European giant could hardly be blamed for focusing on the mass market prize. But as far as the audiophiles were concerned, Philips had fallen at the last hurdle.

Compact disc takes over

As more CD pressing plants came on stream, the cost of making CDs fell, but – with the market still expanding – retail prices did not. This was a honeymoon period, when the public were still in love with CD and prepared to pay for it. The record companies made a lot money. There was also a rather magical opportunity for hi-fi magazines. By doing a deal with a record company and blowing the year's promotional budget in one go, we could (just) afford to get 30,000 CDs pressed and stick them on the cover as a free gift. Since the perceived retail value of a CD – any CD – was at least £10, the cover-mount issue would sell like hot cakes.

Our first free disc, in April 1989, sampled releases from the Virgin Classics label, then just 12 months old. The magazine sold out completely, for the first time since the Crabbe era. over the next few years we gave away sampler CDs from other classical record labels including Chandos, Erato and Hyperion, and eventually Linn Records, the Naim Label and LSO Live.

In the early days the covermount disc came without a booklet or jewel box, so we printed a panel on a page in the magazine which, when cut out and folded, would become a four-page booklet for the CD. We got quite good at this and the 'booklet' for our October 1991 Technics-sponsored Chandos CD, *The Art of the Tonmeister*, was a beautiful piece of artwork. We were gutted to discover that when you'd cut this one out of the page, the back – the inside pages of the four-page booklet – was upside down.

Since there could never be enough in the budget to pay composer royalties, the music had to be by composers who'd been dead for 50 years (today it would 70 years) and thus out of copyright. Despite this, we did manage a memorable non-classical 'freebie' in 1994, thanks to reissue label Ace Records. Ace allowed Ken Kessler to choose tracks by B B King, Isaac Hayes, Dexter Gordon and others for our 'All Time Greats'.

Around the same time, Technics asked KK to choose tracks from the EMI/Capitol catalogue for a CD in its 'Music Lovers' Choice' series. He picked tracks from The Beach Boys, Duane Eddy, Heart, Jimmy Smith and Nat King Cole – but was overruled by the sponsor, who unilaterally decided to omit 'When I Fall In Love'. Ken was enraged, but he was soon proved right. The reissued Cole classic entered the charts a month later.

In 1989, we also came up with a successor to the *HFN/RR Test CD* of 1985. How could we outdo the original? Well, for *Test Disc II*, we flagged up the fact that the disc contained 99 tracks – the maximum a CD player could read – and included a BBC recording of Big Ben striking. The suggestion came from Tony Faulkner, who also helped us to include some truly excellent music recordings.

Test Disc II sold many thousands of copies, but by 1993 we felt it was time to come up with another new package. We enlisted ex-Nimbus record producer Alan Wiltshire, who recorded some specially-commissioned percussion pieces by David Corkhill. It was also Alan who proposed a more human alternative to the usual channel ID signals at the start of the disc, but I still find it hard to keep a straight face on hearing his fruity vocal tones as he does his 'Ambisonic walk-round'.

To make sure the disc really flew, we also reissued our greatest hit – Mike Skeet's spectacular 'Garage Door' ('the dynamic range of real life'), from the 1985 disc. Unfortunately, this time some some unauthorised compression was applied, destroying its impact. We hurriedly remastered, restoring Skeet's terrifying, fist-on-metal banging to its full glory!

Which CD
September 1990 saw the addition of a CD data section, when *HFN/RR* added *Which CD* to the long list of other titles it had absorbed over the years. *Which CD* had started life as a supplement to *Hi-Fi For Pleasure*, but in a reverse take-over, *HFP* had been folded and relaunched as *Which CD*. For those interested in such things, this is pretty much how Haymarket Publishing's *What Hi-Fi?* was born out of *Popular Hi-Fi* in the 1970s. But *Which CD* never had a fraction of the success of Haymarket's mega-mag, and by early 1990 its days were numbered. By then *HFN/RR* and *Which CD* belonged to two different divisions of United Newspapers.

So when *Which CD* was killed off, we were able to take over its monthly CD software and hardware listings. These were generated on a PC by a custom computer program, set up by multi-talented ex-*HFP* editor Trevor Preece. The only people who understood how to run the program and create the data pages every month were Trevor, outgoing *WCD?* editor Nuala Harvey, and a software consultant.

Everything might have been all right if the computer hadn't been crudely decommissioned before shipping to our Croydon office. As it was, we never learned how to get the data pages together without the consultant and (in pre-desktop-publishing days) we couldn't fix the hideous typography either. Readers didn't seem to be particularly turned on by seeing the CD player list repeated every month, so this was dropped. And we realised that we'd rather give readers more reviews than use precious space for the CD software listing, so, regrettably, this had to go too.

The fall and rise of vinyl

The UK's dominant high-street record retailer, W H Smith, had just announced it would no longer stock vinyl LPs when I wrote in a March 1992 editorial: 'Here is a sign of the times: reporting on the Winter Consumer Electronics Show in Las Vegas, KK relegates turntables to the "Bits 'n' pieces" section.' I went on to talk about the listeners to a Las Vegas demonstration of a Rockport/Rowland/Avalon analogue system: 'They weren't exhibiting the signs of concentration and stress that usually go with listening at shows. They were just hanging out. They were listening to the music. They were enjoying it... that friendly, enjoyable vibe took me back a decade and a half to an earlier time of discovery, when the sole purpose of hi-fi was to extract more pleasure from vinyl discs.'

A decade *after* that, vinyl would become 'cool' again. But in the mid-1990s vinyl-playing products were definitely niche-market material, and for a time they got squeezed out of *HFN/RR* altogether, as did valve amplifiers. We made up for this by adding an occasional supplement called *Valve & Vinyl*, which also tied in with a still-growing interest in vintage and retro equipment. At one hi-fi show, with a complete vintage system set up by Chris Beeching, I was able to enthrall a hotel room full of show visitors with Count Basie's 'One O'Clock Jump', recorded in 1937. It sounded so wonderful that some members of the audience refused to believe they were listening to a 78.

For the 40th anniversary issue in June 1996, we seized the chance of an exclusive review on the newly-announced Quad II amplifier reissue – what could be more appropriate? For that 40th birthday issue, we also gave away the first of six *Classic Hi-Fi* supplements – with the title logo and yellow top panel styled to look exactly like the pre-1967 *Hi-Fi News*.

In a way, we did it too well. We got at least one call from a puzzled reader who'd tried to respond to the quaint 1950s ads we'd thrown in; and in the *HFN* office recently, I came across *Classic Hi-Fi* copies that had been filed with the real 'yellow border' issues for the year 1959.

Lifetime Achievement Awards

The last Audio Awards had been presented in 1982, but there was only one Awards-free year before John Atkinson initiated the new *Hi-Fi News* Awards for Lifetime Achievement in Audio. In 1984, Awards were presented to Americans David Hafler, J Gordon Holt and Edgar Villchur as well as to Donald Aldous, Stanley Kelly and, last but not least, Peter Walker – the only man to have both awards. For 1985 there were four recipients: from the UK, Arthur Radford and *Gramophone* audio writer

John Gilbert; and from the USA, Marantz founder Saul Marantz and *The Absolute Sound's* publisher/editor Harry Pearson.

For 1986, Awards went to the influential French audio writer Jean Hiraga, and to Angus McKenzie, to Harold Leak and to Akio Morita of Sony. The next year, our four award winners were John Bowers (B&W), Raymond Cooke, OBE (KEF); Avery Fisher (Fisher Corporation, USA) and Gerry Sharp (Goldring). After this, we gave only two Awards per year, but they were distinguished ones indeed. For 1988, we honoured Alastair Robertson-Aikman (SME) and Sidney Harman. In 1989, it was a pleasure to honour *HFN/RR*'s former Editor John Crabbe; and it was also great to be able to present the award in person to US audio legend Paul Klipsch. In later years, like other magazines, we were driven to give awards to products rather than to people, which I think is rather sad.

As always, running out of space…

I've nearly got to the end of this chapter and I haven't even started to pay tribute to the efforts of all the admirable people who have made up the *Hi-Fi News* editorial team over the years – nor to discuss the hundreds of products we reviewed, or the multitude of fascinating people I've met in the hi-fi business. I've been lucky enough to encounter most of the leading designers and company principals who've enlivened the industry over the past 20 years, on both sides of the Atlantic.

So if I can only mention one product review, it has to be the Finial laser turntable. This was first seen at the Las Vegas CES in 1985, and we pursued it for several years until Finial appointed a UK agent, the late Dennis Wratten, and I was able to secure an exclusive. The review, in May 1990, was a fine piece of work by KK and Martin Colloms. Dennis had hoped to to sell the Finial to the BBC, but they weren't interested because it didn't play 78s (and it cost over £20,000).

More years passed, and Finial was bought by ELP of Japan. In 2001, Michael Fremer reported from an ELP press briefing in New York City. He opened by reminiscing about the Cortlandt Street area, where audio stores and army surplus electronics stores had nurtured the hi-fi industry in the 1950s, mentioning that it had become home to the World Trade Center. Sadly, the timing could not have been worse. Our report went to press before, but appeared on the bookstalls after, 9/11.

A change of name

In the early months of 2000, when *HFN/RR* had been part of the IPC empire for a year or so, we began to plan a major facelift for the magazine.

A quick glance at any bookstall was enough to show that we needed to make the logo bolder and stronger, and to achieve this, the second line of the title just had to go. Along with the new logo came a complete redesign aimed at making the magazine more 'accessible' and more readable.

And of course, the industry was changing fast. High-resolution audio arrived, although not before the SACD and DVD-Audio saga had become the longest and most tedious of all the format wars – it started around 1997 and it's not over yet. Home cinema was now bigger business than two channel audio, and yet there really was a vinyl revival. Now, more than ever before, the hi-fi enthusiast was spoilt for choice. He could have home cinema, also providing music video with respectable sound (thanks to DTS) or he could just listen with eyes closed. He could pursue hi-res digital audio, or content himself with CD, or get back to analogue roots. He could choose 5.1 or even 7.1 channels or he could go back to mono.

But all these choices – the choices of an informed elite called audiophiles – are of perhaps of little consequence against the background of the revolution in the music industry itself, the downloading revolution. We don't know where that will take us, but whichever way the road turns, let's hope that *Hi-Fi News* will still be our guide.

Howard Popeck *of Subjective Audio on Douglas Adams' hitchhiking hi-fi:*

'Douglas Adams was one of our most gracious, humorous, gentle and fun customers. Following the receipt of a 'serious' advance from his publishers for *Dirk Gently's Holistic Detective Agency*, he commissioned me to put together 'almost' the best system money could buy. It was, apart from the turntable, a full Absolute Sounds system including the magnificent but hernia-inducing Micro Seiki CD player and one of the very few pairs of Magneplanar Tympani sold in the UK.

'Installation was a complex affair and during the second day Douglas had to pop out for a bit. He returned later in the afternoon in a taxi, struggling with a number of heavily filled old-style plastic milk crates. In fact, they were packed with over 1000 CDs. He'd been to HMV and they were running some sort of promotion, and they gave him a hundred or so on top of his purchase. It's quite likely that he had purchased the bulk of titles then available in the UK. It was, after all, the early days of CD.

'He cheerfully pointed out that he'd always dreamed of having more music than he could ever listen to. The publishing advance gave him that freedom. His happiness was palpable, and infectious – even when his big American valve amplifiers blew up the moment we switched them on.'

15. Audiophilia

'No matter how rationally they otherwise may behave, and no matter how good their hearing acuity is, most audiophiles need some external confirmation of their purchases to keep themselves sane' **Robert J Reina**

David A Wilson of Wilson Audio, on legendary vinyl.

'Mamie's Record Shop in Sacramento, California's suburban Town and Country Village was a great place to browse the bins and buy LPs in 1960. You would enter the door from the shady Spanish accented walkway and enter a world of quality vinyl wonders lovingly displayed by the store's gracious and knowledgeable proprietress.

'The RCA Red Seals, which I preferred, were $4.98 in quality slipcovers. Black labels were usually a dollar less – seems cheap now, but these were heady prices for a high school kid when gas was $0.24 a gallon and minimum wage was $2.00 an hour. The cruelties of economics forced me to look to the budget labels at $1.98, but even without listening to their music, I knew they didn't sound good. So, you may ask, how did a 15-year-old kid know this?

'Remember the slipcovers? By carefully removing the LP from its jacket and inspecting the grooved record surface, my old friend and technical mentor – especially with his supernatural eyesight – Don Alley and I could see the low-priced LPs' tightly and evenly compressed grooves which betrayed their limited dynamics and filtered bass. Gently flexing the disc revealed the softness of the vinyl, as did the pitch of the characteristic "foink, foink" sound the records made. These were important clues which indicated not only the quantity but also the quality of the PVC used in the discs manufacture. Now, I will confess that some of our fellow teenage classmates thought we were nerds or worse. But we knew better – we knew this was science in the service of music!

'Usually, the sensuously broad low frequency curves of the RCAs' grooves and their tantalisingly wide spacing seduced us into spending the extra cash and buying "shaded dogs". Now, RCA Red Seals weren't the only discs with voluptuous grooving. Some Mercury and London and all Hi-Fi Brand and Audio Fidelity "First Component Series" pressings were even more outrageous than the RCA offerings in terms of sheer vinyl cleavage. Some of the Audio Fidelity liner notes actually listed the cartridges whose tracking prowess was deemed adequate to stay in the groove of that formidable offering. How cool was that? Shures and

Pickerings usually made the grade, while Don's Audio Empire 88 and my Weathers C-501D were usually (and frustratingly) not listed!

'I liked the robust sound of the RCAs, Londons and Hi-Fi Brand productions. With a few notable exceptions, the Columbias were hard, compressed and unsatisfying to me. One of the exceptions, which I literally wore out from use, was E Power Biggs' *Festival of French Organ Music*. The Audio Fidelity offerings usually sounded a little dirty to me; maybe my cartridge just couldn't track them (drat!). I generally liked the airy sweetness of the Westminsters and the direct clarity of the Vanguards (ah, Maurice Abravanel). The forward hardness of some of the Mercury issues was off-putting to me at first, and it wasn't until 1963, when my old friend and music mentor Frank Thompson enlightened me to the joys of Dorati, Starker and Paray, that I really began to appreciate the label.

'But I listened to all my hard-earned LP acquisitions, from beginning to end, and repeatedly I enjoyed sharing the music with others, although my parents hated Bartók. I succumbed occasionally to the game of showing off my hi-fi to the uninitiated using favourite LPs. I even managed to impress a young Sheryl Lee Jamison who would later become my wife!

'Then something began to change. Over a period of a few years, I would put a new LP on the turntable, only to take it off before the side was over. My older LPs became the ones I would go to when I wanted to impress someone with the sound or the music. I bought fewer LPs. The grooves didn't look very exciting anymore. While the liner note "information" provided for RCA Dynagroove, Columbia 360 Sound and some others promised a more technically corrected sound, I didn't hear it that way.

'RCA had chosen a classic example of market-driven versus excellence-driven product development. Presumably, letters from users of dying record changers began to concern the RCA folks in New Jersey. Aunt Tillie's old tone arm, with its certifiably Rigormortised Ronette, was being popped unceremoniously out of the groove during some energetic Reiner finale. Since these folks were unlikely to follow the remarkable recommendation of Consumers Union and fit a Shure M7-N21D cartridge into their record player, RCA saw a technical problem and a marketing opportunity.

'They limited their new LPs' low frequency bandwidth, altered their lathe's cutter-head profile to optimise it for 0.6 mil. diameter styli (which, ironically, most consumers didn't use), dramatically compressed the dynamics (so it would be easy for anything to track), and disingenuously called their creation "Dynagroove". None of the great-sounding RCAs are Dynagrooves. As one who has personally owned and, with the help of some very talented engineers, optimised, an LP mastering room and cutting system, I can tell you that solving a high percentage of consumer complaints of "needle skipping" as well as returns for noisy surface (often vinyl flow fill problems from vertical groove modulation, and the attempt to speed pressing times for higher production rates) could have been achieved by simply "compatilising" (making monaural) the bass at a somewhat higher frequency and dropping peak levels no more than 2dB. The basic quality of the record, though reduced, would have still retained much of its original character.

'Unfortunately, that was not all that was going wrong in the industry. It had entered the world of multi-mono microphone techniques, early solid-state mixers, and the totalitarian rule of unions.

'But that is another story!'

Clement Perry of The Stereo Times (www.stereotimes.com) remembers a Kron jewel:

'I once overheard the late Riccardo Kron, tube maven and manufacturer of KR amplifiers, arguing with Albert Von Schweikert, who was sharing a room at an exhibition using his then VR6 loudspeaker, over room treatments.

'Kron stated, "This room doesn't need acoustic treatment. My amplifiers can *see* the room!"'

Be Yamamura on an electrifying sonic experience:

'It was the peak of quite unbelievable hi-fi bubble, particularly in Italy where I lived. In the mid-1990s, there seemed countless enthusiasts in Europe and for designers and manufacturers, it was a great period to develop and realise some dream systems. However, like every other such phenomenon, it burst. I guess the industry wasn't really mature and it suffered because too many new faces in Giorgio Armani suits and fancy briefcases rushed into the area called "Esoteric".

'One day, I visited my dear friend and fellow enthusiast in Northern Italy. He was unusually hesitant to invite me down to his beautifully-equipped audio room. He always seemed that way when he acquired something new but it was a little exceptional that day. Eventually we went in to listen to some music, and there I saw gorgeously glittering, huge amplifiers spread across his large floor.

'I understood his exceptional shyness and worries about my opinion because it must have cost as much as a nice sports car and looked as big, too. He somewhat nervously put on some music and, already apologising about imperfect balance, it being multi-driver system, he reverently brought out a large white handkerchief as if he was a famous conductor or trumpet player. He then walked towards those glittering amplifiers and started to make careful gain adjustments, always with his handkerchief in hand. I thought they must be so precious for him that he didn't want to leave fingerprints on the shining gold, silver and whatever, despite the sound quality being pretty average. I tried not to notice his handkerchief, but I just couldn't ignore it for long and he was a very close friend. I said, "Isn't it over the top? I've never seen you so nervous."

'He replied, "Of course I'm nervous, because these bloody expensive monsters give me a big electric shock every time I touch them!"'

Robert J Reina on the ultimate audiophile disc:

'No matter how rationally they otherwise may behave, and no matter how good their hearing acuity is, most audiophiles need some external confirmation of their purchases to keep themselves sane. A rave review in a magazine, or a listing of their component in Class A in *Stereophile*'s Recommended Components, or even a visit from a friend who compliments the sound is usually sufficient.

'One day I visited an audiophile friend who had recently built a custom-made house designed around his audio system. I drove up one weekend to hear it and my friend was waiting for his friend, The Famous Audio Writer, to approve of the sound quality of his system in his new super room. He was very nervous. He asked me if I had brought anything I wanted to hear and I handed over a record to him.

'Now, my friend has conservative classical music tastes, and my tastes are rather eclectic. He cued down the expensive moving-coil cartridge and looked at me for my reaction. I stared at him. "What's the matter?" he said. "You don't like the sound? Volume level too low or too high? What's wrong?" My reply: "Bob, I know you're very nervous and I know my taste in music is eccentric, but not that eccentric. You forgot to put the record on. You're playing the acrylic platter of your Goldmund turntable."'

Karen Sumner on The Search for Musical Ecstasy:

'Harvey Rosenberg and I were in love spiritually. We were totally in sync with each other when it came to our reasons for loving this industry. It was all about music, higher states of being, and fun. I first met him when he introduced his OTL amplifiers. He dropped out of sight as far as the industry was concerned after he lost interest in his hybrid MOSFET/tube amps (which came with Pampers packed in the box). I never had the chance to get to know Harvey then except in passing.

'Harvey re-entered the industry about 10 years ago by making an appearance at a *Stereophile* show. We walked toward each other in a show hallway and we both could feel the psychic energy building between us as we approached one another. We talked at length about life, music, and friendship. He told me he was writing a book about high-end audio, *The Search for Musical Ecstasy*, and he wanted me to contribute to it.

'Harvey was really serious about it. He called weekly, and we talked about the transforming power of the aural experience. He wanted me to run for President (as long as he could be Vice-President). He thought that we could make the world a better place. I wrote a chapter for Harvey's book, we stayed in touch off and on until his unexpected death. The world is not a better place without Harvey. I miss him.'

Gene Lyle, Audio Society of Minnesota, on a visit to Audio Research:

'I am reminded of a visit I made to Audio Research Corporation many years ago with a group of people from the Audio Society of Minnesota. This was the first of many visits I made to the company and it was right at the time that audible differences between wires were becoming "hot" topics. Before this, folks just used zip cord or whatever was at hand.

'Part of the demo that evening was the substitution of a trendy carriage trade interconnect (the long-since departed Petersen Emerald, if memory serves) for a standard Radio Shack-type wire between the pre-amp and midrange/tweeter amp driving the towers of an Infinity Reference system. Switching between the two revealed to my then-young ears a noticeable difference, mostly in terms of instrument localisation and focus. The selection was a Faure piece for violin and piano and one of the cables clearly gave a better sense of two instruments in different places on the stage; the other lumped them together. Although we knew what the two cables were, we didn't know which was in the system at any given time.

'There was a gentleman in the audience, probably somewhere in his late 60s or early 70s, who could consistently and accurately identify and describe the differences between the two cables. He was also just about the only person who was not intimidated by the demo, and spoke up immediately when the group was asked to comment on what they heard. Surprisingly, this gentleman wore hearing aids in *both* ears.

'As a budding audiophile, this was my first introduction to the fact that

(a) wire can make a difference, and (b) you can't always assume people with disabilities are disabled. What he heard was what I heard.

'On occasion, I later saw this gentleman at a number of Minnesota Orchestra concerts. I also learned that he had been a music teacher for many years. Both facts help explain his auditory acuity. And for those who might think the Audio Research demo wasn't double blind – it was for him. He was also totally blind.'

Arnis Balgalvis remembers Hy Kachalsky, founder of the Audiophile Society, New York:

'In one major respect, Hy Kachalsky was the antithesis of the prototypical audiophile. While most audio nerds are loners, Hy rarely listened by himself. He needed others to share his listening pleasure. He loved tweaking, but only if others did the work on his system. As a matter of fact, I never saw him do any work on his system. He never once moved an amp, changed a cable, or repositioned a speaker. Instead he made it a community project. He invited his audio cohorts and made it a mini event of discovery. That's not to say he could not hear, or that he used others. The simple truth was that Hy was a social being.

'In the year before he died, Hy set out to broaden the activities of the Society by turning The Audiophile Society Minutes into a national magazine, *The Audiophile Voice*. Despite his illness, which produced fatigue, bone pain, and drowsiness, he assembled a group of talented volunteers to write, edit, and produce *The Audiophile Voice*.

'His zest for living and his love of life will always stay with me. I cannot think of anyone who else who better exemplifies the contribution that a caring and concerned person can make. He will always serve as an example to me that an individual can make a difference.'

Hy Kachalsky in the 10th Anniversary Issue of The Audiophile Society Journal:

'Technology develops ever more rapidly in every area of life. And so it is in high-end audio. There will be no stopping the digital revolution. Rather, we have to influence it to become the equal of analogue, if not better. There will also be changes in the digital format before the dust settles, if it ever does. But the lot of the Audiophile is always to want better, and, by paying for better, inspiring others to make better things.

'So there is still much to do, much to work for, and much to share and appreciate. And so it will ever be. But our love for music, and our love for our fellow man, will ever make our hobby a beloved and enriching one.'

Index

Index ●